D0215019

# The Friendship of
# Florence Nightingale and
# Mary Clare Moore

# The Friendship of
# Florence Nightingale and
# Mary Clare Moore

EDITED BY

## Mary C. Sullivan

**PENN**

University of Pennsylvania Press

Philadelphia

10 9 8 7 6 5 4 3 2 1

Published by
University of Pennsylvania Press
Philadelphia, Pennsylvania 19104-4011

Library of Congress Cataloging-in-Publication Data

The friendship of Florence Nightingale and Mary Clare Moore /
edited by Mary C. Sullivan.
    p.   cm.
    Includes bibliographical references and index.
    ISBN 0-8122-3489-8 (alk. paper)
    1. Nightingale, Florence, 1820–1910—Correspondence.   2. Moore, Mary Clare,
1814–1874—Correspondence.
RT37.N5A4   1999
610.73'092—dc21
[B]                                                                          98-54899
                                                                              CIP

Frontispiece: *Reverend Mother Mary Clare Moore (1814–1874)*, Courtesy of the Sisters
of Mercy, Bermondsey, London. *Florence Nightingale (1820–1910)*, Courtesy of
the Florence Nightingale Museum Trust, London.

# Contents

# Preface

This book records the twenty-year friendship of Florence Nightingale (1820–1910) with Mary Clare Moore (1814–1874), the founding superior of the Sisters of Mercy in Bermondsey, London, whom Nightingale first met en route to their service in the Crimean War. Therefore, some statement of my stylistic and editorial practices may assist the reader. First, a word about names is necessary. In speaking of Florence Nightingale and Mary Clare Moore in relation to one another, I have referred to them by their first names, as Florence and Clare. This of course flies in the face of their own constant practice, at least in their correspondence with one another: Florence Nightingale always calls Clare "Revd Mother," and Clare Moore always addresses Florence as "Miss Nightingale." However, neither of these appellations seemed desirable in a book of this sort, narrating their friendship. When I am referring to Florence Nightingale in contexts other than her relations with Clare Moore, I sometimes use simply her surname, though I cannot vouch for my consistency in this. In general, I try to avoid "Miss Nightingale."

The names of Sisters of Mercy are further complicated. At her reception into the Sisters of Mercy and clothing in the Mercy religious dress, each sister in the nineteenth century (and well into the twentieth century) assumed a new name in religion: a saint's name prefixed by "Mary." Thus Georgiana Moore became Mary Clare Moore. I have sometimes—for example, in initially identifying her—indicated a sister's baptismal name in parentheses: for example, Mary Gonzaga (Georgiana) Barrie. Much more frequently, especially in the case of Clare Moore herself, I have dropped the name "Mary," as is often the practice among present-day Sisters of Mercy. However, for those sisters who chose the names of male saints, I have generally retained the "Mary" to avoid confusion. Thus Mary Gonzaga Barrie usually gets her full religious name, except where Florence Nightingale herself calls her "Gonzaga," or where the use of her full name would be cum-

bersome. Finally, I do not use titles with their names (such as "Sister
_____" or "Reverend Mother _____"), and I do not refer to sisters by
their surnames only, since this would depart notably from common
usage.[1]

In presenting the texts of the letters and other manuscripts included in this volume, I have tried to follow, to the best of my ability,
the spelling, capitalization, and punctuation of the authors, including
their ampersands, dashes, and abbreviations. I have followed their use
of quotation marks, even when it appears inconsistent, and I have used
italics for the emphasis they expressed by underlining. Occasionally,
for the sake of clarity or ease of reading, and only where this would
not affect the meaning, I have slightly altered what I took to be the
punctuation or paragraphing of the original. Nightingale uses both
parentheses and square brackets in her writing; since I have preserved
these, I use double square brackets to indicate my queries and other
editorial insertions in her texts, although I use single square brackets
for this purpose in other texts. While I cannot be wholly confident
that in every instance I have read an author's handwriting correctly, I
trust that, through numerous proofreadings against the original manuscripts, my errors have been kept to a minimum.

In carrying out the research for this book, I have depended on
three main collections of Nightingale papers, in addition to the Archives of the Sisters of Mercy in Bermondsey, London. The Nightingale
Collection of the Florence Nightingale Museum Trust, London, now
preserved at the London Metropolitan Archives (formerly called the
Greater London Record Office), has provided, among many other helpful documents, the texts of nine extant letters of Mary Clare Moore to
Florence Nightingale. I am very grateful to Alex Attewell, Curator of
the Florence Nightingale Museum Trust, for permission to reproduce
these letters and to quote from other Nightingale materials in the London Metropolitan Archives, including the five extant letters to Florence
Nightingale from Mary Stanislaus Jones, a Sister of Mercy who served
with her in the Crimea. Appropriate documentation of these materials is provided in the text. I also offer my thanks to Harriet Jones and
Geoff Pick, who generously assisted me at the London Metropolitan
Archives.

The resources of the Department of Manuscripts of the British
Library have been extremely beneficial to this research, and I am very
grateful to Dr. R. Evans for permission, granted on behalf of the British

Library, to publish the letter of Clare Moore to Florence Nightingale, as well as to quote from numerous other Nightingale documents in the Library's collection of Additional Manuscripts. Appropriate identification of these manuscripts is provided. I also wish to thank Anne Summers of the Department of Manuscripts for a very helpful conversation and for her insights into Nightingale research.

Many letters of Florence Nightingale to her family and other correspondents are preserved at Claydon House in Buckingham, England, the estate of her deceased sister and brother-in-law, Lady Parthenope and Sir Harry Verney. Photocopies made of these documents by Sue M. Goldie are now available for researchers at the Wellcome Institute for the History of Medicine in London. Dr. Richard Aspin, Curator of Western Manuscripts at the Wellcome Institute, has been very helpful to me as I worked with these photocopies and with the Wellcome Institute's collection of Nightingale autographs. I offer him and the Wellcome Institute my sincere thanks. I especially wish to thank Sir Ralph Verney and his family, as represented by the Claydon House Trust, for permission to quote from the Wellcome Institute's photocopies of letters in the Claydon Collection. In citing these materials, I refer to the photocopies at the Wellcome Institute by their assigned manuscript numbers.

The greatest personal assistance I have received in the course of this research has come from the Sisters of Mercy now living and working in Bermondsey, London—in the successor community to Mary Clare Moore's own. The heart of the present book is the texts of the fifty-two letters of Florence Nightingale, most of them to Mary Clare Moore, that these sisters and their predecessors have preserved for almost a century and a half.

In addition to presenting the full texts of these Nightingale letters, I have also—in my own commentaries on Florence Nightingale and Mary Clare Moore and in the narrative links between their letters to one another—frequently quoted from these letters as well as from other letters preserved in the Archives of the Sisters of Mercy, Bermondsey.[2] These include autograph letters from Thomas Grant, Bishop of Southwark, to Mary Clare Moore, and from her to him; autograph letters of Cardinal Nicholas Wiseman, Archbishop of Westminster, to Mary Gonzaga Barrie, and from her to him; autograph letters from Clare Moore and Mary Gonzaga Barrie to one another, or to other Sisters of Mercy; and photocopies or typescripts of letters from Mary

Gonzaga Barrie to her family, and from Florence Nightingale to Mary Stanislaus Jones. Whenever I quote from one of these numerous letters, I try to identify it by date, but I do not provide a specific in-text citation, the source in each case being understood (or stated) to be a manuscript or copy in the Archives of the Sisters of Mercy in Bermondsey, London.

The Annals of the Convent of Our Lady of Mercy, Bermondsey, that is, the yearly accounts of the activities of the Sisters of Mercy of Bermondsey, from 1839 to the present, are also preserved in the Bermondsey archives. I have used the two earliest handwritten volumes: Volume 1, covering the years 1839 to 1856, and Volume 2, covering the years 1857 to 1905. In giving citations to these volumes, which I name simply the Bermondsey Annals, I have put the page numbers in square brackets to reflect my own consecutive renumbering of some duplicated page numbers. Enormous credit is due to the early Sisters of Mercy for the care with which they recorded the events of each year, if not as they were happening, then as soon afterward as possible. Clare Moore herself is often the annalist for the years examined in this study.

I warmly thank the Sisters of Mercy now living on the site of the Convent of Mercy in Bermondsey where Clare Moore lived from November 1839 to her death in 1874 (the original convent was destroyed by bombing during World War II). As a Sister of Mercy myself, I am deeply grateful to this community, not only for carefully preserving the many manuscripts I have been privileged to use, but for offering me such generous hospitality on so many occasions. I thank Imelda Keena, RSM, the Archivist of this collection during the early period of my research, for all her thoughtful encouragement.

But I especially wish to thank my collaborator in this project, Teresa Green, RSM, the Assistant Archivist of the General Archives at the Bermondsey convent, who has done considerable research identifying names and other references in the Nightingale letters and who prepared an early typescript of these letters. She has become a generous and enthusiastic partner in the preparation of this book. It was through her efforts early on that the initial permission to publish the Nightingale autographs in the Bermondsey archives was obtained from Mary Paschal O'Brien, RSM, Superior General of the Institute of Our Lady of Mercy (in Britain), which owns the General Archives in Bermondsey. That permission has now been extended to include all the Bermondsey archival materials used in this study as well as the manuscripts of Mary Clare Moore and Mary Stanislaus Jones found elsewhere, for which the Institute of Our Lady of Mercy serves as executor. I am sincerely grateful to Mary Paschal O'Brien for this permission and for her support of this project.

Finally, the copyright of the letters and other papers of Florence Nightingale, wherever these are collected, lies with the Trustees of the will of Henry Bonham Carter, Florence Nightingale's cousin to whom she bequeathed her papers. I am very grateful to the Henry Bonham-Carter Will Trust, through their solicitors, Messrs. Radcliffes and Company, for permission to publish, in whole or in part, the letters and other papers of Florence Nightingale used in this study.

I also wish to acknowledge the generous help I have received from scholars who have published previous editions of letters of Florence Nightingale. Permission to quote, sometimes at length, from letters or other material appearing in their books has been kindly granted by the following authors: Martha Vicinus and Bea Nergaard, editors of *Ever Yours, Florence Nightingale: Selected Letters* (London: Virago Press, 1989); Sue M. Goldie, editor of *"I have done my duty": Florence Nightingale in the Crimean War, 1854–56* (Manchester: Manchester University Press, 1987); and Vincent Quinn and John Prest, editors of *Dear Miss Nightingale: A Selection of Benjamin Jowett's Letters to Florence Nightingale, 1860–1893* (Oxford: Clarendon Press, 1987), by permission of Oxford University Press. When I quote from these sources, suitable acknowledgment is provided in parenthetical documentation and in the Works Cited. I am very grateful for the availability of these scholarly works and for permission to quote from them as well as for the personal support expressed by Martha Vicinus and Sue Goldie.

I am indebted to Anne Coon and Katherine Mayberry, my colleagues at Rochester Institute of Technology, for their careful reading of the manuscript; to Joseph Nassar, former chair of the Humanities division, and William Daniels, former dean of the College of Liberal Arts, for their generous support of my research travel and typing; and to Ernan McMullin of the University of Notre Dame for his helpful critique of several portions of the book. I have appreciated their questions, suggestions, and help very much, and I sincerely thank them. Linda Henderberg has been the excellent typist of the book manuscript, and my gratitude to her is very great.

The correspondence and other documentation presented in this book will interest those who are researching Florence Nightingale's life and thought, as well as those working on the social or religious history of the Victorian era or on the broader history of Christian spirituality. The book is also designed to be accessible to general readers who are interested in Florence Nightingale's or Mary Clare Moore's life or in the experience of women, including religious women, in the nineteenth century, for the book is the detailed record of the friendship of two influential women—who saw much to admire and support in one another and who contributed uniquely and generously to each other's lifework. But the book will offer special insights to those who are interested in studying Florence Nightingale's spiritual development: the deepening of her theology of God and Christ, her prayer, and her self-transcendent desire to seek and promote the reign of God in human history.

# Abbreviations

The following abbreviations are used in citations of manuscript sources.

| | |
|---|---|
| BA: | The Annals of the Convent of Our Lady of Mercy, Bermondsey, London, England |
| BL Add. MSS: | British Library Additional Manuscripts volume number and folio |
| LMA: | London Metropolitan Archives (formerly, the Greater London Record Office) manuscript reference for the Nightingale Collection owned by the Florence Nightingale Museum Trust, London |
| Wellcome Institute: | Photocopies now available at the Wellcome Institute for the History of Medicine, London, of manuscripts in the Sir Ralph Verney Collection of the Claydon House Trust at Claydon House in Buckingham, England |

# Introduction

No HUMAN LIFE can be reduced to a few paragraphs: so much of hope and regret, joy and sorrow, intention and accomplishment, eludes verbal formulation. Nevertheless, it may be helpful at the beginning of this volume of their correspondence to provide some biographical information about Florence Nightingale (1820–1910) and Mary Clare Moore (1814–1874), the founding superior of the Sisters of Mercy in Bermondsey (London). Readers may thus appreciate the nature and significance of Nightingale's relationship with this little known but valued correspondent whom she had met in late 1854, during the first months of the most harrowing experience of her life, her nursing service during the Crimean War. Since the career, mythic or actual, of Florence Nightingale, is relatively well known, even among the general public, only a brief review of the broad highlights of her life is needed. But because the biography of Mary Clare Moore is generally not known, even among historians of the Catholic Church in England, a more extensive summary of her life is required, if readers are to appreciate the character of the friendship that meant so much to Florence Nightingale's spiritual development.

Having been educated at home by her father, who spared her neither mathematics nor the classics in Greek and Latin, and having then, on her own, acquired some limited nursing experience, Florence Nightingale was at the age of thirty-four chosen by the British government to be superintendent of female nursing in the British military hospitals in Turkey and the Crimea during the war with Russia (1854–1856). Though exhausted when she returned to England in August 1856, she vowed to honor the thousands of soldiers who had died needlessly in the Crimean conflict, by working with medical and governmental collaborators to achieve reforms in the Army Medical Department of the British War Office. But intense research, report writing, correspondence, and personal advocacy further weakened her. By August 1861, Lord Sidney Herbert, the former Secretary at War and her chief ally in reform efforts, was dead, and Nightingale herself, having been ailing since she collapsed in 1857, was now more or less an invalid.[1] Yet she continued to work from her bed for the next thirty years or more, contributing in various substantial ways to improvements in both military and civilian spheres: in army medical training, the keeping of army medical statistics, army sanitation and cookery, public health, nursing and nurses' training, hospital design, workhouse nursing, midwifery, and sanitation in India. From her London quarters, she did research, issued reports, received official and personal visitors on a limited basis, and carried on a voluminous public and private correspondence. Her extant letters are now estimated to number about 14,000.[2]

Florence Nightingale died in London on August 13, 1910, at the age of ninety.[3] To her surprise, she had outlived not only her parents, William Edward Nightingale and Frances Nightingale, but also her sister Parthenope and her sister's husband, Sir Harry Verney. Though she grew to maturity in her family's country homes at Lea Hurst in Derbyshire and Embley in Hampshire, she spent over fifty years of her adult life living in London as an invalid or semi-invalid; forty-four of these years were spent in the house at 10 South Street where she died.

Georgiana Moore was born in Dublin of Protestant parents on March 20, 1814.[4] The Register of the Bermondsey (London) convent of the Sisters of Mercy—Georgiana's future home—notes that she was the daughter of George and Catherine Moore, and that she "was born in the [Church of Ireland] Parish of Saint Anne's." Mary Austin Carroll, a nineteenth-century historian of the Sisters of Mercy, says that Georgiana's father died in 1817, and that "the family continued Protestant until 1823, when Mrs. Moore and her children had the happiness of being received into the Catholic Church" (*Leaves* 2:37).[5] Georgiana was then about nine years old.

Years later Georgiana wrote that she "became acquainted" with Catherine McAuley, the founder of the Sisters of Mercy, in September 1828 and that she "went to reside in Baggot St. on the 13th October."[6] The House of Mercy that Catherine McAuley had built on Baggot Street, Dublin was opened on September 24 of the previous year. The House was not then intended to be a convent, but rather a night refuge for homeless poor girls and servant women, a school for poor children, and a residence for lay women who wished to join Catherine in these works of mercy, as well as in the visitation of the sick poor in their homes and in Dublin hospitals. Mary Bertrand Degnan, a biographer of Catherine McAuley, says that Georgiana, who was then about fourteen years old, "came to Baggot Street in answer to a call for a governess" for Catherine's young niece, Catherine Macauley, and her adopted cousin, Teresa Byrn, ages nine and seven respectively (75).[7]

Eight months later Georgiana left Baggot Street temporarily, evidently in poor health. However, she returned on June 10, 1830, and remained there until 1837, when, at the age of twenty-three, she departed to become the first superior of the Mercy community in Cork. Her sister, Clare Augustine Moore, writing to Bermondsey in 1875, several months after Georgiana's death, says of her: "She entered St. Catherine's [a later name for the Baggot Street house] when she was little more than sixteen, not without a severe mental struggle. How she lived so long is wonderful for her lungs were diseased when she was fourteen and continued so for many years after, I know, perhaps to the last."[8]

In 1830 Catherine McAuley and the community of twelve on Baggot Street, after suffering much clerical and lay criticism of their atypical way of life, made the decision to found a religious congregation of women devoted to the works of mercy. Catherine, Mary Ann Doyle, and Mary Elizabeth Harley then made a required novitiate in the convent of the Presentation Sisters on George's Hill, Dublin and professed their religious vows there, as the first Sisters of Mercy, on December 12, 1831. Georgiana Moore, who had stayed behind on Baggot Street to help carry on the works already begun, was among the first seven who received the habit of the Sisters of Mercy at Baggot Street (on January 23, 1832), and one of the first four who professed their religious vows there (on January 24, 1833). She was then not quite nineteen years old. At her reception of the habit she adopted the baptismal name of her older sister Mary Clare (who would later also enter the Sisters of Mercy, as Mary Clare Augustine Moore) and so became known in religion as Mary Clare Moore. She was, by all accounts, an intelligent, trusted companion to Catherine McAuley and is acknowledged to be the person who most closely assisted Catherine in preparing the original manuscript of the Rule and Constitutions of the Sisters of Mercy.

On July 6, 1837 Catherine and Clare founded a community of Sisters of Mercy in Cork, and Clare became the superior. Then, on November 21, 1839, having left Cork—as she thought, temporarily—

and journeyed from Dublin to London with Catherine McAuley and the rest of the founding party, Clare became the first superior of the Bermondsey (London) foundation of the Sisters of Mercy. This appointment was intended to last only a year, until one of the two English women who had made their novitiate in Cork and come to Bermondsey as part of the founding community was prepared to assume leadership. A year and a half later, Clare returned to Cork, where she resumed the role of superior, leaving Mary Clare (Elizabeth) Agnew as superior in Bermondsey. However, in the six months that followed Clare Moore's departure, Clare Agnew's grave misunderstanding of the ministerial vocation of the Sisters of Mercy threatened to destroy the spirit of the Bermondsey community. Preferring a life more fully focused on contemplative practices, she was removed from the office of superior in December 1841 and subsequently left the community (in October 1842). On December 10, 1841, Clare Moore returned to Bermondsey, at the request of Bishop Thomas Griffiths, Vicar Apostolic of the London District, and was reappointed superior on December 13, 1841.[9] From then until her death in December 1874—except for fifteen months, from June 5, 1851 to September 23, 1852—she was the superior of the Bermondsey community.[10]

The Bermondsey Convent of the Sisters of Mercy, founded in 1839, was adjacent to the Church of the Most Holy Trinity in Dockhead. The old chapel of the parish (the new church was opened in 1835) had long been a Catholic place of worship in this region of London—on the south side of the Thames, east of what is now Tower Bridge, across the river from the old docks of London. In pre-Reformation times the area had been served by Bermondsey Abbey of St. Saviour. The Abbey was surrendered to King Henry VIII on January 1, 1537, and in 1545 the monastic church was destroyed (Whatmore 1–6, 40–50).

The convent had been designed by Augustus Welby Pugin—much to the dissatisfaction of Catherine McAuley, for the building was, in her view, too Gothic in style, with insufficient interior light and poor allocation of space. It was said to be the first new convent for Catholic women erected in or near London since the Reformation.[11] The principal financial contributors to its construction were the late Baroness de Montesquieu and Lady Barbara Eyre, daughter of the Earl of Newburgh, who subsequently became a Sister of Mercy herself. The first ceremony held in England for the reception of the habit of the Sisters of Mercy occurred in Holy Trinity Church on December 12, 1839.

The work of the Bermondsey community was multifaceted. They visited the sick poor in their homes and in Guy's and St. Thomas's Hospitals, instructed adult converts and Catholics who had not been attending church, prepared hundreds of children for their first Communion and Confirmation, conducted poor schools for the female children of the parish and an infant school for toddlers, and assisted the poor in countless other ways, providing both material help and spiritual consolation. Clare Moore was, for almost thirty-five years, the chief organizer of all these ministries, and their inspiration and sustainer. The Bermondsey Annals says of her, quoting an unnamed source: "Her governing powers were extraordinary; as was once remarked of her [evidently by one of the bishops with whom she worked], 'she was fit to rule a kingdom' " (2:[225]).

On October 17, 1854, while remaining superior of the community, Clare with four other Bermondsey sisters went to the Crimea to nurse the sick and wounded English, Scottish, Welsh, and Irish soldiers who were involved in the war with Russia. They went, on three days' notice, at the request of Bishop Thomas Grant of Southwark, in response to a plea for volunteer nurses issued by Sidney Herbert, the Secretary at War. In early 1856 three more Sisters of Mercy from Bermondsey joined them. Clare was assigned to the Barrack Hospital in Scutari, Turkey and worked there until peace was declared. But, having become dangerously ill, she left Scutari before all the wounded had returned home; she arrived back in Bermondsey on May 16, 1856. In the Crimea, the Bermondsey sisters served under the general superintendency of Florence Nightingale. On April 29, 1856, the day after Clare left Scutari to return to England, Florence wrote to her from the General Hospital in Balaclava:

Your going home is the greatest blow I have had yet. But God's blessing & my love & gratitude go with you, as you well know. . . .

. . . You were far above me in fitness for the General Superintendency, both in worldly talent of administration, & far more in the spiritual qualifications which God values in a superior. . . .

I will ask you to forgive me for everything or anything which I may unintentionally have done which can ever have given you pain—remembering only that I have always felt what I have just expressed & that it has given me more pain to reign over you than to you to serve under me. . . .

> Ever my dearest Revd. Mother's
> (gratefully, lovingly, overflowingly)
> Florence Nightingale [12]

During the thirty-five years of her life in England, Clare's remarkable skills—of nursing, consoling, teaching, administering, and writing—served hundreds of people, the neglected and the well known, including the bishops of London and Southwark. It was she, and other sisters from Bermondsey, who "day and night" attended the severely ill, and now almost blind, Bishop Thomas Griffiths, Vicar Apostolic of the London District, before his death on August 12, 1847. Clare herself evidently stayed with him each night for over two weeks. On August 16, four days after he died, she wrote to the sisters in Chelsea, a convent she had founded in London in 1845, to give them "some little account of our good Bishop's illness and death." In her six-page letter, one senses what her presence meant to the dying man. She says: "he told me to suggest to him what aspirations he should make, and what he should be thinking of—but I had no need to do this for he was praying incessantly when he was awake"; "he did not refuse any thing however unpleasant, the vomiting was continual, every thing he took"; "he told me the first day that his sight was gone entirely from one eye and almost from the other"; on Wednesday night, August 10, "as soon as he perceived I had come, he said . . . if I would cause the Holy Name of Jesus to sound in his ears, when he was dying, he would make me hear it at my death"; "his mouth was so parched . . . , and he could only get a teaspoonful [of water] at a time"; "when the sinking of death was coming he asked very often to be raised, and when we could not raise him as much as he wanted, he would say, so quietly, what can you do for a dying man"; "he died so tranquilly that the Priest who was kneeling beside him did not know it." Clare's long, detailed letter, now in the Bermondsey archives, illustrates not only Bishop Griffiths's simplicity but also what the chapter of the Rule of the Sisters of Mercy on the Visitation of the Sick had come to mean in Clare's own life.

Clare also worked with Cardinal Nicholas Wiseman, Bishop Griffiths's second successor and Archbishop of Westminster (1850–1865), and with Archbishop Henry Manning, who succeeded Wiseman. But the bishop with whom she collaborated most closely was Thomas Grant, Bishop of Southwark from 1851—just after the restoration of the English Catholic hierarchy in 1850—until his death in Rome, at the Vatican Council, on June 1, 1870. A wealth of material in the Bermondsey archives of the Sisters of Mercy, including correspondence, documents their relationship. Grant's letters to Clare were always solicitous, and respectful of her judgment. He once wrote: "Pray much for me between now and Friday as I am in great anxiety of mind about two matters in which I have to decide. They do not regard the Convents of course." Their correspondence also reveals that Clare served as a secretary to Bishop Grant, and that others in the Bermondsey community occasionally did copying for him. He once wrote to her: "I hope they will forgive me for troubling them so often with my MSS." Clare herself frequently mentions work that she has received from him, including letters to be translated. Once she reminds him: "I have delayed this, to send, at the same time, the copy of the French letter, but we have not yet received the conclusion which you promised to send by post." Grant evidently also relied on her to respond, when possible, to personal requests that came to him. Thus he writes from Berkshire: "Sir Robert Throckmorton wants a Sister who can speak French and can nurse their governess. Have you any Sisters who could be spared? I do not like one to go alone, and I fear you could not spare two." He asked her to respond to similar requests for nursing care from the Duchess of Leeds, for her husband, and from the Marchioness of Wellesley.

Many passages in the Bermondsey Annals, as well as many letters in the Bermondsey archives, tell of Thomas Grant's helpfulness to Clare, and of hers to him. For almost twenty years, until his death in 1870, their working relationship and mutual respect contributed steadily to the accomplishments of both. It was therefore fitting, as the Annals record, that when Clare was dying in December 1874 Bishop James Danell, the new Bishop of Southwark, "visited her every day and left with her his pectoral cross . . . which formerly had belonged to the revered Bishop Grant" (2:[238]).

Unlike Bishop William Ullathorne, who publicly acknowledged the help Mother Margaret Hallahan, OP, gave to his endeavors in Coventry and Birmingham, Bishops Griffiths and Grant did not write autobiographies, so Clare Moore's many comparable contributions to the mission of the church in London and Southwark have not been historically recognized. Moreover, her own temperament and Bishop Grant's would have worked against public notice. The Bermondsey Annals record that, in a eulogy preached in the parish church on the Sunday after her death, Canon William Murnane described Clare's life as "a humble, unobtrusive life, yet full of sublime self-sacrifice and painful labour in the cause of God, doing far more for him and suffering humanity than the accumulated acts of many others" (2:[240]). However, a close friend of Bishop Grant, probably Bishop Ullathorne, has reported Grant's view of her:

When unusual labor and self-sacrifice were required in his diocese . . . it was to the mother-superior of Bermondsey he had recourse. Over and over he said in my hearing, "She has never yet failed me, never once disappointed me." (quoted in Carroll, *Leaves* 2:256)

During her years in London, Clare Moore and the Bermondsey community founded eight additional autonomous houses in England: Chelsea (1845), Bristol (1846), Brighton (1852), St. Elizabeth's Hospital for Incurables on Great Ormond Street, London (1856), Wigton in Cumberland (1857), Abingdon in Berkshire (1859), Gravesend (1860), and Clifford in Yorkshire (1870)—where they replaced sisters who had originally come from Dublin—as well as a branch house in Eltham (1874). During these years other new foundations of Sisters of Mercy, coming directly from Ireland, were also established in Birmingham (1841), Liverpool (1843), Sunderland (1843), Queen's Square, London (1844), Cheadle (1849), and Hull (1857), as well as in Glasgow (1849), Edinburgh (1858), and Dundee (1859).

St. Elizabeth's Hospital on Great Ormond Street, London—later called The Hospital of St. John and St. Elizabeth, and decades later relocated to St. John's Wood—was founded at the request of Cardinal Wiseman a few months after Clare and the other Bermondsey sisters returned from the Crimea. Thomas Grant wrote to Clare on July 15, 1856, while she was recuperating in Boulogne:

Dr. Manning came here this morning to speak about the plan of having 5 of your Sisters (if possible, Crimean Sisters) for the new Hospital established by the zeal of L[ord] Campden in Westminster. I told him that you were too unwell to attend to business at present, and therefore I will not enter into any of the details beyond mentioning that he thought that it was very important that the experience of hospital work acquired by your Sisters should not be sacrificed.

Four months later, Saint Elizabeth's Hospital for Incurables was opened, the first Catholic hospital in London since the English Reformation. Mary Gonzaga Barrie, who had nursed in the Crimea and would later nurse the dying Nicholas Wiseman for a month before his death, was named superior. However, in 1865, shortly after he became Archbishop of Westminster, Henry Manning sought to remove the Sisters of Mercy from this hospital, and from the convent attached to it, so that he might install the French Sisters of Charity whom he wished to bring to London. In the end he did not succeed, although the hospital itself was closed from late 1866 to late 1868.

While neither the Bermondsey Annals nor Clare Moore's extant letters fully explain this painful three-year episode, the letters of Florence Nightingale from August 1865 to November 1868 frequently decry Archbishop Manning's presumed plan and his treatment of the sisters at the hospital. The Bermondsey Annals simply note that "On November 18th [1867] Sister Mary Gonzaga Barrie returned to this [Bermondsey] Community after having spent eleven years at the Hospital of Saint Elizabeth which she had been sent to found in the year 1856, and where she had held the office of Mother Superior for ten years" (2:[127]). Apparently Mary Gonzaga's voluntary departure from the hospital community was the compromise that resolved the issue, and allowed the other sisters to continue to serve the hospital when it was reopened in 1868. Under these circumstances, it is not surprising that in Lent 1867 Clare Moore became severely ill. Presumably she was suffering a flare-up of her old tendency to pleurisy—brought on by the winter weather, overwork, and worry.

Despite all this, Clare was a solicitous and generous correspondent, and many of her autograph letters are preserved in the Archives of the Sisters of Mercy, Bermondsey. What strikes the reader immediately in the letters to her sisters is her good sense and affection. While still in Turkey in 1856, she writes from Scutari to Mary Stanislaus Jones in Balaclava, to ease the latter's worry over the little opportunity she had for Mass or confession while working near the front (the Irish Catholic chaplain in Balaclava having refused to serve the spiritual needs of the sisters who worked with Miss Nightingale): "You are a good old lady. . . . do not be the least discouraged about your not getting Confession or H[oly] Communion—remember, our B[lesse]d Lord can supply for all." When she finishes the letter the next morning, she writes: "Good morning, Miss Heathen—I ought not to be writing to an excommunicated old woman, ought I?" Mary Stanislaus was then about thirty-four! Like Catherine McAuley, Clare often signs her notes, "Your ever affectionate old Grandmother." On December 11, 1870, she writes to Mary Teresa Boyce in Brighton to congratulate her on the anniversary of her reception of the habit, and of the founding of the Sisters of Mercy (December 12): "We have set many favourite verses of our dear Foundress to music and we shall have them sung after supper with great glee—I wish you could come up to spend the evening with your oldfashioned relatives in Bermondsey—should we not give you a hearty welcome!!" On October 21, 1871, a week after Teresa Boyce's feast day, and while Clare herself is, again, ill in the infirmary, she writes, "to offer you, though late, the most cordial and affectionate good wishes of all at Bermondsey, including pussy and the noisy sparrows."

Mary Austin Carroll quotes from numerous other letters of Clare Moore to her sisters. To one, Clare writes: "Experience is the best teacher—we grow wise through our blunders"; to another: "Do all with an upright intention, and never look back"; to yet another: "We are not angels; faults will be committed, mistakes made. Well, they can be remedied by quiet patience, and cheerfulness above all. Always look on the bright side of everything, and don't let anything trouble you"; and to one who was ill: "Yes, indeed, we must have pity on ourselves, and not believe in half the ghosts we see at such times. Did you think you were to march off to heaven and leave poor old me behind? No, truly; I will pray that you may be a jubilarian!" (*Leaves* 2:251–52, 260).[13]

Clare had a wise sense of administration, a compassionate attitude toward human nature, and a tender devotion to the poor. On October 30, 1856, she wrote to Bishop Grant: "Some of our poor children made their first Communion today and breakfasted here—will you give them your blessing—one poor child must stay out tonight 'till 12, selling onions in the street." In her younger years in Ireland she may have been rather quiet and reticent in conversation (as Catherine McAuley, Clare Augustine Moore, and Clare herself all claimed), but the letters and work of her later years show a remarkably outgoing kindness. For example, the Bermondsey Annals for 1874 report her personal involvement in establishing the Eltham house, nine miles from Bermondsey; this was to be her last major endeavor on behalf of the English poor:

On Sept. 23rd . . . Canon Wenham came, on behalf of the Bishop, to ask Revd. Mother if she would take charge for him of a Girls' Industrial School at Eltham, which had fallen into a very deplorable state, through neglect and mismanagement. . . . They went thither accordingly . . . and found the place in even worse condition than they had anticipated. . . . On Sept. 30th Revd. Mother, accompanied by Mother M.

Camillus Dempsey and Sister Francis, lay sister, went to Eltham to take possession and begin the new work. No words can describe the dirt and disorder that everywhere prevailed. . . . The place had been stripped of everything but 25 bed steads with their miserable straw mattresses and thread-bare coverings. There were 25 neglected looking girls, who had hardly a change of clothing. The house with everything in it was thoroughly cleaned and all necessaries speedily procured. The poor children were provided with good clothing and good food, and their numbers increased so fast, that in a very few weeks there were over sixty. (2:[222–24])

Clare was to live only ten weeks longer. As the Annals indicate "the labour and anxiety entailed upon her by this new work, together with the fatigue of the constant journeys between Bermondsey and Eltham in the unusually severe weather, soon produced fatal effects" (2:[225]). On December 2, 1874, she caught a cold, but claiming that "a cold doesn't last for ever," she rallied for a couple of days (Carroll, *Leaves* 2:268). However, on December 6, the doctor diagnosed her condition as pleurisy, and on December 14, 1874, she died in Bermondsey, in her sixty-first year.[14]

About a month before her death, Clare had written about the Eltham situation. In this letter one sees both her generosity and her sense of humor:

. . . we have been obliged to take from our own barely sufficient quarter's income almost half. We had to buy necessary furniture, and you would be amused at the scanty supply; clothing for the poor children, whose garments are next to rags; bed-covering and food, besides begging three months' credit from butcher, baker, grocer, etc.; afraid to light fire enough to warm us or cook our provisions. . . . One [child] only eight years old had stolen a perambulator with a baby in it; another a waterproof,[15] which she sold at a rag shop. What a blessing for these to be with us, but what an anxious charge for us! . . . I have been there six or seven times—no little cross to me, who do not care for travelling. We must accept our cross whatever it is made of, even a railway carriage. (quoted in Carroll, *Leaves* 2:268)

Like Catherine McAuley thirty-three years earlier, Clare had had her "surfeit" of traveling, but this letter also manifests the same enlivening zeal which had led Catherine herself to proclaim: "Hurra for foundations, makes the old young and the young merry" (Neumann, ed. 289). On November 14, 1874. Clare wrote to "My very dear Children" at Eltham, telling them she was thinking of "getting up a Library" for them: "I thought if we had a book for each of the children marked for the charges [assigned chores] they might be the first contributors and by degrees we might have a very large Library of nice books to read on Sundays. You could write me a few letters to tell me what you would like."

This cheerful attention to ordinary human needs was but one facet of Clare's rich personality. For the same Clare Moore who just a month before her death wrote to poor children, promising "nice books to read on Sundays," also authored three very important documents on the early history of the Sisters of Mercy and the life story of Catherine McAuley: a set of five letters about Catherine, which she wrote to her sister, Mary Clare Augustine Moore, from August 23, 1844 through August 26, 1845;[16] a long biography of Catherine McAuley entered into the Bermondsey Annals for the year 1841;[17] and the first compilation and publication of *A Little Book of Practical Sayings, Advices and Prayers of Our Revered Foundress, Mother Mary Catharine [sic] McAuley* (London: Burns, Oates & Co., 1868).[18]

In light of the apparent similarities and differences in these two interwoven lives, the specific purposes of the present book are two-fold: to offer an analysis of the quality of Florence Nightingale's friendship with Mary Clare Moore as revealed in their correspondence, particularly as this friendship influenced Nightingale's spiritual development; and to present—in nearly all cases, for the first time in published form—the forty-seven extant letters Florence Nightingale wrote to Mary Clare Moore, five she wrote about Clare to other Sisters of Mercy in Bermondsey, and two letters Nightingale's Aunt Mai Smith wrote to Clare Moore. These letters are supplemented by the ten known letters of Clare to Florence; by excerpts about Florence Nightingale taken from the Annals of the Sisters of Mercy in Bermondsey; and by excerpts from Clare Moore's and Florence Nightingale's other writings and correspondence which further illumine their friendship.

Two general purposes of the book are no less important. First, the record of this friendship presents aspects of Florence Nightingale's personality and character, especially her religious sentiments, which few were privileged to see and which often are not treated in her biographies. When Florence, an Anglican unenamoured of church-going, writes to Clare, a Roman Catholic sister, she reveals a side to her mind and heart that markedly supplements her public persona and the view of her presented by some of her critics. Here Florence is humble, grateful, selfless, and profoundly religious.

Second, Florence Nightingale's friendship with Clare Moore stands in sharp contrast to her brief but unfortunate relationship with another Sister of Mercy whom she met during the war in the East: Mary Francis Bridgeman, superior of the Sisters of Mercy in Kinsale, Ireland, and superior of the second group of Sisters of Mercy, fifteen in number and mostly Irish, who in December 1854 came to nurse in the Crimea, accompanied by Mary Stanley. It is a sad irony of biographical writing that attitudes and relationships that are strikingly negative in character, even though ephemeral, sometimes receive more detailed narrative attention than those that are positive and enduring. Florence Nightingale's several angry letters about "Reverend Mother Brickbat," as she occasionally called Mary Francis Bridgeman, have contributed to this emphasis.[19] Thus her conflict with the Irish contingent of Sisters of Mercy has enjoyed considerably more play in biographies about Nightingale and in published editions of her letters than has her life-long and mutually helpful friendship with Clare Moore and the Bermondsey Sisters of Mercy.

This friendship, though limited in its range of expression by Florence's work and illnesses and by Clare's work and community obligations, nonetheless flourished through correspondence, some of which is probably no longer extant or remains undiscovered. Clare apparently burned most of the letters Florence had labeled "Burn," as she assures Florence in one of her own extant letters. Florence evidently did the same, except for the series of Clare's letters in 1862 and one letter in 1858, although it is possible that more of Clare's letters to Florence may yet be found in the various Nightingale collections. The fact that Mary Clare Moore's correct name has not been generally known among Nightingale researchers—she has sometimes been called "Revd. Mother Bermondsey" or "Mother Mary Grace Moore"—may offer some hope that among the thousands of Nightingale papers in the British Library, in the Wellcome Institute's manuscript collection as well as its photocopies of the Sir Ralph Verney collection at Claydon House, and in the Nightingale Collection of the Florence Nightingale Museum Trust at the London Metropolitan Archives—to name the major sources I have examined—additional letters from Clare Moore may one day come to light.

Meanwhile, the correspondence presented in this book is more than sufficient to portray the nature and depth of their friendship. These letters also serve well to illustrate the personal lives and spiritual struggles of two highly influential women living in Victorian England: the one working to achieve military and governmental reforms; the other designing and implementing new church-related services for the poor; both bound together by their devotion to those who were neglected, by nursing and other skills they had learned the hard way, by mature Christian faith, and by their lively affection for one another, born of mutual respect and ease of communication. It is little wonder, then, that when Clare lay dying on December 12, 1874, Florence wrote: "It is we who are left motherless when she goes."

The Epilogue of the book seeks to summarize some of the effects of this friendship on Florence Nightingale's thoughts and feelings, especially on her religious views and aspirations. Specifically, it proposes that, while Nightingale's *Suggestions for Thought to the Searchers after Truth among the Artizans of England*, written mainly in the early 1850s and printed privately in 1860, represents her earlier religious views, certain strands of her religious convictions evolved during the decade of the 1860s, particularly her own personal hunger to live a truly spiritual and Christian life. I am very grateful to have had Michael D. Calabria and Janet A. Macrae's edition of *Suggestions for Thought* to consult in this regard.

Believing in 1868 that she was "only quite in the infancy of serving God," Nightingale turned in the early 1870s to a project she unfortunately never completed: the compilation, with her own extensive commentary, of numerous excerpts from the writings of religious authors, mostly Christian, many of them saints. The majority of these excerpts, which she had begun to collect in the preceding decade, were taken from books that Clare Moore had lent her. In this draft anthology, which she titled "Notes from Devotional Authors of [the] Middle Ages, collected, chosen & freely translated by Florence Nightingale" (BL Add. MSS 45841), Nightingale reveals a growing spiritual companionship with some of the most articulate representatives of the tradition of Christian spirituality, notably Saints Gertrude of Helfta, Catherine of Siena, Teresa of Avila, and John of the Cross. The collection as a whole—with all its inserted scraps and the penciled revisions of her commentaries—constitutes a remarkable revelation of Florence Nightingale's religious spirit at this stage of her life, a spirit influenced in no small measure by her friendship with Mary Clare Moore and by the books Clare had given her to read.[20]

Although the primary purpose of this volume is to present the extant correspondence of Florence Nightingale and Mary Clare Moore, I have quoted extensively from Nightingale's draft anthology. Together, the letters and the draft anthology contradict the unqualified claims that "Nightingale did not pray. . . . She read the Christian mystics, only to disagree with their passivity. . . . She did not believe, in any orthodox sense, in the Incarnation, the Atonement, Revelation, or Salvation through faith or works."[21] Nightingale's lifelong struggle to understand and to express the meaning of the Christian scriptures as well as to live an authentic Christian spiritual life was far more nuanced than such claims would allow. Her letters to Clare Moore describe this personal struggle, and are, for this reason alone, an important source of biographical insight.

# The Friendship of
# Florence Nightingale and
# Mary Clare Moore

FLORENCE NIGHTINGALE'S MEMORY of Mary Clare Moore's dependable service during the Crimean War (1854–1856) and of her calm manner throughout that searing experience remained vividly alive through all the years of their correspondence, until Clare's death on December 14, 1874, and long afterward. Moreover, in the years after their return from the Crimea, Clare's understanding and support of Florence—expressed through frequent letters, occasional visits, and loans of religious books—evidently responded to a spiritual need in Florence's life which she acknowledged to few. For this sensitivity on Clare's part Florence repeatedly expressed her gratitude.

Clare's practical, working faith—her not simply basking in the comfort of religious theory, but her *acting* for the good of other human beings—corresponded fully with Florence's own sense of the purpose of religious understanding. As she wrote to Benjamin Jowett in 1862:

The most religious mind I ever knew was that of a R. Catholic Revd. Mother, who was so good as to go out with me to the Crimea. After we came home I found her one day cleaning out a gutter with her own hands. I know she did it on no theory. I think she had much better have employed a man to do it, but that is what I mean by a true idea of religious life, and she the only R. Catholic too I have ever known who never tried to convert me. (BL Add. MSS 45783, f. 12)[1]

Later that year Clare wrote to Florence: "I have never felt restraint in speaking with you, or rather, you are almost the only one, dearest Miss Nightingale, to whom I can speak freely on religious subjects—I mean my own feelings on them" (LMA, HI/ST/NC2—V31/62).

The respectful affection that characterized their friendship was based on and sustained by several factors: among them, their mutual capacity for spiritual depth and mystical grasp of religious truth, not as an end in itself, but as a guide and motive for work and service; their common desire to lead a truthful, selfless life and to seek the will of God with a pure heart; and their thoughtful gifts to one another.

Indeed, their shared theology, their desire for purity of heart, and their mutual generosity created strong bonds between these two women whose lives were in other respects very dissimilar. After the Crimean War, Florence was generally an invalid who did most of her work from her bed or couch; Clare was a socially engaged public worker, managing a community and various works of mercy, walking the streets of London, and traveling to many parts of England. Florence was disenchanted with many aspects of church life and worship, whether Anglican or Roman; Clare was a devout practicing Catholic who treasured the sacraments, devotions, and ministers of her church. Florence was sometimes inclined to verbal expressions of paranoia, anger, and self-pity; Clare seems to have absorbed or transcended provocations to these feelings. Florence was, it may be conjectured, permanently scarred by the frustrations of her work, both in the Crimea and afterward; Clare, who endured far fewer directly personal disappointments and harassments, was not so damaged. Florence was, by nature, intense and passionately prone to see conflict and effrontery; Clare was calm and, from all that is known of her, more objective. As Florence herself wrote to Clare in 1865: "I am not like my dear Revd Mother who is never ruffled."

Yet it would be inaccurate and misleading to overdraw these apparent differences in their personalities and development, as if their life experiences and the influences on their lives had been the same, and only their reactions were different. In many respects, Clare's life was simpler and easier than Florence's. Moreover, Clare enjoyed one lifelong benefit that Florence seems not to have experienced, at least not to the same degree. She had the affectionate presence, and later the animating and consoling memory, of a woman—a mentor and model— whose virtues and mode of life were a constant source of support and inspiration to her: Catherine McAuley, the founder of the Sisters of Mercy. In fact, it is not fantastic to suppose that in some analogous sense, though severely limited by the lateness of their friendship and the diverse circumstances of their daily lives, Clare Moore became a Catherine McAuley to Florence Nightingale. This possibility may underlie Florence's claim, on December 15, 1863: "I have had all your dear letters. And you cannot think how much they have encouraged me. They are almost the only earthly encouragement I have."

In 1862 Clare evidently sent Florence a copy, perhaps her own original manuscript,[2] of the Life of Catherine McAuley that she had earlier composed and inserted in the Bermondsey Annals, as well as copies of some of Catherine McAuley's letters. On October 10, 1862, she wrote to Florence: "I am so glad you are pleased with our dear Revd Mother—as I always call her, she seems to be living to me—her words & ways come so often before me. One of the Sisters in Baggot Street copied out some of her *poetical* letters from foundations—they will amuse you & I venture to send them in their untidy state" (LMA, HI/ST/NC2—V25/62); and on October 13 she adds: "I forgot to say that you could keep our dear Revd Mother's life as long as you please, and our Rule . . . if I might be allowed to offer it" (LMA, HI/ST/NC2—V26/62).

In sending these documents, Clare may have hoped that the example of Catherine's life and the reading of her words might help Florence to overcome her discouragement and bitterness about the inactivity in the War Office's work of reform, following Sidney Herbert's death in August 1861.[3] With shrewd insight Clare wrote on September 17, 1862: "our dear Foundress used to say Mercy is more than charity—it adds forgiveness of even the worst ingratitude to the benefits bestowed" (LMA, HI/ST/NC2—V23/62). To forgive was very difficult for Florence, especially at this time when her memory of the injustices she had seen and of the reforms that had been needed in the Crimea—and were still needed more generally in the military—was so vivid, and her determination to see them addressed so great.

## A Shared Theology

In her penciled drafts, written about 1872–1873, for the projected anthology of religious writings that she tentatively titled "Notes from Devotional Authors of [the] Middle Ages"—and which may be regarded as a later development of some of the ideas originally presented in her *Suggestions for Thought*, printed privately in 1860—Florence Nightingale sets forth the main strands of her evolving personal theology, her "Stuff," as she called it. Here she repeatedly explains that the earth has been designed according to God's will (plan), as revealed in laws which humans can and should discover with God's help; and that true religious communion with God is to live and work in respectful alertness and fidelity to these laws, ever seeking, through research and genuine prayer, to know them more precisely and act upon them more thoroughly. In one of her drafts of a Preface to this proposed anthology, she writes:

Positivism is thus the handmaid of mysticism—by Positivism meaning the truth that God acts by universal Law—by Mysticism meaning personal communication with God. For we don't wish for a false communication with God but a true one. And the true one must be based on the manner of His acting, i.e. His character. In this sense, therefore, Positivism is an initiatory doctrine—not an antagonistic one—to true religion. . . .

. . . We are told that the religion of Law must be dull.

Why?

Because its idea of prayer is the same as that of the highest Christians—viz. that it is to be a means of bringing our will to God's, not His to ours?

Litanies (did we know more, should we not call them irreligious?) are to tell God what to do, to teach God. Whereas we think prayer is for God to tell us what to do—to teach us, which He does by His laws. (BL Add. MSS 45841, f. 30)

## Earlier in this same draft Preface she says:

"The idea is God"—or at least the most practical way of living with God is living with ideas—not merely thinking about Ideals, but doing & suffering for Ideals. . . . if, as Christ said: he was the "bread of life," our religious feeling is not 'bread' for our *lives* it had better not be there at all. If we make no "provision for the *permanence*" or the embodying in real actual life of our spiritual Ideal, we had better have none. If we live our lives apart from our Spiritual Ideal, & keep the Spiritual Ideal for Sundays or for prayers, it is like people who go to hear Bach's Passion Music at Westminster Abbey, & think their enjoyment devotional feeling. . . .

If these Mystical feelings are true, must we not have them *always*, inspiring *all* our work?

An "Ideal" is a poor thing unless it be the Ideal of every minute. . . .

. . . And how much more must this be the case with the spiritual Ideal! People who have not the courage or the perseverance of their Ideal end by having no Ideal at all. . . .

The "mystical" state—by which we understand the drawing near to God by means of—not Church or Ceremony but—the state in which we keep, through God's Laws, our own soul—is real & should be permanent. The "ecstatic" state is unreal, & should not be at all.

The "mystical" state is the essence of common sense if it be real; that is, if God be a reality. For we *can* only act & speak & think through Him; and what we need is to discover such laws of His as will enable us to be always acting & thinking in *conscious* concert or co-operation with Him. We cannot conceive that this, the very best gift we *can* have, can be the gift of arbitrary caprice on the part of our Almighty Father. But if we find out that He gives us 'grace'—i.e. the "mystical" state, in accordance with certain laws which we can discover & use—is not that a truth & common sense?

These old Mystics [[of the 13th through 16th centuries]],[4] whom we call superstitious, were far before us in their ideas of God & of prayer—that is, of our communion with God—in their knowledge of who God is—in their understanding of His character, in short.

Where they failed was supposing this world not to be what God has given us to work upon.

There will be no heaven unless we make it.

And it is a very poor Theodiké which teaches that we are not to 'prepare' *this* world—but only to 'prepare for' another.

Must we not 'possess' God here, if we wish to 'possess' Him hereafter? (BL Add. MSS 45841, ff. 11, 15–18)

Such thoughts had been forming in Florence's mind as early as July 1862, when she wrote to Jowett in response to his enquiry about the "Stuff":

I think I could teach it *viva voce* to a few working men. What I am so afraid of is that even if anybody would listen to it, it would lead to nothing but a philosophical school, not a religion. I should like to say to them—now it does not signify in the least whether you believe this or the reverse, unless you put it into practical truth in your lives. . . .

If I were what I was 8 years ago, I would have a Working Men's Children's School . . . to teach them all the laws of Nature (known) *upon this principle*, that it is a religious act to clean out a gutter and to prevent cholera, and that it is not a religious act to pray (in the sense of asking).

I have such a strong feeling that he who founds a Soldiers' Club (to keep them out of vice) is doing more than he who teaches abstract *religious truth*, that I would not teach "the Stuff" if I could do anything else practical—but I can't now. . . .

This is not to say that I consider the Stuff a *pis aller* [[a last resort]]. In as far as it says a grain of truth about the Character of God, that surely has immeasurably more importance than anything else.

I speak for myself—if it were not for the Character of God, I should shirk work. I could not go on for the sake of mankind doing the immeasurably little I can for them, if I did not believe myself part of a plan by which God is doing the immeasurably much for them. . . .

. . . Now nothing but a study of the Character of God cd. make one think that still one's little work was part of the infinite plan to bring everyone to perfect happiness, and that His is the only plan by wh. it can be effected—therefore I think the study of His character must always be of the first importance. . . .

I would not be supposed to mean that the cleaning out of the gutters is to be all our religious acts. I [[mean]]⁵ that might be some manifestation . . . of our feelings toward our Creator, some "religious" service, in short, whether a *form* of religious service I know not. . . .

. . . I don't want the "Stuff" to enter anyone's mind without its having for a result to settle what to say to God, and I am sure I cannot do this, at least for others. I don't want the Stuff to enter anyone's mind without improving his life.

I always recur to the *working* religious orders, as being the only people who have said, that is what we think God says to us. We are going *to do it*.

Now the only satisfactory result of this (or of any) "Stuff" would be to do something like that. The most religious mind I ever knew was that of a R. Catholic Revd. Mother, who was so good as to go out with me to the Crimea. (BL Add. MSS 45783, ff. 7–11)

Clare Moore shared Florence Nightingale's belief that authentic devotion to the will of God manifests itself in work on behalf of the needy, not simply or primarily in private expressions of religious faith. As one of Catherine McAuley's earliest associates, Clare had developed a religious conscience akin to hers. The founder of the Sisters of Mercy had always believed that the public works of mercy in which the sisters were engaged—"the service of the poor, the sick, and the ignorant"⁶—while deriving strength and character from the depth of their prayer and meditation on the life of Jesus, possessed an urgent priority which not only superseded that of their religious exercises, but, in fact, gave depth and honesty to those private devotions. In a handwritten essay which has come to be known as "The Spirit of the Institute," Catherine wrote:

We learn by visiting prisons and hospitals, and by reconciling quarrels what misery there is in the world, and come thereby to have a greater esteem for our vocation . . . and all the occupations which our holy state enjoins, so far from being any occasion of remissness, that on the contrary they help to keep us more carefully on our guard and to excite us more and more to virtue and perfection. . . .

. . . if a great reward has been promised to such as administer to the corporal wants and miseries of their fellow beings, what may we not justly hope for those, who being constantly engaged in the spiritual instruction of the ignorant, which is far more important, add to it also whatever temporal relief and comfort they can procure by all the exertion in their power. . . .

We ought therefore to make account that our perfection and merit consists in acquitting ourselves well of these duties, so that though the spirit of prayer and retreat should be most dear to us, yet such a spirit as would never withdraw us from these works of mercy; otherwise it should be regarded as a temptation rather than the effect of sincere piety. It would be an artifice of the enemy, who transforming himself into an angel of light would endeavour to withdraw us from our vocation under the pretence of labouring for our advancement. We ought to give ourselves to prayer in the true spirit of our vocation, to obtain new vigor, zeal and fervor in the exercise of our state, going on with increasing efforts so that we may say with holy Job—"If I go to bed to sleep I will say, when shall I rise again, and in the morning I will be impatient until the evening approaches" (Job 7.4) [7]

Clare Moore, who carefully preserved this manuscript in the Bermondsey archives, shared Catherine McAuley's belief in the priority of actions of mercifulness. On October 13, 1862, in one of the handful of her extant letters to Florence Nightingale, she writes of her visit to two sick families on her way home from transacting business with Thomas Grant:

I went to St. George's Church this morning to bring home my writing to the Bishop . . . on my way back I felt I must go out of my way to see a poor family; the children have been obliged to stay from School on account of small pox—five had it—one died—a dear little child of six—her younger sister greeted me by pulling out from a dreadful piece of rag a halfpenny for the poor—"for Katie's soul!" I could not well describe their own wretchedness, for the father has been in a dying state for months. We had five shillings to give them—a small fortune—but I could not help feeling it was the dear child's selfdenial & faith which drew me there, for I hesitated to add to my walk—already very long for me.

We then went on to a poor young man in the last stage of consumption, his only child of two years old lying at the foot of his bed in small pox of the worst kind, his poor wife making sacks, or rather unable to make them on account of the child's illness—poor man, he was very ignorant & inattentive to religion—now full of joy having received all the Sacraments. It is a great pleasure though a sad one to be devoted to the Service of the Poor. (LMA, HI/ST/NC2—V26/62)

Elsewhere in her writings, Clare explicitly or implicitly says that the test of authenticity in one's religious faith and devotion lies in humbly doing the work that needs to be done for the sake of one's neighbors in this world, especially the most vulnerable and needy. In notes for her lecture to the Bermondsey community on the first Sunday of November 1870, she writes:

Now perfection does not consist in sitting with our hands before us and saying we wish to be like our Lord, or in merely fulfilling the ordinary duties of the day; for had we stayed in the world, we might have taught, or swept, or dusted as we do now. It matters little how much we do, if we have not *humility*. . . .

. . . If we only look at the example of our Lord we shall see in Him everything (if we might use the word) which could be called obliging. He—God—was at the beck and call of everyone—to cure this one of disease—to raise that one to life—He truly fulfilled His own sacred words—"I am in the midst of you as one that serv-

eth." Even when worn out with labours, He thought not of himself but of others &
forgetful of Himself gave His assistance & relief.

We may also draw from our Divine Lord's miracles a very practical lesson, viz.:
to employ the talents & abilities God has given us, for the good of others, not for
ourselves. We do not find our Lord working a miracle to supply His own wants,
but those of others; in the same way we must be glad to employ our abilities for
the service of our neighbour. . . .

. . . Our divine Lord could have spent His hidden Life in those higher works of
art and have attracted the admiration of thousands,—of the whole world, we know.
He could; but He would be employed in labour of the hardest kind.[8]

Living in a religious community where she experienced the daily
joy and help of the Mass was, in Clare's view, clearly a benefit Florence
did not and could not enjoy. Yet Clare made no fundamental distinc-
tion in her assessment of their mutual capacity for union with God. In
her October 13, 1862 letter to Florence, she says:

I wish we could meditate as we ought—I might add, I wish I could meditate at all;
it is such a confusion to be full of distractions during the brief space one can give
to prayer—but it is also a comfort to feel that our poor efforts are joined with the
prayers of God's holy ones by our union with them in the Church, to feel still more
that our prayer is united with that of our most loving Lord & that this union with
Him becomes stricter and more intimate each time we approach the Sacraments,
especially the Holy Communion. I have so often wished you could have that joy—
you who are working so much harder than I do for God's sake—& making such
great sacrifices—but I do feel that our Blessed Lord will give you that union with
Himself which your heart seeks for so sincerely & I do pray for you constantly as
well as I can. (LMA, HI/ST/NC2—V26/62)

Evidently Florence Nightingale never seriously considered becoming a member of the Roman Catholic Church, although hopes
to this effect and rumors about its likelihood arose among Catholics
and persisted, as a consequence of her early friendship with Henry
Manning and Catholic admiration of her after the Crimean War. Clare
Moore was undoubtedly aware of these suppositions, but there is no
evidence that she was ever an active agent in promoting such a decision on Florence's part. On the contrary, as Florence herself wrote
to Benjamin Jowett in July 1862, Clare was "the only R. Catholic . . . I
have ever known who never tried to convert me" (BL Add. MSS 45783,
f. 12). Yet some letter of Clare to Florence in late 1862—perhaps that
of October 13 noted above, or another one not yet discovered—caused
Florence pain on this point. On December 28, Clare wrote her a not altogether clear letter responding to some complaint on Florence's part

having to do with a communication from Bishop Grant. Clare says: "although since I have spoken with yourself I felt that your faith in our Divine Lord's mysteries was the same with mine—yet it was a comfort to me that you should *say so*—& though apparently you are not a member of the Church, your most upright will & heart makes you such, for if you knew of any thing more you could do to please our Heavenly Father, you would do it unhesitatingly." Later in the same letter Clare says:

I have made a long explanation, and I have not said all I wish—yet I hope our Divine Lord will make you know it all, for it is before Him I think about you & that my heart seems to be with yours. In loving & labouring for Him you are far before me, though I have my advantages over you in the grace of the Sacraments & the direction of His holy Church. I think of you so much at Holy Communion & I wonder what is your faith there—but I am not asking nor do I wish you to tell me anything of yourself—it is very clear that our Lord loves you very much & that you love Him with your whole heart & mind & strength—I wish I could say I did, & I am trying with His grace to do better—

Again I must ask you to believe that our good Bishop meant kindly—he is most kind & anxious for the welfare of all—but probably some one said those things which caused him to write so—

I feel ashamed to take up your time and I beg pardon for many failings in your regard, but not for failing in love and gratitude. (LMA, HI/ST/NC2—V31/62)

Although researchers have only the correspondence and other writings of Florence Nightingale and Clare Moore as firsthand evidence for comparing their theological views, these seem sufficient to demonstrate the overall similarity, not of their doctrinal beliefs point for point, but of their personal assessment of the fundamental imperative of Christian faith. This imperative was, in their view, active, wholehearted work for the good of one's neighbor, lovingly undertaken in fidelity to God's will, and dependent for its efficacy not finally on human exertion but on the indwelling Presence of God.

Thus Florence could write, in the draft Preface to her proposed anthology of excerpts from "Devotional Authors": "Mystical books are for hard-worked people like you & me who have not time to read them—not for young ladies & old gentlemen who have nothing else to do" (BL Add. MSS 45841, f. 6). In a later draft of this Preface, in a gloss on Jesus' claim, "My meat is to do the will of him that sent me and to finish His work" (John 4.34), she says:

What is this but putting in the fewest & most striking possible words the meaning of all real Mystical doctrine; namely that, for all our actions, all our words, all our thoughts, the food upon which they are to live, the life in which they are to have their being, is to be the indwelling Presence of God, the union with God (that is, with the Supreme Power of Goodness & Wisdom,) in performing every act of our lives, from the highest prayer to the most every-day need, such as cleaning out a drain. (BL Add. MSS 45841, ff. 13–14)

Cleaning out a drain or gutter had become for Florence a concrete and worthy symbol of "doing the business of the world" (see her letter to Jowett quoted earlier), and, as she argued in a later footnote on the above passage, "an essential part . . . in a divine scheme, as much as a priest administering the sacrament to a dying man" (BL Add. MSS 45841, f. 33).

Like Catherine McAuley, Clare believed in "The Perfection of Ordinary Actions" (the title of a chapter in the original Rule of the Sisters of Mercy). She was convinced that "the perfection of the religious soul depends, not so much on doing extraordinary actions, as on doing extraordinarily well the ordinary actions and exercises of every day" and that "actions the most trivial, when accompanied by [a 'pure and upright intention'] become valuable and meritorious of Everlasting Life" (Rule 5.1 and 5.3, in Sullivan, ed. 300–301). Speaking of the hundreds of children in their poor schools in Bermondsey, she urged her sisters to remember that "We are their mothers while they are entrusted to us, and they should find us such by our kindness and earnestness in teaching them" (Carroll, *Leaves* 2:266). Her fidelity to the work at hand—whether it was copying or translating letters for Bishop Grant, writing a children's play, opening a hospital or an orphanage, building an infants' school for poor young boys, transforming a wretched, run-down industrial school for girls, or cleaning a gutter—explains the steadfast helpfulness Florence found in her in the Barrack Hospital at Scutari, as well as Florence's later willingness to accept Clare's friendship and with it Clare's long-term influence on her own spiritual development.

## A Common Desire for Purity of Heart

On the surface, Florence Nightingale's life and Clare Moore's appear vastly different, except for the two years they spent together in the Crimea. Yet, ironically, it is the intention underlying their going to and serving in the Crimea in the first place that best explains the essential similarity of their lives after 1856. For despite all that may be claimed about Florence's thirst for power or her need for fame, whether during or after the war with Russia, her surviving letters to Clare Moore reveal a much more fundamental desire for selflessness and a persistent yearning for true peace of heart, as the necessary foundation for any authenticity in her reform efforts.

Clare's daily life both before and after the Crimean period was chiefly occupied with administering a religious community of women dedicated to the instruction of poor children and adults, the visitation of the sick poor, and the sheltering of girls and women in distress—and hence, with all the ecclesiastical, financial, and other business arrangements needed to establish and support these works of mercy. Florence's life after August 1856 was chiefly occupied with writing reports and proposals on military practice, medical and nursing training, workhouse management, and sanitary conditions at home and abroad—and hence, with all the research and governmental, parliamentary, or other communications needed to bring these reforms to fruition. Still, despite all their diverse activity they had a common desire for purity of heart, for what Florence called "seeking first the kingdom of God," and a common recognition that, finally, after their own full labor, the worth of what they were trying to do rested wholly on God. This desire for purity of heart gradually deepened in Florence over the course of her friendship with Clare.

For beneath Florence's occasional public and private sputterings, harangues, exaggerations, and impatience, just as beneath Clare's generally calm and peaceable manner, was the goal they shared: to do God's will in this world, selflessly and truthfully, without regard to their own personal loss or benefit. As Florence wrote to Clare on September 8, 1868:

Alas! dear Revd Mother, you ask after me. I feel as if I was only quite in the infancy of serving God. I am so careful & troubled & have such a want of calmness about His work & His poor—as if they were *my* work & *my* poor instead of His. . . . I know you pray for me. *Offer me* to Him, that His will may be done in me & by me. I feel, you know, that, if I really believed what I say I believe, I should be in a "rapture" (as St. Teresa calls it) instead of being so disquieted. And therefore I suppose I don't believe what I say I believe.

I *think* I seek first the kingdom of God & His righteousness. But I am sure I don't succeed in being filled with His righteousness. And so I suppose that I regard too little Himself & too much myself. I should like to try to listen *only* to His voice as to what He wishes me to do, among all His poor. . . .

It is 11 years last August since I have been a prisoner more or less to my room.

It is 7 years last August since Sidney Herbert died. You know what a terrible break up that was to what we were doing in the War Office. Still God has pleased to raise up the India work & the Poor Law work since that. And I ought to be very thankful.

But it does me good, I assure you it does (tho' I can't bear myself), if I think that your dear Reverence is offering me to God, that whatever He wills may be carried out in me.

I have so little of the only true patience.

Perhaps it was the contrast in their exterior manner that, in part, drew these two women to admire one another. Some time after Thomas Grant's death in June 1870, Clare wrote to a sister in another Mercy community: "Our late revered bishop said we never rightly become friends with some people till we have had a good quarrel with them" (Carroll, *Leaves* 2:259). There is no record of a "good quarrel" between Florence and Clare, but there were certainly the makings of one: in Scutari, the treatment of the Bermondsey sisters by Florence's good friend Selina Bracebridge (who, according to the Bermondsey Annals, "was always averse to Catholics, and who lost no opportunity of annoying the Sisters and hindering their being employed in Hospital work" [1:255]), and Florence's unbridled language about Mary Francis Bridgeman, who was, after all, an Irish member of Clare's own religious order; and in later years, Florence's delay, at least in 1862, in responding to Clare's requests to visit and her tendency to rail against Archbishop Manning (when even she recognized that Clare didn't like her "to say these things").

Clare undoubtedly had sympathy for Florence's temperament. She may have seen in her something of her own earlier behavior, which she had overcome only with great effort. Her sister, Clare Augustine Moore, writing after Clare's death, says of her as a child: "At that time she was chiefly remarkable for a very violent temper, great beauty with a very decided appreciation of that fact, & great anxiety about who & when she would marry," and she notes that "Till nine years old she was educated a Protestant & was quite a little bigot." Clare Augustine also reports an instance of her sister's "animal courage" as a young girl:

Our hall door was being painted when the workman ran to a public house for a draught of porter & did not return so hastily. Meanwhile [Georgiana], being then just turned of eleven & lately recovered from fever, wishing to fetch something from her bedroom went up stairs, when just as she got halfway up the last flight to the second floor she perceived a coarse-looking woman with a large bundle about to descend. Without [fear Georgiana asked][9] the occasion of her being there and what she carried & the woman daunted by her firm tone and demeanour dropped a collection she had made of all our outdoor wraps, shawls, furs & mantles which hung on racks on the upper landing. The child then told her to pass down & the woman passed her very meekly as she stood still halfway up the flight of stairs with her back to the balustrade. She saw the wretched creature out of the house & shut the neglected hall door before returning to the room where her mother sat at work. When she was remonstrated with on the danger she incurred of being thrown over the balustrade (which had the woman half the courage of the child she might have done & escaped with her prey for there were no street police then) she coldly answered, she "did not mean the house to be robbed."[10]

As a young Sister of Mercy in Dublin, Clare had been, according to her sister, "very reserved" and "avoided giving an opinion." Yet when another young sister expressed a scruple about not being able, while she was serving table, to follow the reading that accompanied meals, Clare simply answered: "I never attempt it. I always fix my attention on my present duty."[11] This realism grew as Clare matured, and with it greater kindness and deeper personal peace. The letters of the last two decades of her life are remarkable not only for their affectionate encouragement, but also for their calm acceptance of human realities. While she shared Florence's idealism and worked hard to achieve high goals in her own life and in that of her community, she was nonetheless patient and charitable toward human frailty, whether in herself or in others. She did not often complain about people, and she did not speak ill of them. She was, in this respect at least, unlike the Florence who appears in some of her letters written during and after her experience in the Crimea War. Yet Clare understood the positive wellsprings from which Florence's impatience arose, and she appreciated the more-than-ordinary strains that Florence's life—as the young superintendent of the female nurses in the war hospitals, and later as a working invalid—placed upon her. Thus Clare wrote to her in September 1862:

I have thought of you so much. Your hardest task seems to me the knowledge of so much misery, vice & degradation. The thought seems to blacken every thing & almost every one—& we begin to forget there is any thing good or any thing pleasing to God in the world. . . . I am sure you do look on the bright side of the picture—only I judge by myself, for it makes me very sad when I hear or k[now] of wicked people—& I know & hear of so little. Our divine Lord's Heart was oppressed with a[nguish?][12] because our sins were always in His sight. May He help you in your efforts to remove those [these?] evils. (LMA, HI/ST/NC2—V23/62)

Clare Augustine Moore says of her sister: "She was wonderfully courageous and strictly truthful. I never knew her to be guilty of the smallest lie or even of an equivocation. She always detested detraction and even while a child would reprove it very sternly in grown persons as well as in her companions."[13] This difficult combination, of truthfulness and charity manifested in a peaceable demeanor, may have been what most attracted Florence to friendship with Clare, and what most led Clare to respect, sympathy, and love for Florence.

After Clare's death Florence called her "the purest soul I ever knew" (LMA, HI/ST/NC1—75/2). But Clare also saw in Florence a deep struggle to achieve purity of desire, a certain fierce—and unalloyed and elemental—innocence of heart. Thus in 1862 she assured Florence: "I do indeed pray for you—it is all I can do—and I trust your desire is the prayer our most loving Lord now asks from you— you have spent yourself for His sake—you cannot have the energy of younger days. This is no comfort—as I well know—but there is the comfort of seeking to do God's will & trusting that He will come to heal and help us in His own good time" (LMA, HI/ST/NC2—V25/62). Florence evidently did not feel this "comfort" within herself. In January 1865 she acknowledged to Clare both her desire and the absence of feeling associated with it: "The greatest blessing is to know & *feel*, as you say, that one is doing His will. I never am in full possession of this *feeling* tho' I have nothing left at all in this world, except to do His will. But I have not deserved that He should give me this feeling which is the greatest strength of all." Were Clare's letters of this period available, one would probably find her pooh-poohing any talk of deserving, and instead stressing the value of Florence's desire to serve God, over that of mere feeling, whether present or absent.

## Mutual Generosity: Clare's Gifts to Florence

Gift-giving cannot of itself create friendships. But when the gifts indicate understanding of another's need and symbolize a desire to help, they can reveal the potential grounds for friendship, and can later deepen it.

Florence Nightingale fully and humbly acknowledged the gift Clare Moore gave to her in the East in 1854–1856: the gift of dogged, reliable, uncomplaining work in the Barrack Hospital at Scutari. In her most frequently published and quoted letter to Clare—the letter written on April 29, 1856, as Clare, still weak from fever and pleurisy, departed for home—Florence says: "Your going home is the greatest blow I have had yet. . . . You were far above me in fitness for the General Superintendency, both in worldly talent of administration, & far more in the spiritual qualifications which God values in a superior. . . .what you have done for the work no one can ever say." She signs this letter: "ever my dearest Revd Mother's (gratefully, lovingly, overflowingly) Florence Nightingale." In a private letter to Lady Cranworth, written earlier that year, Florence listed Clare and two others (Mrs. Roberts and Mrs. Shaw Stewart) as "my main-stays through this terrible work" (BL Add. MSS 43397, f. 75). Seven years later, on October 21, 1863, still mindful of Clare's "conduct in the Crimean War," Florence wrote to her: "I always felt you ought to have been the Superior & I the inferior. . . . I always felt how magnanimous your spiritual obedience in accepting such a position . . . & how I should have failed without your help. . . . I always wondered at your unfailing patience, sweetness, forbearance & courage under many trials peculiar to yourselves, beside what was common to all. . . . I wondered so much that you could *put up* with me—that I felt it was no use to say to your face, either then or since, how I admired your ways."

But Clare's gift to Florence in Scutari was not only her patient, imperturbable manner, but her intelligent hard work in grim and unprovided circumstances. The legendary shortages of food, clothing, bedding, and medical supplies that greeted their arrival at the Barrack Hospital on November 5, 1854, and persisted for months afterward, as well as the constant need to provide clean beds, clean clothing, fresh dressings, rations, and extra diets to the incoming wounded, constituted a situation in which "sweetness" was plainly not enough. At various stages of their two-year ordeal, Clare stuffed pillows (to serve as beds), superintended the washing of soiled laundry, managed some or all of the linen stores, managed the Extra Diets Kitchen, had charge of Florence Nightingale's own private stores, from which necessities were purveyed when army-issue supplies were non-existent or locked in red tape, and—at night—tended the sick, wounded, and dying soldiers in the hospital wards.

The Bermondsey Annals, in Clare's own handwriting, report that "The Barrack was built round a square, the courtyard in the centre being 220 by 194 yards. The Corridors and Wards surrounding, of one flat and part of two other flats occupied by the patients, whose number in the winter of 1854 to 1855 varied from 1900 to 2500, were filled with beds which, measured across with the intervals between them, extended over a space of from three to four miles" (1:[226]). It was in this setting that Clare and two of the four other Mercy sisters who had come from Bermondsey, Mary Stanislaus Jones and Mary de Chantal Hudden, set to work after their arrival. And when, as the Bermondsey Annals record, the "crowds of wounded men in the worst stage of destitution" began to arrive on November 9, after the fatal engagement at Inkerman, "The Sisters were now almost overworked preparing the wards and beds, and, according as the wounded arrived, helping them, dressing their wounds & comforting them" (1:[228]).

The Bermondsey Annals for 1854, 1855, and 1856 devote over eighty pages—all in Clare Moore's handwriting, but narrated in the third person—to recording the experiences of the Bermondsey sisters in Turkey and the Crimea, including transcriptions of letters they had written home or to one another when they were separated by new hospital assignments. Occasionally these accounts focus on Clare's work. For example, citing Florence Nightingale's own reports after the war (which she prepared using Clare's records), the Annals note that, in the three months from November 10, 1854 to February 15, 1855, Clare issued from Florence's own store " 'Cotton Shirts, 10,537— Flannel d[itt]o, 6823—Drawers, 4607—Socks and Stockings, 6173'— other Hospital Clothing, furniture & utensils in proportion"; and in the Extra Diets Kitchen, where Clare "had the sole charge of supplying demands made by Medical Officers, Nurses, etc.," the average daily issue was " 'Twenty five gallons of Beef Tea—Fifteen gallons [of] Chicken Broth—Forty gallons of Arrowroot & fifteen of Sago—240 quarts of Barley Water:—275 portions of Rice Pudding: 40 Chickens— 21 Bottles of Wine—though sometimes even 100 bottles of Port were mixed in the proportionate quantity of Arrowroot in one day.' Jellies, rice, etc. were also abundantly supplied" (1:[248]).

Such labor was the daily gift Clare gave in Scutari—foremost and directly, to the wounded men; but also, secondarily and indirectly, to Florence herself, who was six years her junior, whom she had never known before their meeting in Paris on October 22, 1854, and yet who bore the central and public burden of their collective nursing assignment. Clare recognized from the start that Florence "had her difficulties, the nurses were discontented & troublesome, the Medical Officers opposed her having care of the sick, [and] the Purveyors were unwilling to place the Hospital Stores & Clothing at her disposal," so she quietly did the many jobs she was assigned, even when, at first, "the bread was sour & often mouldy, the meat was of the worst description & divided in a manner only fit for animals," and "the want of water was a suffering greater than can be expressed" (BA 1:[227–28]).

In the years after Scutari, Clare's gifts to Florence were far less daily and exhausting, but none the less thoughtful. Chief among them were her frequent letters of encouragement, her occasional visits, and the numerous religious books she loaned for Florence's reading. While only ten of Clare's letters to Florence have so far been discovered— all but one of them in the London Metropolitan Archives—Florence's letters to her frequently refer to letters Florence has received from "dearest Revd. Mother." In December 1863, she describes Clare's letters as "almost the only earthly encouragement I have"; and in December 1866, as "almost the greatest earthly support I have." In October 1864, Clare evidently offered to nurse Florence in her home in London or to send a sister to nurse her, for Florence writes on October 31: "I never can forget your kindness. To think of your being willing to leave your most important post to come & nurse only me, or to send me one of my dear Sisters. I feel as if I never could, God only can, tell you how grateful I am. But I must not take advantage. I am not looking out for a Nurse, as you heard. I shall 'scrat on' as well as I can, as long as I can work at all. And then I shall go, please God, to where I mentioned to you." (Florence here refers to her plan, later abandoned, of going to a ward in St. Thomas Hospital when she could no longer work.)

In a letter to Clare that was apparently never posted, Florence recalls their Crimean days and names the particular aspect of Clare's presence that she found most helpful: "I always felt with you that you understood without my telling you, from similar experience at home, a great many of my trials which none of my other ladies did & which I never told to you or to any one. And I cannot tell you what a support your silent sympathy & trust became altho' I never acknowledged them. I felt that you knew the real difficulty of my position" (Vicinus and Nergaard, eds. 194). Perhaps it was Clare's capacity to understand more than was said in words and her ability to convey this wider sympathy that Florence most treasured in her letters. As she told Clare on September 3, 1864: "You see I always count upon your sympathy & tell you our doings—tho' I think you are the only Revd Mother in the world who would, or could, hear them with indulgence." When Clare worried earlier that year, during a lull in letters from Florence, that her own letters might be troublesome, Florence wrote in June: "No: dearest Revd Mother, you can't think that your letters would ever 'trouble' me. And I know how little time you have to write which makes me all the more grateful. On the contrary, they are the greatest refreshment I have. But answering is often beyond me." In September 1868, after a gap in Clare's correspondence due to her illness, Florence wrote: "I was so thankful to see your handwriting again."

That Clare occasionally visited Florence at her residence in London is evident from both sides of their correspondence. When Clare was dangerously ill with "pleurisy and inflammation of the lungs" in April and May 1858 (BA 2:[13]), Florence wrote: "I need not tell you how happy it would make me to keep you *here*, quite quiet with one Sister—and I do not think you would see much more 'of the world' here than at home. But I am afraid you would not go anywhere but to a Convent." Clare did not accept this invitation, but went instead to St. Elizabeth's Hospital in June to regain her strength.

Presumably she visited Florence before 1862, probably more than once, but in September 1862 they were again planning an overnight visit. Clare writes: "You are too good to think of the Chapel for me, but unless I had a companion or that I remained a longer time, I think I should prefer hearing Mass in spirit, as I did when I was with you, although I should have been very glad if I could have got to Mass without going out." She then adds: "You made me feel a little proud because I am to go to you again. I was afraid I had been too stupid & tiresome—for I had had a cold just before, & my teeth were bad." Toward the end of this letter Clare says she will come to visit after September 24, and she will then be able to tell "how grateful I am both to you & your household, & how afraid that I made myself too much at home for their ideas of Nuns who of course ought to walk up in the air!" (LMA, HI/ST/NC2—V23/62). Perhaps Clare still had not visited Florence by October 28, for she writes: "I have been longing to hear when I may go to you"; however, her comment in this letter about Florence's mother may suggest that she had recently met her at Florence's: "She seemed to be so like yourself, full of tender pity for all and seeking to do good to all" (LMA, HI/ST/NC2—V27/62). On November 19, Clare playfully asks again: "Am I doing wrong in writing to remind you of your promise to allow me a little visit sometime during this month—I got afraid that your guardian angel did not think I was trying to be good enough & so he would not put it into your mind to send for your Ever loving & grateful Sister M. Clare" (LMA, HI/ST/NC2—V28/62). Probably a visit occurred in late November or early December, because a year later, on December 15, 1863, Florence writes from 32 South Street: "I am here, as you see (my brother in law's house—where you were so good as to see me last year—to think of that being more than a year ago) & have been here a good bit. But I have had all your dear letters."

Obviously, Clare appreciated the rare opportunities to visit as much as Florence did, but she respected the peculiarities of Florence's health, life-style, and work schedule. Like other friends of Florence, she persisted in offering and asking to visit, and in sending letters that were sometimes not answered. Throughout 1863, Florence was heavily engaged in "harassing" and "heart-breaking" work, most of it on sanitary reform in India. Probably there was no visit that year. On January 3, 1864, reminding Clare that "You are busy too at these seasons," Florence offers an indirect apology: "Dearest Revd Mother, if I did not ask you to be so good as to come to see me, if you could—it was not because I see other people at Christmas time, but because I am so busy. We are always very busy for two months before the meeting of Parl't [[Parliament]] (in February). But this time much more than usual, because of the India business." She acknowledges that when they were in London recently she was able to see her sister Parthenope for only "10 minutes; & my good brother in law, who is one of the best & kindest of men, not at all—nor his children." Toward the end of the letter, she writes, almost wistfully: "I am glad you are going to Sister M. Gonzaga. It will be a great comfort to her. What a comfort it would be to me."

But later that year, on September 3, Florence wrote from Hampstead:

This is the first day, the very first day that I have felt I was getting ahead of my business, instead of my business getting ahead of me, miles, miles ahead, over my head & ears.

You see I am come down here. And would you come & see me? This next week I have less to do. Would you come on Monday, 5th? or would you come on Friday, 9th? I know well how much you have to do—& that it is always difficult, sometimes impossible, for you to find even one hour. And should that be the case next week, I will ask you to name your own time any day these next two months. And I will say sincerely if *I* can't manage it.

I would send a carriage for you, whatever time you said. And I could give my dearest Revd Mother a bedroom, & one for a Sister, if more convenient to bring one, & if you really can arrange to sleep.

And I would ask you in that case to have the carriage to fetch you so as to be here that I might see you a little before your dinner, which I think is 4 o'clock—& that I might see you the next morning, before you started, if you *can* sleep.

I know that it is a great favour for a Revd Mother to grant. But it is not the first time *my* Revd Mother has granted me favours.

Presumably this visit took place. They may have discussed, among other things, Clare's need to borrow copies of the recipes Alexis Soyer had used in the Crimea, for on September 24, Florence writes: "I was never able till yesterday to hunt in my stacks of papers for these things. . . . your friends may keep them as long as they like. And pray do not *you* trouble yourself with them."

Whether Clare visited Florence again is not known. Although their extant correspondence over the remaining ten years of Clare's life does not refer to such occasions, it certainly does not rule them out. Florence's continuing gratitude for Clare's sympathy and support is repeatedly expressed. On September 8, 1868, she writes: "I often pray God that He would give me the opportunity of being able to show you the gratitude I feel to you. But you see He does not."

The most permanently helpful gifts Clare gave to Florence were the many spiritual books she loaned her. Throughout the mid-1860s, Florence frequently refers to these books and quotes from them in her letters to Clare. Many of the excerpts in her draft anthology of "Notes from Devotional Authors" no doubt came from the books Clare had sent. The fact that most of these authors were Catholics writing after the Reformation, or saints particularly honored in the Catholic mystical tradition, may explain Florence's reluctance to give their names in her anthology. An intriguing paragraph in her draft Preface rationalizes this omission: "I do not dare to mention the names of the works from which these Notes have been translated—some for the first time into English. But, if any one reads them, & any one wishes to know the authors, I shall be happy to publish a key" (BL Add. MSS 45841, f.3). In a later revision of this paragraph Florence wrote: "Notes have been translated—some of them for the first time into English—from Spanish & other mystical writers. It has been thought that they might have a fairer chance of acceptance now, if the names of their authors were not at first given" (BL Add. MSS 45841, f. 3).

Florence was grateful for and admired what these writers had said, but in a manuscript intended for eventual publication, in the un-ecumenical climate of her day, she was unwilling to demonstrate pub-

lic appreciation of "Catholic" thinkers. Fear of renewed efforts to convert her, or of renewed claims that she was already converted, may also
have motivated her silence about the names and background of those
who had proved to be such a source of comfort and inspiration in her
own religious life. As it turned out, the anthology was never published.

Among the books Clare loaned her were the lives and writings
of Saints Catherine of Siena, Catherine of Genoa, Gertrude of Helfta,
Teresa of Avila, John of the Cross, Francis de Sales, Francis Xavier, and
John of Avila. That these books brought Florence insight and consolation is clear from her letters to Clare, especially over the years 1863 to
1868. In December 1863, she writes: "I have felt so horribly ungrateful for never having thanked you for your books. S. Jean de la Croix's
life I keep thankfully. I am never tired of reading that part where he
prays, for the return for all his services, Domine, pati et contemni pro
te. I am afraid I never could ask that. But in return for very little service, I get it. . . . I have always, with all my heart & soul, offered myself
to God for the greatest bitterness on my own part, if His (War Office)
work could be done." A year later, in January 1865, she is still reading this French edition of the life and writings of John of the Cross:
"I am quite ashamed of keeping S. John of the Cross so long. . . . I
am often afraid that I have not so much as entered into the first Obscure Night. Yet that Obscure Night does seem so applicable to me. I
have never found S. John of the Cross mystical or fanciful. On the contrary, he seems to have had the most wonderful practical knowledge
of the ways of God in the heart of man." On December 17, 1866, she
writes to thank Clare for praying for her on the feast day of St. John
of the Cross (November 24): "I think my troubles are always greater
at Christmas than at any other time, tho' I do desire humbly to follow
in the footsteps of S. John of the Cross. And I constantly read over the
Life & some Extracts I made from what my dearest Revd Mother sent
me. And I thank her from the bottom of my heart for offering me to
God on the day of S. John of the Cross." In the following March, after
"an attack on my Chest, so that for 17 nights I could not lie down"
and "could scarcely get on with my work," she once more refers to the
consolation this Spanish reformer and mystic is to her: "I read over &
over again your little S. John of the Cross—& many Extracts which I
made from your books."[14]

Apparently Florence found in John's life and writings not only
a way to interpret her own loneliness and dark discouragement, but

also the courage to continue to press for needed reforms, even in the face of direct opposition and official evasion. The Calced Carmelite leaders in Spain who obstructed the new Discalced Carmelite reform that Teresa of Avila and John sought to establish were Florence's War Office and Parliament. John's persistence in doing what he took to be the will of God was a constant beckoning to her own self-sacrifice—as she interpreted her present vocation.

In a similar way, Florence drew support from the books on Catherine of Siena, Catherine of Genoa, and Teresa of Avila that Clare loaned her. These three women had also embarked on great reform efforts despite considerable opposition from men in positions of authority: Catherine of Siena, to reform the church and the papacy, despite the contrary advice and influence of powerful cardinals; Catherine of Genoa, to reform medical care of the sick poor, especially the plague-stricken and lepers, contrary to the attitudes and current practices of hospital workers; and Teresa of Avila, to restore Carmelite convents and monasteries to contemplative prayer and strict simplicity of life, after decades, if not centuries, of widely accepted relaxations on the part of Carmelite and other church leaders. Each of these reformers was an ardent, hard-working, prayerful woman whose spirit of humility and steadfast service of God and God's people inspired Florence.

On December 15, 1863, she wrote to Clare: "I return the life of St. Catherine of Genoa. I like it so much. It is a very singular & suggestive life. I am so glad she accepted the being Directress of the Hospital. For I think it was much better for her to make the Hospital servants go right than to receive their '*injures*' [[insults]], however submissively—much better for the poor Patients, I mean." Ten days later, on Christmas Eve, she reminds Clare: "May we all believe in Our Lord's 'goodwill towards man'—the same today as 1863 years ago. As S. Catherine of Genoa says, when she thinks that Dieu s'est fait homme in order to make l'homme into Dieu. I like those words so much—that belief in perfection."[15]

In the same letter, Florence quotes a long prayer of Catherine of Siena in which Catherine offers her bodily sufferings "pourveu que je voye la réformation de la saincte Eglise." Florence says: "I often say that prayer," and then notes: "St. Catherine did not see the reformation she desired. And I shall not see the reformation of the Army. But I can truly say that, whatever I have known our Lord to desire of me,

I have never refused Him (knowingly) anything. I can feel the same now." In her January 23, 1865 letter to Clare, while commenting on the near-death experience of Cardinal Wiseman during his last illness, she recalls "what St. Catherine of Sienna calls God's withdrawing from the body & restoring to the body the soul 'tousiours avec plus grande peine une fois que l'autre.'" She concludes this letter, again quoting Catherine: "Dearest Revd Mother, I thank you always 'tousiours une fois plus que l'autre' for your goodness in writing to me."[16]

Evidently Clare had lent Florence a large-sized, two-volume French edition of the *Life* and other writings of Teresa of Avila.[17] Florence's letters repeatedly apologize for her delay in returning these books. In December 1863, she says: "I am quite ashamed to keep Ste. Thérèse so long. But there is a good deal of reading in her. And I am only able to read at night—& then not always a large, close-printed book. Pray say if I shall send her back. And I will borrow her again from you perhaps some day." A month later, she writes: "I meant to have written you a long letter about St. Teresa (of whom I have still the first Vol.). . . . But I really cannot. The books I returned looked as if I had been reading them through the back, as those impostors of clairvoyants pretend to do. But I assure you I did not make those nibblings in the backs—nor the cats!" By January 1865 Florence had returned both volumes. Although she does not quote from Teresa of Avila in her letters, several excerpts from Teresa's writings appear in her "Notes from Devotional Authors."[18] One can presume that she found in Teresa a kindred spirit, a companion whose passionate temperament, arduous undertakings, and down-to-earth prayer gave her solace in her own difficult work.

Numerous references to other books Clare had loaned her appear in Florence's letters. In January 1864, she says: "I try to remember what St. M. Magdalen de Pazzi says, that she finds God even more in the most distracting business than in prayer. Alas! the time I find him *least* is, when I am quite exhausted with His business & can neither read nor pray. That is the hard part of my lot, I think." In the same letter she says: "I sent you back St. Francis de Sales, with many thanks. . . . I like that story where the man loses his crown of martyrdom, because he will not be reconciled with his enemy. It is a sound lesson. I am going to send you back S. Francis Xavier. His is a life I always like to study as well as those of all the early Jesuit fathers. But how much they did—& how little I do."[19]

By June 1864 Clare had already sent a new batch of books, two
of which Florence was now returning "with a great parcel of thanks."
Her critique of these books, by seventeenth-century French writers on
the spiritual life, reveals something of her own rhetorical preferences:

Boudon's P. [[Père]] Seurin is indeed as full of demons' tricks as a pantomime.
But I like very much certain parts of it, particularly the chapter on *pureté de coeur*,
Chap. 2, Book 3—& all that he says about P. Seurin's not only submitting but offering himself to the humiliation of madness, (if the will of God,) is so striking, it puts
it quite in a new light. There is so much that is morbid in a solitary imprisonment
like mine, with sickness into the bargain—so much that is quite unavoidable—that
I am glad to look upon it, as P. Seurin, as a humiliation to which one should offer
oneself willingly, if it presents itself clearly in the path of God's will.
  But I like the other book of P. [[Père]] Lallemant's better still. How curious is the
absolute brief compressed precept of the part by P. Seurin, when compared with
Boudon's flowery pantomime. I think it far more striking. Indeed I think P. Lallemant & all that we have of P. P. [[Pères]] Rigoleu & Surin so singularly sublime—in
this—that there is not an effort to dress up their high & noble doctrine or to make
it attractive with flowers of rhetoric. It is as brief & dry as it is possible to have it.
And I should never be tired of reading P. Lallemant. I am so much obliged to you
for letting me keep them so long.[20]

By early 1865 Florence was reading Clare's copies of Frederick
Faber's *Spiritual Conferences* and a biography of John Olier.[21] She found
Faber's essay on "Wounded Feelings" especially interesting. On February 3, in a postscript, she says: "I did not tell you that there is much
in Dr. Faber's book which you were so good as to lend me, that I like
very much indeed—tho' it is impossible not to laugh when he says so
quaintly, 'Religious people are an unkind lot.'"[22] On February 28, she
writes: "I am very much obliged to you for sending M. Olier's life. I
shall read it with the greatest interest." In July she thanks Clare "for
your St. Gertrude, which I read with the greater pleasure, because it
comes from my dear Revd Mother. I hope I shall be able to profit by
it. For indeed it contains great lessons."[23] In December 1865 she sends
"Many thanks for the Advent Meditations."[24]

By August 1868 she is back with the Spanish mystics, reading a
French edition of the writings of Blessed Juan d'Avila.[25] She says she
regrets the pain felt by the Mercy community awaiting the re-opening
of Saints John's and Elizabeth's Hospital on Great Ormond Street, "but
as B. Jean d'Avila says, how are we to prove the 'modération et tranquillité de notre esprit' except under 'contrariétés'?" Three weeks later
she tells Clare: "I have not learnt yet the first lesson of His service. 'Je

m'en vais à Dieu: cela seul doit m'occuper,' as B. Jean d'Avila says—
meaning, of course, in serving Him."

Considerable research remains to be done to analyze in detail the
contents of the religious books Clare loaned to Florence, and to discover, in Florence's unpublished letters and notes, their further influence on her thought and aspirations. At the very least, the character
of these books and of her known references to them reveals the inner
depth of religious hope and struggle that underlay her public work
throughout the decade of the 1860s, and, perhaps, until her death in
1910. To no one other than Benjamin Jowett, with whom she also shared
her religious views, was Florence so explicit about her spiritual desires
and efforts as she was to her trusted "Revd Mother." In the trust she
felt with Clare, she was able to let down her old "War Office" guard,
to explore her own religious feelings, and to enter deeper Christian
realities of the heart.

## Florence's Gifts to Clare

Over the twenty years of their friendship Florence Nightingale's many,
many gifts to Clare Moore, and to the Bermondsey Sisters of Mercy,
were equally thoughtful and generous. During their common ordeal in
Turkey and the Crimea she was always solicitous of their health and
spiritual needs—perhaps more so because they did not make an issue
of these matters or ask for special consideration. She knew their desire
for the sacraments, and, as some of her letters of this period show,
she facilitated arrangements for them whenever she could. Moreover,
when Mary Martha Beste was severely ill in Balaclava with "Crimean
fever" (probably typhus), Florence herself sat up at night. Her letter to Parthenope on April 22, 1856—part comedy, part melodrama—
records one such occasion:

Would not you like to see me hunting rats like a terrier-dog? Me!
  Scene in a Crimean Hut
  Time midnight
  Dramatis Personae—
  Sick Nun in fever perfectly deaf
  me the only other occupant of the hut
  except
  rat sitting on rafter over sick nun's head

& rats scrambling about.
Enter me, with a lantern in one hand & a broom-stick in the other (in the Crimea,
terrier dogs hunt with lanterns in one paw & broom-sticks) me, commonly called
"Pope" by the Nuns, makes ye furious Balaclava charge, i.e. the light cavalry come
on & I am the Russian gun.
   Light cavalry ensconces itself among my beloved boots & squeak—
Desperate Papal aggression.
   Broom-stick descends—enemy dead—"Pope" executes savage war dance in tri-
umph, to the unspeakable terror of Nun (& of himself)
   Slain cast out of hut unburied. (Goldie, ed. 260–61)

Earlier, when a bigoted pamphlet appeared in England, complaining
about the Bermondsey sisters' serving under the nursing authority
of Miss Nightingale and decrying—inaccurately, as to the facts—the
alleged impropriety of "Catholic Nuns transferring their allegiance
from the Pope of Rome to a Protestant Lady,"[26] the Bermondsey sisters,
especially the playful Mary Gonzaga Barrie, began to call Florence
"Your Holiness" and "Pope." Florence entered into the joke and designated Mary Gonzaga "my Cardinal." These titles continued to enliven
their correspondence long after the war was over.

   It is possible that Florence visited the Mercy convent in Bermondsey more than once, before she became virtually house-bound. Her
first and only known visit to Bermondsey was, however, singularly
touching: the quiet morning hours she spent there on August 7, 1856—
the day she landed at Portsmouth on her return from the Crimea. This
visit was, to Clare and the community, a privileged gift of trust and
affection. On July 23, Florence had written to Mary Gonzaga Barrie
from Scutari: "I shall not stop in London at all, but go to Bermondsey
to call upon Revd Mother & then sneak quietly out of the way. . . . I
shall come to see dear Revd Mother, not on business but on pleasure,
& shall have but a flying taste of her, both for her sake & my own."
The Bermondsey Annals for 1856 record this visit:

Revd. Mother returned from Boulogne in time to begin the Retreat with the Community, on the second day of which, August 7, Miss Nightingale accompanied by
her Aunt [Mai Smith], came directly upon her arrival in England to see the Sisters & take some hours rest. It was a joyful & yet a sad meeting, for they felt that
she who had been so benevolent & full of tenderness for her fellow creatures, &
whose religious sentiments approached so nearly to their own, was not to enjoy
with them the rewards & happiness which they possessed as members of the True
Church. But her friendship continued & still goes on undiminished, as her kind
communications and frequent presents testify. (1:[309])

In the years that followed, Florence's gifts to Clare and the community in Bermondsey were very generous: vegetables, fruit, meat, port wine and brandy, Christmas greens, flowers, and artistic or instructional materials for the children in the poor schools. Over and over—in Florence's letters, in Clare's, in the Bermondsey Annals—one finds reference to the most recent delivery of gifts. Florence often received baskets of food and flowers from friends or from her parents at Embley or Lea Hurst, and then passed some or all of these on to Clare and the Mercy sisters. In May 1858, when Clare was sick, Florence wrote to Liz Herbert: "I must thank you my own self for your grapes. . . .'Revd Mother' (of Bermondsey), whose name you will remember, has been and is dangerously ill. She has had all her food from here, and your grapes have almost kept both her and me" (BL Add. MSS 43396, f. 59). The reference to "all her food" is undoubtedly an exaggeration, although the food Florence sent was certainly finer than the Bermondsey community could or would have bought for themselves.

Clare herself wrote in May 1862: "you know I never can tell you how grateful I feel, and when the Sisters see all you send me they can only say, dear Miss Nightingale, how good she is! Shall we not pray for her—and that is truly the only way in which I can thank you—only I would like to be beside you and tell you so—yet that would be but a passing joy—and we must look on beyond this earth" (LMA, HI/ST/NC2—V16/62). In July, Clare thanked her for "the nice pictures and the book of Prints" which "the Sisters as well as the children will value" (LMA, HI/ST/NC2—V19/62), and in October, "for all your kind presents last Friday" (LMA, HI/ST/NC2—V26/62). On May 15 of the following year Florence wrote to her mother: "Do you think you would make up a fine hamper of home produce for Revd Mother of Bermondsey & send it to me by Tuesday. . . . I generally buy her a flitch of bacon two or three times a year. A leg of pork, apples, nothing comes amiss. What I buy is not so good as what you send. And plenty of your American flowers to make show for her children on Whitsunday—please" (Wellcome Institute, photocopy, MS 9000/102). On Christmas Eve that year, Florence sent honey from Malta for the children, noting that "A little child, tasting this honey, said, If I were a bee, I would live at Malta."

Each year until Clare's death, and for long afterward, the gifts came: in 1864, "6 bottles of Port Wine" for a sick sister, brandy for the same purpose, "five little books," including a copy of the "*Combattimento . . .* a great favourite with me,"[27] and boxes of food for the sisters at Saint Elizabeth's Hospital; in 1865, "a copy of the (English) S. John of the Cross" for the thirty-third anniversary of Clare's clothing in the Mercy habit (January 23, 1832), a copy of "the Manual for the Sisters of Charity," and "three other manuals"; in 1867, "a few little things, which I *insist* upon Sr. Gonzaga's making you eat yourself," and perhaps "some wine"; and in 1868, "a little offering for your poor." Sometime in the late 1860s, during one of Clare's bouts of illness, Florence wrote to her sister Parthenope: "Revd Mother of Bermondsey has been dangerously ill with Pleurisy & Fistula. [Mrs. Bracebridge says Manning will kill her.] All my Embley things, including flowers, have recently passed on to her—besides Gunter's Turtle Soup. She understands that I shall never forgive her, unless she becomes as fat as a Lord Mayor with time & soup" (Wellcome Institute, photocopy, MS 9003/21).

As her portrait testifies, Clare was not built to be "as fat as a Lord Mayor"—and she may not have cared for turtle soup—but she did recover. In fact, despite another serious illness in 1870, she was actively involved in direct service of the poor until two weeks before her death. But on April 13, 1873, Mary Gonzaga Barrie died of typhus contracted while visiting a sick family. Her death was a deep personal loss to Clare, and to Florence, who wrote to Mary Jones: "A very dear friend of mine who went thro' the Crimea with me died at Bermondsey, after 4 weeks' struggle. . . . And tho' I could not wish her back, O no, yet 19 years of troublous recollections pass away for me with her" (Vicinus and Nergaard, eds. 344).

A year and a half later Clare Moore herself was dying—of pleurisy and of over forty years of unrelenting work on behalf of the poor and needy. Florence's gifts to the community at this time were utterly simple and practical. On December 12, 1874, two days before Clare's death, Florence wrote to a sister in the community: "Perhaps she is at this moment with God. But this we know: She could scarcely be more with God than she was habitually here: & therefore all things are well with her, whether she be there or still here:. . . . I send 2 or 3 Eggs for the chance. And I have got a little game which I send: for I think you, & perhaps others, must be so worn out with watching & sorrow that perhaps you cannot eat. And you know she would wish you to eat." Three weeks after Clare's death Florence wrote to Mary Aloysius Booker, the acting superior of the Bermondsey community:

My Aunt, Mrs. Smyth, whom you may remember at Bermondsey, & who was with dear Revd Mother at Scutari, has written to me, sending £5, which she wishes me to lay out in any manner that would be most satisfactory to dear Reverend Mother. I thought of it as a contribution to her Monument at Kensal Green. Then I thought her heart was very full of the children at Eltham, & that a contribution to them would be most satisfactory to her. . . . But you will know best; please tell me— (quoted in BA 2:[241–42])

It is not known how Mai Smith's gift was spent, but given the sisters' great new expense of running the dilapidated industrial school for girls at Eltham, the money probably went for food and clothes for them, not for a monument for Clare Moore's grave at Kensal Green Cemetery.

On December 1, 1856, Florence had written to Clare: "Please don't brush out any more gutters (like a cat) this cold weather," and two years later she had written of Clare to Liz Herbert: "she is . . . a woman in whom is no one earthly failing that I ever could discover" (BL Add. MSS 43396, f. 59). But Clare had kept on cleaning out gutters, both literally and figuratively. And through their friendship with one another they both came to realize a little more deeply that earthly failings, whether visible or not, are not the whole story of individual human lives. As Clare once wrote to Florence, "When the ways of Providence become clear to us, we shall see how blessed were the hardships we repine at, how they have saved souls who would have lost themselves had they not been so afflicted" (LMA, HI/ST/NC2—V27/62).

\* \* \*

In her extant letters to Clare Moore, Florence Nightingale refers twice to Saint Gertrude the Great of Helfta (1256–1302), whose writing she was reading in a book Clare had lent her. Gertrude, whom Nightingale identifies as a Benedictine, was a nun in the Cistercian- or Benedictine-inspired monastery in Helfta, Germany. Her life there coincided in part with the lives of two other women saints living in the Helfta monastery: Mechtild of Hackeborn and Mechtild of Magdeburg.[28]

Gertrude of Helfta evidently wrote several works; of these, two Latin texts of spiritual theology attributed to her have survived: *Legatus divinae pietatis* (*The Herald of Divine Love*) and *Exercitia spiritualia* (*Spiritual Exercises*).[29] Florence Nightingale as well as Clare Moore would have encountered Gertrude's *Legatus* not by this title, but in a translation of the manuscript assembled by Johannes Lanspergius in the early sixteenth century and published under the title *Insinuationes divinae pietatis.* This work, often also translated as the *Life and Reve-lations of St. Gertrude,* contains five books, including a biography of Gertrude in Book One and other writings by and about the women of Helfta. Gertrude's account of her mystical experiences is Book Two, although her other writings and insights evidently contributed to the compilation of the other books.[30]

Florence Nightingale's most numerous references to Gertrude appear not in her letters to Clare Moore, but in her draft anthology of "Notes from Devotional Authors" (BL Add. MSS 45841), where she frequently quotes Gertrude and comments approvingly on her theology.[31] The passage from Gertrude's writing that struck a special chord in Florence's spirit is the brief chapter 17, "The Divine Self-Restraint" (as titled in Barratt's translation of the *Legatus*). In her draft anthology, Florence does not transcribe the precise setting of Gertrude's question, but only Gertrude's account of God's response. In the opening scene of the passage in the *Legatus,* as Barratt presents it, Gertrude relates that

One day, when I had washed my hands and was about to go to eat, I was standing around with the other members of the community and noticed the brilliance of the sun shining with all its strength. This gave me pause for thought, and I said to my-self, 'If the Lord who created that sun and at whose beauty it is said that the sun itself and the moon are filled with wonder, the Lord who is also a consuming fire, were really and truly with me as he so often presents himself to me, how could it possibly be that I could lead my life among human beings with such a chilly heart, and so devoid of human warmth, or rather, so full of evil?' (144)

Then follows the response Gertrude heard, as Florence transcribes and comments on it:[32]

*The Lord*: How should I shew myself Almighty save by the power of hiding myself in myself wherever I am, so that I be neither known nor perceived, except in as far as is convenient according to the circumstances of place & time & person? For since the beginning of the creation of heaven & earth until now, in the whole work of redemption, I have used far more the cunning of my love than the power of my might. And it is still the guidance of this same love which is shewn particularly in my patience, bearing with the imperfect until I bring them, still keeping intact their free will, into the way of perfection.

By a Benedictine nun
13th century

[It seems that, in a few words, the ways of God in history could not be better indi-cated.] (BL Add. MSS 45841, f. 67)

On the two folios that follow, Nightingale writes:

And is not this exactly what the Benedictine says has been God's course in history since the beginning? His plan is not to reveal Himself suddenly & completely by the "force of His power". . . . men are far from being unable even now to recognize the love of God, to try to imitate His goodness as far as they can:—but to understand him entirely? not yet. . . .

But the Benedictine is wiser than we are who wonder at these things. She says: how *can* God reveal himself except according to the *times* & to the man? And how marked it is that the attribute of a Perfect God is to reveal Himself, not by His power but by His love—that is, conducting men by their own powers or "free will," (as it is commonly called), to discover God, no matter how slowly. . . .

. . . The Perfect God (in whom there can be no contradiction, "neither shadow of turning") is educating man to be able to "see Him as He is." (BL Add. MSS 45841, ff. 68, 69)

In endorsing Gertrude's theological view of God's accommodation to human capacities as they evolve, Nightingale clearly focused on its universal application to humankind as a whole, and the gradual discovery of God's "laws" in the wide embrace of human history. But she was not unconscious of its particular personal relevance, as an explanation of her own spiritual and religious development: God's slow, patient education of her own imperfect self. By September 1868 she was well aware that she had not "learnt yet the first lesson of His service," and she was willing to admit to Clare that "I regard too little Himself & too much myself. . . . I *think* I seek first the kingdom of God & His righteousness. But I am sure I don't succeed in being filled with His righteousness."

That Mary Clare Moore's encouragement and guidance served to support and even to enhance Florence Nightingale's spiritual development during the decades of their friendship is evident in Florence's letters to her. Clare's example, advice, and prayer, as well as the character of the books she loaned Florence, apparently provided both the solace and the insight that, in part, enabled Florence to embark, during her semi-invalid years, on the least known of her accomplishments during those years: the deepening of her own spiritual life and the purification of her prayer. Her comment as Clare lay dying: "It is we who are left motherless when she goes," is a gracious summary of the effects of their friendship, a friendship often mediated through the wisdom and spiritual companionship of writers such as Gertrude of Helfta.

# The Correspondence
## 1855–1874

## Introduction

The friendship of Florence Nightingale and Mary Clare Moore covers a period of twenty years, from their first meeting in October 1854 en route to the Crimea to Clare's death in December 1874. Their extant correspondence covers a period of thirteen years, from 1855 to 1868. However, references in their letters to other correspondents indicate that the last date of the extant Nightingale-Moore correspondence does not signify the end of the correspondence itself, which clearly endured through Clare's final illness. Moreover, for at least three more decades Nightingale continued to correspond with other Sisters of Mercy who had worked with her in the Crimea. These letters show that the memory of her friendship with Clare—"now a Saint in Heaven"—remained deeply active in Nightingale's mind and heart, almost to the end of her own life.

The extant letters presented below have been arranged chronologically in six groups, framed according to the nature of the correspondence during each period: 1855–1859, 1860–1862, 1863–1864, 1865–1866, 1867–1868, and 1869–1874. All but three of the twenty-three letters in 1855–1859 were written by Florence Nightingale: twelve in 1855–1856 while she was in Turkey or the Crimea, five in October 1856 through January 1857, and three in May 1858; two were written by Nightingale's Aunt Mai Smith, and one (in 1858) by Clare Moore. Since all but four of these 1855–1859 letters deal with the Crimean War experience, they form a natural grouping; the four letters in May 1858 flow out of that experience as it might have been applied to proposed hospitals in Mauritius.

The correspondence of the years 1860–1862 is unusual for two reasons. The nine extant letters of this period were all written by Clare Moore, and all in 1862, there being no extant letters of Florence Nightingale from 1858 to 1863. However, Clare's letters imply the other side of the correspondence—which she was asked to "burn"—and indirectly reflect the "blackened" state of mind and heart Florence experienced after the deaths of Sidney Herbert on August 2, 1861 and of Arthur Hugh Clough on November 12 of that year.

The twelve extant letters in 1863–1864 were all written by Florence Nightingale (as was the rest of the correspondence presented in this volume). Despite Nightingale's heavy involvement in work for the Indian Sanitary Commission, these letters begin her more explicit and intimate sharing with Clare on religious and spiritual topics, prompted no doubt by Clare's loaning her some books by John of the Cross, Teresa of Avila, Catherine of Genoa, and Catherine of Siena, among others. The eleven letters of 1865–1866 continue these themes, but are also preoccupied in early 1865 with the illness and death of Cardinal Nicholas Wiseman and then later in the period with Archbishop Henry Manning's attempt to remove the Sisters of Mercy from Saint Elizabeth's Hospital on Great Ormond Street. The key Sister of Mercy in both of these events was Mary Gonzaga Barrie, Clare's longstanding friend and one of Florence's beloved companions from Crimean days.

There are seven extant letters from Florence Nightingale in the years 1867–1868, six to Clare Moore and one to Mary Gonzaga Barrie. These letters deal with the hospital situation, not fully resolved until late 1868; Clare's prolonged illness, in Lent 1867 and again in late 1868; Florence's successful and unsuccessful efforts to reform workhouse nursing; and her humble estimate of her own "infancy" in serving God. In the five years before Clare's death, 1869–1874, there is apparently no extant correspondence between Florence Nightingale and Clare Moore, though their correspondence evidently continued, for Florence notes elsewhere the death in April 1873 of her "very dear friend" Mary Gonzaga Barrie, and Clare, writing in October 1874, says that she "had a very kind letter from Miss Nightingale." These years end with two extant letters: Florence's heartbroken letter to an unnamed Sister of Mercy in Bermondsey on December 12, 1874, as Clare lay dying, and a second letter to Bermondsey, in early January 1875, forwarding Mai Smith's contribution toward a monument for Clare in Kensal Green Cemetery, London.

The extant correspondence of Florence Nightingale and Mary

Clare Moore is arranged below in the six chronological groupings just described, since these periods reflect the developing phases of their friendship itself and of the content of their letters. As the years pass, one sees the increasing mutual trust and helpfulness of the two correspondents as well as the growing depth of Nightingale's self-revelations and spiritual aspirations.

The first group of letters is preceded by an account of the events of late 1854. Florence Nightingale's extensive correspondence with officials, friends, and family in England, from November 1854 onward—as presented, for example, in the generous selections of her letters edited by Sue M. Goldie and by Martha Vicinus and Bea Nergaard—more than amply describes the harrowing and frustrating experiences she and those with her encountered as they nursed the sick and wounded in the Crimean War. The purpose of the somewhat extended introduction to the first group of extant letters to Clare Moore is not, therefore, to repeat Nightingale's vivid accounts published elsewhere, but simply to set the opening scenes of the friendship, and of the correspondence that followed, and to do so from the perspective of Clare Moore and the Sisters of Mercy from Bermondsey, as recorded in their own Annals.

On Saturday evening, October 14, 1854, Thomas Grant, Bishop of Southwark, came to the Convent of Mercy in Bermondsey to hear the sisters' confessions. Afterward, he told Clare Moore, the superior: "I have plenty of work for the Nuns now: to go and nurse the sick & wounded soldiers" (BA 1:[210]). Although Londoners were suddenly becoming aware of the disastrous lack of proper care of the sick and wounded in Turkey and the Crimea, the Bermondsey sisters apparently had not yet seen correspondent William Howard Russell's shocking dispatches from the Crimea in the *Times*. Grant asked for three volunteers, although he was not sure any of them would be accepted by the British government. If they were, he did not think Clare Moore should be among them, given her many responsibilities in Bermondsey.[1]

However, by late afternoon on Monday, October 16, the matter was settled: passports for five had been secured, and the party was scheduled to depart by train from London Bridge at 8:10 the next morning. Grant had sent three letters to the Bermondsey community that day: urging them to "provide warm clothing" and still thinking it "impossible to spare" Clare; recognizing that "the lot of those who go will be the more difficult"; and finally, after struggling with the question all day, deciding that Clare should go and promising to "bring the money before six this evening" (BA 1:[212–13]).

Peter Collingridge, the parish priest, bought "a coarse Railway wrapper & small travelling bag for each," and Grant, "fearing that the Sisters might not be allowed to wear the Religious Habit, wished them to provide some secular dress, but the only articles of apparel which could be procured were black net caps which they packed up in simple obedience," hoping never to wear them. Grant came in the evening—and wept. When he was asked for advice, the only words he could speak were, "Nothing, do the best you can" (BA 1:[213–14]). After he left, the community worked until midnight, packing their few articles of clothing and their prayerbooks in the small bags they would carry. The next morning, after Mass and breakfast, Clare blessed and embraced all those who would be left behind, and then the five set out: Mary Gonzaga Barrie,[2] Mary de Chantal Hudden,[3] Mary Stanislaus Jones,[4] Mary Anastasia Kelly,[5] and Clare herself. Clare was forty years old; the average age of the other four was twenty-nine.

They reached Paris late that night and were put up at the Hôtel Clarendon. On October 18, Clare received a telegram from Thomas Grant, asking them to wait there for Florence Nightingale. On October 20, he wrote again, saying that he had assured the government "there would be no difficulty" in the sisters' cooperating with "Miss Nightingale as Superintendent of the Nurses . . . provided the Sisters were free *as Nuns* to act under their own Superior. Of course, *as Nurses*, the Sisters have no objection to be distributed by her over the Wards (two Nuns at least being always together, although not necessarily both of the same Institute, e.g. you might allow one of your Sisters to be with a Sister of Charity)." In this letter Grant also gave his interpretation of the one restriction the government placed on their work: "Do not *introduce* Religion to any but Catholics, but if others speak do not be afraid to answer. When you can, suggest an act to the dying of Contrition, Faith, etc., but avoid beginning the subject of *controversy* with those who are not dying unless they are Catholics, to whom speak quite freely always. The regulations of Miss Nightingale specifies [sic] that you are not to introduce Religion to any but Catholics, and act very prudently in this matter." About Miss Nightingale herself, he noted parenthetically, without further comment: "She has been prayed for before now as being likely to become a Catholic" (BA 1:[217–19]).

Florence Nightingale and the party of twenty-eight nurses traveling with her from England arrived in Paris on Saturday, October 21. On the following day she visited the Sisters of Mercy, who found her "simple demeanour & unaffected kindness . . . a source of comfort in their new and trying position of being associated with Protestants & Nurses from public hospitals" (BA 1:[219]). Protestant-Catholic relations in England were, to say the least, strained in this period, following the restoration of the Catholic hierarchy in 1850 and several notable conversions to the Catholic Church in recent years.[6]

For her part, according to the Annals, Florence Nightingale "expressed her gratitude & satisfaction at the readiness with which the Sisters promised to concur with her and to take whatever portion of the work she might see fit to mark out for them, for she foresaw that in others she would not find the same compliance" (BA 1:[219]). She told them they would depart for Marseilles on Tuesday, October 24, and gave them a letter she had brought to them from Bishop Grant. Enclosed in it was a copy of the agreement he had worked out with the government. The full text of this agreement, addressed to Sidney Herbert, Secretary of State, is transcribed in the Bermondsey Annals:

St. George's Oct. 20, 1856

Sir,

Having learned that you are willing to include among the Nurses, now about to proceed at the expense of Government to the Military Hospitals in the East, a number of Sisters of Mercy, I have offered five of those under my spiritual care, and I now beg to express my acceptance for their guidance of the conditions which have been laid down as follows.

1. Her Majesty's Government having appointed Miss Nightingale to be Superintendent of the Nurses Department, it will belong to her Office to regulate all the Duties of the Nurses in the Hospitals, their employments, hours, places in the wards, & in general all that falls under the head of Hospital regulations. The Sisters of Mercy will therefore place themselves in these respects under her sole direction.

2. Inasmuch as the Sisters of Mercy or others depend on their respective Superiors in England & Ireland for directions in the matter of their religious duty, it will be requisite that one of their number be appointed by competent authority in this country to act as Superior in this respect while they are employed abroad.

The Superintendent of the Nurses will communicate with them through their Superior; and in the event of any of them being judged by the Superintendent incompetent to the duties of nursing, the Superior will at once intimate to her the cessation of her employment in the Hospital.

If the Superior, on her part, should find it necessary that any of their number should return to England, the Superintendent will arrange for her passage home.

3. As no one will be admitted as a Nurse in the Hospitals without the sanction of the Government, those who accompany the Superintendent from England will receive their approval from her; and any Sisters who may hereafter be sent will be approved as Nurses by Dr. Andrew Smith, if they are in London; or by a Medical Officer appointed by him in the neighbourhood of their residence if they are out of London.

4. The greatest caution being necessary on all hands, in the matter of religion, the Sisters of Mercy will hold themselves free to introduce such subjects only with patients of their own Faith.

I have already mentioned that the Sisters now proceeding through France with Miss Nightingale have been taken from the Convent of Mercy under my charge: and as the Sisters of other houses who may be required will be presented by their respective Superiors, I have endeavoured in this short space of time to communicate with them, and from the answers received, I have every reason to believe that they will fully acquiesce in these conditions.

(Signed) + Thomas Grant<br>(BA 1: [220–21])

As Florence Nightingale soon realized, she was fortunate that Clare Moore was designated the superior of all the Catholic sisters in this first contingent. As she eventually also discovered, she was fortunate that Clare and her sisters had their wits about them in Paris: they had visited the Sisters of Charity at St. Roch's Hospital and, on their advice, purchased "cases of surgical instruments used in the Military Hospitals, which afterwards proved a most valuable addition to their little stores & recommended them to the Medical Officers under whom they worked at Scutari" (BA 1:[222]).

The Norwood Sisters arrived in Paris on October 23. They were five additional Catholic sisters recruited by Bishop Grant from an enclosed religious congregation, called the Sisters of the Faithful Virgin, who ran an orphanage in Norwood in the Diocese of Southwark. They were, consequently, often called the "Norwood Sisters." Thus the entire party traveling to Turkey with Florence Nightingale numbered thirty-eight, of whom ten were Catholic sisters. The party departed from Paris by train for Lyons on October 24.[7] From Lyons they took a steamboat on the Rhône to Avignon, and from there traveled by rail to Marseilles, arriving on the night of October 25. After some delay they embarked on the *Vectis* on Friday evening, October 27. Beyond Malta, where they had stopped on October 30 to take in coal, they encountered the worst storm of their voyage: "the Deck Cabins were washed away, & the vessel all but lost." Clare, who had been severely ill since they left Marseilles, was now "full of grief for the Sisters whom she had left in Bermondsey, and for those who were sharing her trials" aboard ship (BA 1:[225]). However, the wind soon abated and they reached Constantinople on Saturday, November 4. The five Norwood Sisters "accepted the invitation of the Sisters of Charity at Galata to remain with them until they recovered the fatigue of the voyage," but the five Sisters of Mercy chose to press on, crossing the Bosporus to Scutari with Florence Nightingale.

Their landing at Scutari, the desolate condition of the Barrack Hospital and their quarters, the lack of provisions, the fresh arrival of hundreds of wounded men, and their work during the first month are all graphically described in the Bermondsey Annals. These pages, recorded after the war by Clare Moore, are notable for their precise detail, their expressed affection for the soldiers, and their restrained references to difficulties. They begin with the landing at Scutari:

The news of this uncommon arrival brought crowds of spectators, through whom our weary Sisters passed carrying their scanty luggage, scarcely able to climb the steep hill from the landing place to the Barrack. . . . This immense building (the Turkish Barrack), capable of accommodating about five thousand men, had been generously given by the Sultan as a Depot for the English Troops. He also gave the Hospital belonging to it, large enough for two thousand, and his own Summer Palace, "Haida Pacha," which was occupied as a Hospital in January following. . . . The quarters allotted to Miss Nightingale were in the North West Tower (there was one at each angle of the building) consisting of a Hall with some rooms adjoining, one of which was for Mr. & Mrs. Bracebridge, a very small room or closet for Miss Nightingale, a large room for the twelve Hospital Nurses with a Matron, and another room for the ten Religious. There were two rooms above; the first floor was given to seven members* [*Footnote in the Annals: Eight left England, but one was so ill that she was obliged to return at once—and, three or four weeks later, two were sent back by Miss Nightingale] of a Society formed by a Miss Sellon under the name of Protestant Sisters of Mercy; the second floor to six Nurses from St. John's Training Establishment; they were of a more respectable class than the Hospital Nurses.

It is scarcely possible to describe the extreme desolation of these apartments. The room given to our Sisters had no furniture except an old chair without a back, which served them for a table. The windows completely broken admitted the piercing air, for it was then bitterly cold & there was no means of procuring a fire. The Commandant, Major Sillery, most kindly sent in mattresses & such bedcovering as could be spared, & the Soldiers gave part of their rations, no provisions having been laid in for this unforeseen addition.

When the different divisions of the little band had thus taken possession of their new dwelling, the next thought was to provide some refreshment, for they had had but a small allowance on board the "Vectis," its stores having been quite exhausted. A can of warm water therefore from the Barrack Kitchen was procured into which some tea was put; & a small cup full, without milk or sugar, was measured into copper basins for each; this with a scanty portion of bread was their supper: and this kind of privation, which they felt the more on account of their feverish state after such a trying journey, continued for many months. . . . the Purveyors were unwilling to place the Hospital Stores & Clothing at [Miss Nightingale's] disposal. However, before the end of the first week she succeeded in obtaining leave to send Nurses to the General Hospital, a building similar in design to the Barrack, the number of patients being above a thousand; the distance was about a mile over a bleak rocky hill, beset with wild dogs. Miss Nightingale appointed to this charge Sister M. Gonzaga & Sister M. Anastasia with a party of nurses. Revd. Mother with Sister M. Stanislaus & Sister M. de Chantal had work in some of the Wards of the Barrack Hospital when suddenly the news of the fatal engagement at Inkerman came, and this was quickly followed by crowds of wounded men in the worst stages of destitution on the 9th November and the succeeding days. The Sisters were now almost overworked preparing the wards and beds, and, according as the wounded arrived, helping them, dressing their wounds & comforting them. The want of changes of linen being one of the greatest miseries, Miss Nightingale undertook to have the Soldiers' shirts washed and mended, and she purchased a supply of shirts & flannels, the men having all lost their kits on the field. They had also been without the means of washing themselves for weeks and were therefore in a most sad state, so that those employed for them in any way were covered with vermin. Miss Nightingale gave the charge of the linen and of her own Store Room to our Revd Mother, who also went round through the night to the Wards & Corridors: very soon after she appointed her to give out the extra diets in a room which she fitted up for a kitchen. . . .

. . . it would be difficult to describe or even to imagine their many privations both temporal and spiritual. In the severest cold, when the snow lay deep on the ground, they never had a fire; their food was so bad & so sparing that they were often faint from hunger—the bread was sour & often mouldy—the meat was of the worst description & divided in a manner only fit for animals. The want of water was a suffering greater than can be expressed: during the first weeks (as before noticed) they were parched with thirst occasioned by their feverish state after so trying a voyage & only one very small cup of tea was measured into their copper basins—and they were unwilling to seek remedy or redress as the others did, feeling how important it was for them to give an example of patient endurance & conformity with prescribed regulations. Even for washing so little water was to be had & so destitute were they of all conveniences that they were forced to wash in the same water, & in the same basin to wash also their linen, making contrivances both for washing & drying which could scarcely be credited. They had been able to take with them but one or two changes of under clothing & had no second Habits or veils, so that any who were caught in the rain, which fell there in torrents, had no alternative but to remain in bed, while through the kindness of the Soldiers employed as Orderlies their clothes were dried at their own kitchen fire. This accident however happened but rarely, as only Sister M. Gonzaga & Sister M. Anastasia who went out to the General Hospital had the advantage of going into the open air for some months after their arrival. In these and similar difficulties the Soldiers were truly devoted & attentive to alleviate the hardships of the Sisters, and resented deeply the unpleasant treatment to which they saw them subjected from the Matron & others.[8] (BA 1:[225–29])

On December 3, 1854, Mary Gonzaga Barrie, now working at the General Hospital a mile from the Barrack, wrote home to Bermondsey. Her letter, transcribed in the Bermondsey Annals, betrays her own share of the Protestant-Catholic tensions and competition existing in Scutari, and, at this time, in the English consciousness generally. The letter also provides some insight into relations between the nurses and Florence Nightingale:

I think I have told you all our adventures up to the present; now we are tolerably settled to our work, though nothing here is very settled. Miss N. is very kind to us & prefers us to all the rest. Revd. Mother is a general favourite with all parties & is invaluable for keeping peace, rather a difficult thing in these parts. The Nurses are always wrangling with each other, and only make common cause to abuse the poor Anglicans or Sellonites—much as I dislike them, I believe we are the only people who are tolerably civil to them—they seem thoroughly self relying sufficient Protestants & are very proud of themselves. At first they talked of "us Nuns", but, I suppose, finding they could not establish their character as such, they always now speak of us as "the Nuns". I have now three of them in the General Hospital & one of them paid me a compliment yesterday, saying we had got on so well together they had hoped we should go over there. I shall certainly pity them if they go over with the Nurses, all of whom are quite determined to resist their authority. This is a strange place, I only wonder how they get on at all coming out for such motives as most have. I am not without hopes we may convert some, about five seem inclined, thanks to the misrepresentations that have been made, and which seeing us has opened their eyes to. The ministers are very zealous, especially in Tract-giving, but they have no sympathy from the men. One dying man assured me he much preferred listening to what I said, to having the minister read a chapter, for that was all he could do—and this seems the general feeling with the Protestants; as to our own people, they are quite triumphant at having us. You would be surprised at the nice feeling the men shew, they are so cautious in their manner, and never utter a bad word, nor an oath before us. If any chance to say what the others think too free in our presence the whole Ward cry out "hush"—sometimes when I cannot imagine what they are calling out for. The men are over grateful for the little we can do for them, and generally very patient. . . . The other day I was dressing a gangrened wound in a man's leg, and he tried to draw a plan of Sebastopol on it to explain the fighting to me. I cannot say I was much the wiser, for the wound occupied all my attention. However, I made out that there are seven ships sunk across the harbour. Some die as they are carried from the landing place, some as we change their clothes when brought into Hospital. (BA 1:[229–31])

In this inauspicious setting, surrounded by these human difficulties, began the close friendship of Florence Nightingale and Clare

Moore, as well as Florence's friendships, and later correspondence, with Mary Gonzaga Barrie (her "Cardinal") and others in the Bermondsey community.

## 1855–1859

The earliest extant letter of Florence Nightingale to Clare Moore was written in November 1855, from the Castle Hospital at Balaclava, on Florence's second trip to the hospitals on the Crimean peninsula. She had gone there to try to resolve matters with Dr. John Hall, the Principal Medical Officer in the Crimea, and with Mary Francis Bridgeman, the superior of the mostly Irish contingent of fifteen Sisters of Mercy who, having arrived in Scutari in December 1854, were now nursing in Balaclava. Mary Francis Bridgeman's relationship with Florence Nightingale had been tense from the beginning. It is not possible to rehearse here the detailed understandings and instructions with which this second group of Sisters of Mercy had come to the Crimea — especially as regards the responsibilities and authority of Mary Francis Bridgeman as their religious superior, and as regards their conversations with the sick and wounded on religious topics. Nor is it possible here to describe in detail the reasons for Florence Nightingale's refusal to welcome them to Scutari, her initial insistence that they be subordinate to the religious authority of Mary Clare Moore, her suspicions about their conversations with the wounded, and her general unwillingness to incorporate them gratefully into her nursing plans.[9]

On November 6, 1855, Florence sent a set of instructions back to Scutari, presumably to her Aunt Mai Smith; in it she said of Clare: "At present, Revd Mother must take all the Linen Stores, with Miss Ecuyer under her. For Revd Mother does the business far the best" (Wellcome Institute, photocopy, MS 8995/68). Now, writing to Clare herself, Florence says nothing directly about Mary Francis Bridgeman, but requests that Clare ask for more volunteers from Bermondsey:

## 1. To Mary Clare Moore

*Castle Hospital*
*Balaclava*
*Nov. 19/55*

My dear Revd Mother

Would you like to have three more of your Sisters out from Bermondsey to serve in some other of the Hospitals which we serve — & would you consent to their being at a distance from you, altho' under your Superintendence — as at the General Hospital, for instance?

As they would not be with you, I should prefer that they should not be very young Sisters.

If you would think this desirable, will you write to me & also write home to your House?

I must communicate with the War Office, for it is not certain that they will sanction the measure.

I cannot express to you, dear Revd Mother, the gratitude which I and the whole country feel to you for your goodness.

You have been one of our chief main-stays & without you, I do not know what would have become of the work.

With love to all my Sisters, believe me, dear Revd Mother, ever yours affectionately & gratefully

Florence Nightingale

*Autograph: Archives of the Sisters of Mercy, Bermondsey*

Responding to Clare's request on behalf of Florence, three more Sisters of Mercy arrived in Scutari from Bermondsey on January 24, 1856: Mary Helen Ellis,[10] Mary Martha Beste,[11] and Mary Joseph Hawkins.[12] In February, Clare suffered "a bad attack of dysentery" (BA 1:[278]), and on March 15 she was seized with "dangerous pleurisy." Florence, now back in Scutari, "at once called in the Principal Medical Officer, and the remedies he prescribed abated in some degree the violence of the pain, but the patient lay all that week in almost a dying state" (BA 1:[280]).

Florence received her wished-for clarification of the scope of her nursing authority in the General Orders of March 16, 1856. Her superintendence was now not even implicitly restricted to Turkey. On Good Friday, she set out again for Balaclava — with Mary Stanislaus Jones,

Mary Helen Ellis, and Mary Martha Beste, who were destined for hospitals at the front.[13] Arriving in Balaclava on Easter Monday, March 24, she met with Mary Francis Bridgeman and her party—Florence was by now regularly calling them the "Brickbats." Rather than accept Florence Nightingale's authority over her work in the General Hospital in Balaclava, Francis Bridgeman privately submitted her resignation to Sir John Hall. She and the Irish Sisters of Mercy subsequently left for home on April 11.

Florence had apparently sent a letter to Clare the day after she arrived in Balaclava, as she notes in instructions sent back to Scutari. But three days later she wrote Clare another long letter:

## 2. To Mary Clare Moore

*Balaclava*
*March 28/56*

Dearest Revd Mother

It is the greatest consolation I could have to hear that you are better. I *beseech* you to take all the means which are recommended for the recovery of your health & to remember how valuable your life is to this poor world. I do not say this because I think that that life can be very valuable to you in it—but because we cannot spare you yet. Have you changed your room?

I want my Cardinal very much up here. But I do not mean to have her till you are quite well.

The Sisters are all, thank God for it, quite well & quite cheerful. They have made their hut look so tidy, & they put up with all their cold & inconveniencies with the utmost self-abnegation. Everything, even the ink, freezes in our huts every night.

I have been very anxious since I have been here. But I am sure you will pray for us. And God has really prospered our hands. All yesterday I was in Balaclava with the Doctors & Purveyors, & could not see our Sisters. But I was able to send up to them from our Stores or the Purveyors', every thing that they wanted, & to settle with the Doctors, which was the main thing, that we should be allowed to do the needful for the sick, give all the Extras (& cook them), all the medicines, & the wine and brandy—& see to the cleanliness of the Patients. These four things, the Extras, medicine, stimulants & cleanliness were the chief points.

Sir John Hall made a great difficulty about the Extras—but by conceding to him the drawing of the Requisitions, he has conceded that we should do the cooking & serving. For here there are no kitchens but ours for the sick, which can be called such.

I have no fear now but that the sick will be benefited, while the health & comfort of our Sisters will be secured. We have been allowed to draw our Rations like Medical Staff Orderlies, which was the only way I could feed us, while I have taken care that such comforts should be supplied *privately* to the Sisters, as they must require, & Orderlies cannot be supposed to want.

I have been with the Sisters today till dark—have gone round the Hospital with them, & each has got her ward, & her arrangement with the Dr. as to serving Extras & stimulants. I think nothing can be better. And I have no doubt of the good which will be done.

I did not leave the Sisters till after dusk. And then I rode into Balaclava & landed Mrs. Barker & the two from the General Hospital, Scutari, from the "Ottawa," quite safe, & brought them to the Castle Hospital.

I shall take Mrs. Barker the first thing in the morning to Sister Helen as her cook. (It is about 5 miles from the Castle Hospital to the L.T.C.)[14] They will then be complete, all but my Cardinal or one nurse. They have been so good as to wash for themselves, as an accident prevented our washing for them, just for this week.

We are building Extra Diet Kitchens to both Hospitals. And I have brought up three stoves for each. Mr. Soyer[15] will help us.

We are not quite so well established at the Left Wing Hospital, owing to an accident. Mrs. Shaw Stewart is in charge of this. I have been there today also, divided all the Stores, & sent over to our Sisters the larger half of all these Stores, as they are less used to this rough & hostile Crimea than she is.

God has however been very propitious to us, & I think we have cause to trust that our undertaking will be blessed to the Sick Men. The Drs. were really glad of us, for they were frightened. For these poor L.T.C. Hospitals were the only ones in distress.

Pray let Vickery & my Aunt send us up 6 doz. Brandy directly. There must have been some mistake. For, while we have 9 doz. Port, we have only 6 *bottles* Brandy. I desired 6 doz. Port, 4 doz. Brandy to come.

Sister Stanislaus has been most useful.

I am afraid we shall have a little difficulty at the General Hospital, B'clava. The War Office has chosen to replace matters where they were before (relative to the Nursing of Military Hospitals) & to make me Gen'l Supt. of all these. I immediately went to Mrs. Bridgeman & told her that I purposed making no change in her arrangements, & that she was only replaced where she was at the beginning. She however wrote to Sir John Hall & resigned, telling me that I might meanwhile refer the case to him, without telling me that she had done this.

This morning she told me what she had done. I entreated her to reconsider her decision—& to take nine days to consider of it. She has consented to do this, & to let me know at the end of that time her decision, at the same time telling me that she will submit to any "socrifice" & to any "humiliation". I do not know what are the "humiliations" or "socrifices" which I call upon her to "submit to".[16] But I hope she will maturely consider before she brings such a scandal upon the work, as resigning, because she is replaced where she was before. Meanwhile I assure you, Revd Mother, that for your sake, I have taken up my cross with her, & for the sake of the work.

I entreat you to take care of yourself, who are our chief anxiety & our chief support, & to believe me ever yours faithfully and gratefully

F. Nightingale

*Autograph: Archives of the Sisters of Mercy, Bermondsey*

The Treaty of Paris, ending the Crimean War, was concluded on March 30, 1856, though it would be four months before all the wounded were returned home.

Clare, still ill with pleurisy, began to recover slowly. But she was grieved by news coming from the Crimea: the inability of Florence Nightingale and Mary Francis Bridgeman to resolve their differences, and a Catholic chaplain's written refusal to hear the confessions of the Bermondsey sisters working with Florence because he "disapproved totally of their coming to the Crimea" under Miss Nightingale's authority and "could not connect himself with the transaction in any way whatsoever" (BA 1:[282]). The Rev. Michael Duffy, a Jesuit who supported the Irish sisters in their conflict with Florence Nightingale, not only censured the Bermondsey sisters in the Crimea, but later sent word of his opinion to the Rev. O'Dwyer, the Catholic chaplain at Scutari, who then also "expressed his displeasure warmly, and informed the Sisters [in Scutari] (Revd. Mother was still too ill to be spoken to) that he would make known to Dr. Grant his resolution to have no connection with them in any way" (BA 1:[283]).

All in all, it was a sorry picture of Roman Catholic partisanship, in its clerical form. In the midst of this, Florence wrote to Clare:

## 3. To Mary Clare Moore

*Balaclava*
*April 1, 1856*

Dearest Revd Mother

Your precious health is the chief of my cares. I beseech you to go to Malta with Sister Gonzaga or Anastasia or both, if it were only for 2 or 3 weeks, when Dr. Cruickshanks recommends it. Please do not neglect his advice, or I shall be obliged to come back & tyrannize over you.

Your Sisters here are perfectly well, very efficient & very cheerful. After mature consideration, owing to my unwillingness to trouble you when you are so far from well, I have concluded to consult you about two things—

1. the letter of the Revd Mr. Duffy to the Sisters, which will be enclosed to you by this post with their own account of the transaction. I will therefore not enter farther into it. They are not in the least depressed in spirits about it. Mr. Cuffe was very kind.

2. Mrs. Bridgeman appears determined to leave—& next Saturday. I have done every thing which in me lay to keep her, but in vain. For every reason, I think it best (*indeed essential*) to replace her with our Sisters, replacing them again at Scutari with more Sisters from Bermondsey if you can grant them. I have no time to enter into all the details of this singular business. But the best course at present appears to me to be for you to come up here yourself (*after* you have been to Malta, *if* then quite recovered, & *if* it is sanctioned by your Medical Officer)—& *meanwhile could you trust me* with your *other* three Sisters up here? I will stay with them till you come. I will not leave the Crimea till then. And they shall have Mrs. Roberts & two of the steadiest Nurses with them. There are only 200 Patients in Mrs. Bridgeman's Hospital, & this pomp of attendance upon 200 men, where so many Hospitals are suffering, is to me inexplicable. But we are surrounded with spies, & I cannot tell you how essential I think it to our work to do this Hospital well.

Miss Morton will replace you in the Linen Stores at Scutari—pro. temp. —with some Nurses.

Can you have three more Sisters out from Bermondsey?

I am sure you will know that it costs me much more than it does you to trouble you in illness as I am obliged to do. But the night cometh when no man can work.

Ever dearest Revd Mother's
faithful & grateful
F. Nightingale
*Autograph: Archives of the Sisters of Mercy, Bermondsey*

Three days later, on April 4, Florence sent another set of instructions to Scutari. Although the autograph letter, now in the Bermondsey archives, has no salutation, it was presumably addressed to her Aunt Mai, her assistant in Scutari since the fall of 1855, after the departure of her original traveling companions, Charles and Selina Bracebridge. In this letter, Florence again expresses her concern over Clare's convalescence:

I trust Revd Mother will send me two Sisters immediately, or three, according as she keeps one or two with her.

The party at the General Hospital sail tomorrow. I must fill their places directly, & am going today to take two or three, of the three who came up with me, according to Sister Helen's interpretation of Revd Mother's wishes.

I cannot describe to you what it is to me to trouble her now, as I know this will trouble her. . . .

If the Army stays here 4 months more, I shall ask for more Nuns from Bermondsey, as I have already said to Revd Mother.

You must please to communicate with Drs. Linton, Lawson, Revd Mother and Miss Tebbutt upon all these things, *as from me*, alledging my inability to write to all.

Of course, as the Crimean Hospitals contract & the Scutari enlarge, I shall be able to throw back my Nurses upon the latter. But for the moment I must have the Sisters here.

Tell Revd Mother it will not be for long. We shall soon be all together again.

Whatever Revd Mother determines upon in regard to herself, she *must not* go into the Stores till I come back. (Autograph: Archives of the Sisters of Mercy, Bermondsey)

Although Florence refrained from burdening Clare with her feelings about Mary Francis Bridgeman's attitudes and decisions, and with her own prejudices about the Irish and Roman Catholics, she was not so restrained on April 5 in writing to Lieutenant Colonel John Henry Lefroy at the War Office. Her letter to him exposes what the Bermondsey sisters in the Crimea certainly knew about the situation in Balaclava and Father Duffy's treatment of them, and what they had no doubt privately, though much less harshly, communicated to Clare:

As the old Whig families are said always to have the heir-apparent a Tory, in order to be "*in*" both ways, so the Roman Catholics always have one set of priests & nuns with the Govt. & one against it.

The split between the "secular" & "regular" priests, older than Ignatius Loyola, & always repeated in the R. C. Church in one form or other, obtains even in Krim Tartary.

Mrs. Bridgeman & her 11 Irish Nuns & the 6 Jesuit Priests here are against us— the Secular priests & Bermondsey Nuns for us.

As Peace was imminent, there was no time to lose in making a martyrdom.

Mrs. Bridgeman & her 11 Nuns have been instructed to resign & go home, in consequence of the "General Order". And this they do next week. I have piped to her & played the Circe, but in vain. I have proposed to her a "Novena" or "nine days' prayer", to reconsider her decision, to which she assented. But also in vain. I was in hopes she would have a vision. But no.

"*Ho imparato un po' del mestiere*", as the policeman said to the "*ladro*", when picking his, the "*ladro's*" pockets (in the "*Promessi Sposi*",) so also had I, in the "Novena" matter, "*imparato un po' del' mestiere*".[17]

But it was all of no avail. For, as Mrs. Bridgeman herself informed me, it was a matter resolved upon months ago.

So "*ladro*", "Novena", all, has alike failed.

I shall fill their places immediately with Bermondsey Nuns, of whom I brought up some with me.

Two more instances of the R. C. split. 1. The Revd. Mr. Duffy, Jesuit, has been instructed to refuse Confession & therefore Holy Communion to, or even to visit those Bermondsey Nuns, whom I brought with me to one of the Land Transport Hospitals, & he writes to them, among other things, that they are a disgrace to their Church. For none so coarse as an Irish R. C. priest.[18]

2. Cardinal Wiseman has recalled the Senior R. C. priest here, a secular, "under these circumstances".

On the other hand, the Secular priests repudiate the Irish Nuns & do the civil by the Govt. & me & the Bermondsey Nuns—& even *Father Cuffe*[19] who used to call me "Herod" in the Irish papers, now licks my hand, as the Provost Marshal says, "like a good 'un."

"Irish Regulars are little else than Rebels," is said here.

Deputy Purveyor-in-Chief Fitzgerald has *forgotten*? the Rations of the Bermondsey Nuns during 10 days—during which I have had to feed them by hook or by crook.

I have written a Despatch to Lord Panmure upon Mrs. Bridgeman's resignation. But I should be truly obliged to you, if you would communicate to him the real circumstances explaining the case. I cannot express to you the sorrow & anxiety it has caused me, nor the pains I have taken to avert it.

I so deeply regret that the "General Order" should have produced this consequence.

I can only add that I thought most seriously of resigning the "General Hospital", at Balaclava; for the sake of peace.

But last year's experience was quite sufficient to prove to me the necessity of the "General Order" in question. The Govt. had now put this tool in my hands, & if I laid it down again, the consequences would be my fault, not theirs—viz. the impossibility of preserving discipline or morality among Nurses, if, as soon as they rebelled, I resigned, or of having one rule for R. Catholics & another for Church of England, like myself. And you expressed, yourself, much more tersely than I should have done the undesirableness of a Medical Officer appointing one whom the Female Supt. had thought it necessary to discharge, be she Lady, Nun or Nurse. (BL Add. MSS 43397, ff. 228–30)

On April 8, Florence again wrote to Clare, requesting that she send three more Sisters of Mercy from Scutari, keeping only Mary Gonzaga Barrie with her at the Barrack Hospital. When the Irish sisters left for home, Florence evidently intended to place Bermondsey sisters in the Balaclava General Hospital:

## 4. To Mary Clare Moore

*Balaclava*
*April 8/56*

Dearest Revd Mother

I was so glad & thankful to see your own dear hand again, & I trust that God will preserve you yet some time to us & to His work.

Our Sisters are quite well & cheerful, & most efficient & useful. Dr. Taylor[20] expressed to me yesterday, in the strongest words, his feeling of the reform they had worked in his L.T.C. Hospital. They do more than medicine, he said.

All our Hospitals are going on well, thank God. Our crosses have been many, & very sad ones, as you may perhaps know. But God prospers the work.

I must now urge you, dear Revd Mother, to send me *two* or *three* Sisters without delay, if they have not already sailed. I cannot tell you how it grieves me to break up your nice arrangements at the Barrack Hospital. But it will not be for long. The Crimean Hospitals will soon contract, & we shall then be replaced at Scutari.

It is now, however, of the utmost importance to keep up the "General Hospital" at Balaclava, owing to its being the nearest point to embarkation. And Sister Helen will tell you how, (as soon as Mrs. Bridgeman is gone, which will be probably tomorrow,) we thought that it would be more according to your wish for Sisters Stanislaus and Martha to accompany me there with

Mrs. Roberts, Logan & two washerwomen, and Sister Helen to remain at the L.T.C., till reinforced by you. The Sisters, whom you send, will go to whichever Hospital you direct, either giving back Sister Helen her own Sisters, or replacing them.

Believe me, ever my dearest Revd Mother's
grateful & loving
F. Nightingale

*Autograph: Archives of the Sisters of Mercy, Bermondsey*

Two days later, Florence again wrote to Clare, still concerned about her health, but modifying her earlier request that three more sisters come out from Bermondsey:

## 5. To Mary Clare Moore

*Balaclava*
*April 10/56*

My dearest Revd Mother

Many, many thanks for your three letters—all of which I received last night. The mails are late & irregular.

I am afraid that I have written very hastily & not very perspicuously, a great fault in a Supt. But I assure you that my letters have been the result of thought, not hasty but anxious thought.

The great distance of the Hospitals from each other in the Crimea, & having to settle much "Ration" & other business with officials, converts her Holiness into a tramp and makes her "rescripts" scrawls.

But first, about your dear health, which must be the most anxious thing to us at present.

I can easily understand & I am afraid cannot remove the reasons which would prevent your going to Malta. At the same time, I do earnestly hope that you will go, if possible. And I hope that you do not think that you would be allowed to go at the charges of your Community. General Storks will give you passages. And I enclose a Cheque for £100, which any house at Malta would cash. Dr. Trench, whom Sister Gonzaga will remember at the General Hospital at Scutari, has *asked* to take charge of any of us going to or at Malta, & he will meet you on board the vessel & provide for you medically and comfortably. Dr. Cruickshank [[sic]] will know whether he is at Malta now, &

write to him before you go, that you may be comfortably put up on arriving. I hope that you may also know Catholics there.

Dear Revd Mother, I hope that, whatever you determine upon, you will do no work at Scutari. A slight imprudence might have such consequences. I have begged my Aunt to let me know if you begin to work, or to do anything imprudent. And, if you do, you know I must come back. Your life is the most precious thing we have, both for the work's sake & for the Community, & to peril it for the sake of C Store or for any store would break our hearts.

Mr. Wills will take C Store for the present.

The Linen Divisional Stores Miss Morton will take, with such help as we have planned.

Sister Gonzaga will keep the Extra Diets till you go to Malta, if you go, or till you come to the Crimea. But that must not be yet—Balaclava would not suit you yet. Pray do not do the Extras yourself—Miss Morton will take them, when Sister Gonzaga leaves with you.

And all these arrangements will be understood to be but temporary, while you & I are away—and the bustle of moving 70,000 men makes the Hospitals uncertainly full or suddenly empty.

I cannot decide quite at present about another Nurse from Scutari—tho' I fear we shall have to make some changes. But we shall be truly thankful for the three Sisters, whenever they come. Mrs. Bridgeman & my Birds are not yet flown from Balaclava—so that I shall have the consolation, I hope, of not separating the Sisters at the L.T.C. Mrs. Roberts, Mrs. Logan and I shall go in with the three Sisters from Scutari. You will direct which is to be "Revd Mother".

The Sisters are well & cheerful at the L.T.C. & very busy. Sister M. Martha has a slight cold, but nothing more. And as, at the other Wing, Sister Stanislaus taxed me with saying that Mrs. Skinner "gives in", & that Mrs. Holmes "has an affection of the heart", she wishes to know which malady I think that Sister M. Martha has. They have never seemed to take their troubles much to heart. And I believe Sister M. Helen and I are the most anxious ones.

On the 20th, the Commander in Chief expects to have his orders, & I think we shall then be able to make some kind of plan, & to know whether it will be desirable to give more Sisters from Bermondsey the trouble of coming out. I only wished to prepare you for the possibility of its being asked, & misexpressed myself if I implied it as desirable to write off directly.

I saw however the Director General of the L.T.C. yesterday, and his opinion was (but it is only an opinion) that we shall be 5 months moving out of the Crimea, & the L.T.C. Hospitals and the General Hospital at Balaclava will be kept up last of all. But all this will depend, of course, upon conditions of which we know nothing as yet. It may be that we shall be out of the Crimea before you & S. Gonzaga will have time to come to us.

> Believe me ever my dearest Revd Mother's
> grateful & affectionate
> F. Nightingale

*Autograph: Archives of the Sisters of Mercy, Bermondsey*

Mary Francis Bridgeman and her party left Balaclava on April 11, 1856. The next day Florence wrote a brief letter, without a salutation, presumably to Aunt Mai. The accuracy of her report on the condition in which she found the General Hospital in Balaclava cannot now be verified, although one can reasonably suspect exaggeration:[21]

We moved in here yesterday, my birds having flown yesterday & (for the furtherance of the comforts of the patients) *without giving any notice*—accordingly there was no time to lose, & Sister Stanislaus, Mrs. Roberts, Mrs. Logan & I came in within 1/2 an hour. Into such a pigstye I *never* came, though it has been my lot to make many *foundations* and all my letters must be left unwritten, because besides Hospital Duty, we must whitewash, scrub, scour, to prevent fever.

The three Sisters quite well. Sister M. Martha has had a slight feverish cold, but is well again. The patients here are in the most disgraceful state of dirt & filth & bed sores—They might have been taken out of the Streets of London, Alas! (Wellcome Institute, photocopy, MS 8996/46)

Before Florence's letter of April 10 reached Clare, the three sisters Florence had earlier requested from Scutari were dispatched, on April 11: Mary de Chantal Hudden, Mary Joseph Hawkins, and Mary Anastasia Kelly. They reached Balaclava on Sunday, April 13, and on Monday, Mary Joseph was sent to the Land Transport Hospital in Karani to replace Martha Beste whose illness had worsened. On Tuesday, Florence wrote to Clare:

## 6. To Mary Clare Moore

> *General Hospital*
> *Balaclava*
> *April 15, 1856*

My dearest Revd Mother

I had the comfort of receiving our Sisters quite well & safe on Sunday afternoon, as they will tell you. And we have arranged thus—Sister Mary

Joseph went yesterday to join Sister M. Helen at the L.T.C. Hospital—Sisters M. Stanislaus, M. de Chantal, & M. Anastasia stay here doing work. Sister M. Martha is, I am sorry to say, at present laid up here with a feverish cold. As soon as she is able, she will join Sister M. Helen. I am not sorry that her illness (or rather unwellness) should be here, as we have greater facilities of nursing her. And the Dr. is such a very clever one.

I am afraid that you would rather have mixed the two parties of Sisters, so that the recent ones should not be all together at one Hospital. I see the objection myself. But my reason was this: Every thing we do at Karani is right—every thing we do here is wrong. Sister Stanislaus is very brave & has already charge of the Extra Diets here which are very disorderly, & which you will manage so beautifully, if you come. Sister Anastasia is such a very steady, quiet worker. She has seven Sick Huts, & Sister de Chantal is commanding & courageous & not easily daunted. Of course whatever we do will be blamed. I do not mean that the recent Sisters would be less likely to go on with their duty steadily, with a single eye to God, altho' evil eyes are all around them. But it requires very good spirits to bear being always misconstrued without being a little depressed. And these old Sisters are very cheerful & used to be "abused"!

Mrs. Roberts & I, Mrs. Logan & Mrs. Skinner are also here. We sleep in one half a Hut & our sick Sister in the other half. The three other Sisters in the next Hut. We have hardly had time to make any arrangements yet for ourselves.

I hope that you will not think of coming up here for three weeks, at least. Thank God you are better! Perhaps then it will do you good. But there will be time to talk of that.

Ever my dearest Revd Mother's
grateful & affectionate
F. Nightingale

*Autograph: Archives of the Sisters of Mercy, Bermondsey*

A week later, Florence wrote again, responding to Clare's suggestions about the placement of her sisters and registering her distress that Mary Francis Bridgeman did not inquire after Clare when she passed through Scutari. In this letter, Florence also comments encouragingly on Martha's illness (which evidently was typhus), even though, on the same day, she sends her sister Parthenope a more dramatic account of nursing Martha at night—"Sick Nun in fever perfectly deaf . . . rat sitting on rafter over sick nun's head & rats scrambling about" (Goldie, ed. 260–61). Florence knew that Clare had seen plenty of rats in Scutari, but she apparently did not wish to cause her worry:

## 7. To Mary Clare Moore

*General Hospital*
*Balaclava*
*April 22/56*

Dearest Revd Mother

When I received your last letter but one, which expressed your wish that Sr. M. de Chantal should be with Sr. M. Helen, I consulted with Sr. Stanislaus who is in charge here & Sr. Helen who is in charge at Karani. Sr. Helen said at once that she would rather have Sr. de Chantal & Sr. M. Joseph (who *is* with her) & leave Sr. M. Martha with Sr. Stanislaus when she recovers. But we came to the conclusion that, as the only change we could make at present would be to exchange Sr. M. Joseph for Sr. de Chantal (our hands being full here at present—& S. M. Martha requiring some one constantly with her, tho' she is much better, but still suffering from a bilious feverish attack) you would prefer that no change should be made, but that we should stay as we are till Sr. de Chantal could go on to Karani. Sr. M. Martha gives us little uneasiness now. But the hut being at a few yards distance from the Hospital, we cannot leave her by herself in the hut in bed.

The weather here is so very trying, —very cold, very hot, very damp— that I hope you will not come up, dear Revd Mother, till it is really thought that the change will do you *good*. I am sure it is cruel (and I feel it) to make the Sisters stay here without you. But you must not risk a relapse. And I really do not know what my Aunt would do without you—for she would have no one to consult with amid all these changes. She says, it is such a comfort to have Revd Mother's advice to go to.

The Sisters are perfectly well and cheerful—all but Sr. M. Martha who is better.

They will have told you that they were able to have help from Mr. Gleeson on Saturday.

I am truly distressed that Mrs. Bridgeman did not, at least, send to enquire after you when at Scutari. She knew you were ill.

God bless you, dearest Revd Mother, & reward you.

Ever your grateful & affectionate
F.N.

*Autograph: Archives of the Sisters of Mercy, Bermondsey*

At this point, the Bermondsey Annals record, in Clare Moore's hand, an extended account of Martha Beste's illness, the rats in Balaclava, the buildings at the General Hospital there, and the deaths suffered earlier by two members of Mary Francis Bridgeman's party of sisters: Mary Winifred Sprey of cholera on October 20, 1855, and Mary Elizabeth Butler of typhus on February 23, 1856. Here and elsewhere in the Annals one sees evidence of Clare's regret that Francis Bridgeman and Florence Nightingale had not been able to develop a working relationship:

Sister Mary Martha's illness which Miss Nightingale so kindly tried to make as light of as possible was a severe attack of fever, during which she received the last Sacraments. Miss N. herself would be her nurse, sitting up with her at night & attending her with unremitting care. It happened one night that while she watched by her bedside, fearing that her illness might terminate fatally, she was alarmed still more by the appearance of a huge rat on the rafters over the poor suffering Sister's bed. With her usual calm presence of mind Miss Nightingale succeeded in knocking down the rat & killed it with her umbrella.

The General Hospital at Balaclava was in the town itself, which lay contiguous to the harbour; it consisted partly of a stone building in which were three large Wards & a small room for the Superintendent, and partly of a number of huts lying close by. When the Sisters, under Mother M. F. Bridgeman's care, undertook the charge of this Hospital, three Huts were erected for them on the hill above the town, and the Soldiers, by making a kind of foundation with broken glass, contrived to exclude the rats from them altogether. All other places were overrun with them, and they were more formidable & daring than at Scutari, for they would pull down entire loaves and roll them along to their holes, when the Sisters were present, or knock off the shelves a bottle full of wine, with similar depredations in the Extra Diet Kitchens, both at Karani & Balaklava, so that it was a real advantage to be exempt from them in the Sisters' Huts. After Mo[ther] M. F. Bridgeman quitted the Crimea, Miss Nightingale got possession of two of their huts, one of which she gave to our three Sisters, the other she occupied with three of the Nurses, & gave half of it as an Infirmary during Sister M. Martha's illness, who, when recovered, took Sister M. de Chantal's place in the Balaclava Hospital work, while this latter was transferred to Karani, where Sister M. Joseph was laid up with bad rheumatism, & one of the Nurses had caught the fever.

The resolution which Mother M. F. Bridgeman had taken to return to Ireland, rather than remain in the Military Hospitals subject to Miss Nightingale's superintendence, was regretted by all parties. The Sisters had been greatly beloved by the Soldiers, they had laboured efficiently among them, had gone through immense hardships, and a second of their number, Sister Mary Elizabeth Butler, an aged Sister from the Convent in Liverpool, died in the Spring of this year. She had endeared herself to all, and her indefatigable attention to the Sick made her death be felt with the deepest grief not only by her Religious Sisters but by the Soldiers, who requested to bury her with Military honours, and they erected tombs over the graves of both the Sisters who died there. (BA 1:[292–93])

In her letter of April 22, Florence had anticipated that Clare herself would come to Balaclava when she was sufficiently recuperated. But, unbeknown to Clare, one of the Catholic chaplains in Scutari, the Rev. John Bagshawe, had written to Bishop Grant about Clare's health, telling him that "Dr. Cruickshanks considered her return to England as absolutely necessary & the only hope of saving her, as her health was seriously impaired." Grant wrote immediately to Clare, asking her "to obey the Medical Officer." His letter arrived on April 22, and Dr. Cruickshanks subsequently decided that she should leave Scutari in the *Victoria* on Monday, April 28. In the Annals, Clare notes that "It was a hard struggle with her feelings, both towards the Sisters & Miss Nightingale" (BA 1:[297–98]).

On Friday, April 25, she wrote to Florence and to the sisters in the Crimea, informing them of her imminent departure from Scutari. The letter to Florence has not so far been discovered among her papers, but the letter to the sisters is transcribed in the Bermondsey Annals:

You will see by the Bishop's letter, which our dear Miss Nightingale will shew you, that I am obliged to return to Bermondsey, and perhaps on Monday. It is indeed a painful separation, but we know it is *best* to do God's will, & we know it to be His holy will since it is the direction of our Superior. I felt one thing, not being able to see you all & our good friend Miss Nightingale—but again I felt that such a parting would be only more sad than now, when we are already separated almost as much as if I were at Bermondsey.

Sister M. Helen being Senior, all will have deference for her & she will in a manner take my place, but in each little party the Senior Sister will be a kind of *head* or responsible person, just as all goes on now—and I need not tell you *my wishes*, dear children, you know them. Be united, & happy, & cheerful, & humble, loving God and trusting in His care, without a shadow of mistrust, and asking our dear Blessed Lady to shew herself a Mother to you in all things, and then if you should make some mistake, have no anxiety. You may be sure our Blessed Lord will not allow you to do any thing contrary to His honour & glory. And now I will only add, be good & faithful, work away merrily, and what a hearty welcome I shall have for you all when you come home to dear Bermondsey, which may be much sooner than you imagine. May God bless you & our Dearest Lady and Mother protect you. Pray for me. (BA 1:[298])

Having gone to the Crimean peninsula toward the end of March, Florence had not seen Clare for over a month. While she certainly knew that Clare was seriously ill, she no doubt hoped for her complete recovery in Scutari or Malta. Thus news of Clare's immediate departure must have come as a shock. Clare's letter to her probably arrived in Balaclava on April 28 or 29. Florence's immediate response, presumably sent to Bermondsey, is a generous, humble statement of her gratitude:

*8. To Mary Clare Moore*

*General Hospital*
*Balaclava*
*April 29/56*

My dearest Revd Mother

Your going home is the greatest blow I have had yet.

But God's blessing & my love & gratitude go with you, as you well know.

You know well too that I shall do every thing I can for the Sisters whom you have left me. But it will not be like you. Your wishes will be our law. And I shall try & remain in the Crimea for their sakes as long as we any of us are there.

I do not presume to express praise or gratitude to you, Revd Mother, because it would look as if I thought you had done the work not unto God but unto me. You were far above me in fitness for the General Superintendency, both in worldly talent of administration, & far more in the spiritual qualifications which God values in a superior. My being placed over you in our unenviable reign of the East was my misfortune & not my fault.

I will ask you to forgive me for everything or anything which I may unintentionally have done which can ever have given you pain—remembering only that I have always felt what I have just expressed, & that it has given me more pain to reign over you than to you to serve under me.

I have now only to say that I trust that you will not withdraw any of the Sisters now here, till the work of the Hospitals ceases to require their presence, & that I may be authorized to be the judge of this—unless the health of any of them should make her return desirable, in which case I will faithfully inform you.

I will care for them as if they were my own children. But that you know, and now it is a sacred trust from you.

Sister M. Martha is, thank God, quite convalescent.

Dearest Revd Mother, what you have done for the work no one can ever say. But God rewards you for it with Himself.

If I thought that your valuable health would be restored by a return home, I should not regret it. But I fear that, unless you give up work for a time, which I do not well see how you can at home, your return to Bermondsey will only be the signal for greater calls upon your strength.

However, it matters little, provided we spend our lives to God, whether like our Blessed Lord's, they are concluded in three & thirty years, or whether they are prolonged to old age.

My love & gratitude will be yours, dearest Revd Mother, wherever you go. I do not presume to give you any other tribute but my tears. And as I shall soon want a "character" from you, as my respected S. Gonzaga would say, I am not going to offer you a "character".

But I should be glad that the Bishop of Southwark should know & Dr. Manning (altho' my "recommendation" is not likely to be of value to you but the contrary,) that you were valued here as you deserved & that the gratitude of the Army is yours.

Pray give my love to S. Gonzaga & thanks for her letter.

Mrs. Roberts sends many messages of respect & of sorrow.

Will you thank the Bishop of Southwark with my respectful remembrances for his very kind letter to me?

Will you ask one of the Sisters at home, I dare say S. Gonzaga will do so, to write to me about your health.

And believe me ever, whether I return to see you again in this world or not,

ever my dearest Revd Mother's<br>(gratefully, lovingly, overflowingly)<br>Florence Nightingale

*Autograph: Archives of the Sisters of Mercy, Bermondsey*

Three days later, still trying to help the sisters in the Crimea to gain access to the sacraments, Florence wrote from Balaclava to Helen Ellis at the Land Transport Corps Hospital in Karani:

## 9. To Mary Helen Ellis

[May 2, 1856]

Dear Sister M. Helen

The Revd Mr. Unsworth thinks, & our Sisters here agree, that it would be very desirable, if you like it, for you to go to confession here. (*You* must play

Revd Mother & join first.) You will have the Revd Mr. Gleeson.[22] I will send an ambulance for you *tomorrow* at *1/4 before 1*, (our carriage being gone to Bakshi-Serai) in order that you should be here, in case you like to come, by 2 o'clock, when our Sisters go to Confession.

I hope you will come.

Revd Mother went on Monday with S. Gonzaga in the "Victoria," the finest ship on the line.

She has written to all. But Sisters say that you have not sent them back her *last* letter.

Sister M. Martha quite convalescent & Lawfield not in danger.

Will you please, if you come, bring us some sweet biscuits, if you have any, & some old linen.

Believe me ever yours
F. Nightingale

2/5/56

The Revd Mr. Gleeson hears Confessions here every Saturday, from 1 to 4—if you like to come. Sisters send you their love & *duty*.
*Autograph: Archives of the Sisters of Mercy, Bermondsey*

On April 29, Clare wrote to Mary Anastasia Kelly, telling her that "two hundred & ten invalids, a troop of Artillery with their officers, a number of invalid officers, some doctors, ladies & children" were aboard the *Victoria* when they left Scutari, and that the ship had picked up more invalids at Renkioi. On May 1, she wrote to Mary Stanislaus Jones at Balaclava and to Helen Ellis in Karani. To the former she said:

Although very sick I will try to write to you, having little to say, except that after a most prosperous beginning, we both became very ill on Tuesday night and all yesterday—today not much better, but able to be on deck.

Well, I hope you are all going on nicely and cheerfully—and I know you will be glad to think that I am safe at dear old Bermondsey (when we arrive there) although we are sent off in a Transport with scarcely two days notice. Dr. Cruickshanks was so determined that I should go in this ship, he ordered me on board with the invalids in the steam tug at 10, but Vickery[23] would not consent to our going until three. And now I must tell you that on last Saturday he [Vickery] *would* take Sister Gonzaga & me over to Stamboul, all through the Bazaar—he could not consent that I should return home without having been even once in Constantinople. In the Bazaar we bought some beautiful blue silk damask to make an Antependium for Our Lady's Altar—also a Turkish Pipe for Jack (the former Sexton at Bermondsey), a pair of Candlesticks for the 88th who are getting up some grandeurs in their hut for Rosary. (BA 1:[300])

To Helen she acknowledged:

I felt deeply leaving as I was forced to do, but I felt also that I could not be more
sure of doing God's holy will in all circumstances, as well as regards myself as
Sister M. Gonzaga—who of course would have preferred going to the Crimea &
remaining there until the work was done, as I should have wished myself. . . .
      . . . All was arranged for us. I might have objected to going all the way by sea, but
I thought best to leave myself to others' care, and I am glad I did so, for although
very sick we are going on better than we hoped we should have done. (BA 1:[301])

Clare Moore and Mary Gonzaga Barrie reached Bermondsey on
May 16. Clare found Florence's farewell letter of April 29 (see above)
waiting for her. Although she had probably written to Florence in the
intervening month, Florence's next extant letter to her responds to a
letter written at the end of May:

*10. To Mary Clare Moore*

*General Hospital*
*Balaclava*
*June 14, 1856*

My dearest Revd Mother
      I will only now thank you for your dear letter of May 26 & say how very
much I hope that you are taking the means to recover your very precious
health—precious for the sake of so many.
      My *business* now is to say that, in consequence of the Sisters' Hospital at
the Land Transport Corps [[in Karani]] having been (suddenly rather) closed,
owing to the removal of that Detachment, in consequence of the difficulty,
of obtaining passages home, now becoming so serious that the Chief of the
Staff has interfered on our behalf & insisted on our taking, without delay,
passages in the "Thames", & in consequence of
                              Sister M. Helen
                              Sister M. Joseph
                              Sister M. Martha
appearing not to stand this climate very well, altho' there is nothing to cause
the slightest uneasiness as to any permanent injury to their health—we have
decided, not without very serious consideration & thought, that these three
Sisters shall return home by the "Thames" on Tuesday, the 17th, where accommodation has been set apart expressly for us by orders from Head Quarters.

Thirteen others from our Staff will accompany them. Such an opportunity is
not likely to occur again.

The circumstance of the Revd Mr. Cuffe & the Revd Mr. Molony[24] being
both about to sail for England today makes the parting with our Sisters to me
less painful, because I think there would have been positive difficulty about
their Spirituals, had they remained here.

I trust that you will allow us to keep

Sister M. Stanislaus

Sister M. de Chantal

Sister M. Anastasia

till the last. I should be sorry indeed to part till then—the partings are painful
enough. But I expect that all will be home before August. They are quite well
& cheerful.

Many, many thanks for your dear letter & believe me

ever my dearest Revd Mother's

grateful & faithful

F. Nightingale

*Autograph: Archives of the Sisters of Mercy, Bermondsey*

Helen Ellis, Mary Joseph Hawkins, and Martha Beste reached Ber-
mondsey on July 9. On July 7, Florence wrote from Scutari to say
that the last three sisters, who had sailed with her from Balaclava on
June 29, were now headed home to England, while she remained in
Scutari, "winding up accounts." This is Florence's last extant letter to
Clare from the Crimea; a restrained sense of closure pervades it:

## 11. To Mary Clare Moore

*Barrack Hospital*

*Scutari*

*July 7/56*

My dearest Revd Mother

Almost before you receive this, you will have received the last of our
dear Sisters. They will explain to you why the proceedings of us all were a
little changed at the last, & it was thought best at once that I should bring
away with me all that remained in the Crimea, in number 13, & that none
should be left with me at Scutari, excepting my Aunt & Mrs. Roberts. I am
now winding up accounts as fast as I can.

I do not yet know when I shall come home. But when I do, I shall come as quietly as possible, see no one in London but you, dear Revd Mother, & go straight into the country to my father's house, whence I shall report myself to the War Department.

Dearest Revd Mother, I am sure that no one, even of your own children, values you, loves you & reverences you more than I do. Take care of your precious health, do.

In closing this work, I can never sufficiently express how much I feel all that you & your Sisters have been to it. It is beyond expression.

Believe me ever, dearest Revd Mother,<br>Your grateful & loving<br>Florence Nightingale

*Autograph: Archives of the Sisters of Mercy, Bermondsey*

Mary Stanislaus Jones, de Chantal Hudden, and Anastasia Kelly arrived home in Bermondsey on July 24. They had traveled on the *Ottawa* with "a hundred sick on board in whose service they were engaged . . . giving comfort to the poor patients, two of whom died & another was left at Malta in a dying state" (BA 1:[307]). On July 23, Florence wrote her last letter from the Crimea to Mary Gonzaga Barrie, giving plans for her return to England and her visit to Bermondsey:

*12. To Mary Gonzaga Barrie*

*Scutari*<br>*Barrack Hospital*<br>*23/7/56*

Dear S. Gonzaga

Again I return to my Sisters my dearest Revd Mother's letters, but this time I had a letter from her all to myself.

You do not give me a good account of her. But do not write again—for I shall soon be home now.

I shall not stop in London at all, but go to Bermondsey to call upon Revd Mother & then sneak quietly out of the way.

And this reminds me to ask you to look out, if Revd Mother will allow it, any Requisitions or Lists which she may have left, belonging to this place, also her Inventory of the wine expended, as I shall have to add up & furnish Abstracts of all these things. All her papers concerning this place will be necessary.

She kept all her Books so beautifully that I trust this will cost her no trouble at all. And I almost expected to find that she had left these documents in the hands of my aunt for me.

Perhaps you will have them ready for me when I come—as I shall come to see dear Revd Mother, not on business but on pleasure, & shall have but a flying taste of her, both for her sake & my own.

Dear Cardinal Gonzaga, this comes with best love from your

poor old Pope

The last of our Invalids go home today.

*Autograph: Archives of the Sisters of Mercy, Bermondsey*

As was discussed in the first part of this volume, Florence stopped at the Mercy convent in Bermondsey with her Aunt Mai on the morning of August 7, on her way home to Lea Hurst in Derbyshire. Presumably she got the records she needed, as well as a good conversation with Clare.

Immediately after the community's spiritual retreat ended on August 15, Clare set to work on plans for the Catholic hospital Cardinal Wiseman wished to establish on Great Ormond Street in Westminster, London. The hospital was to be founded by Lord Campden, and the Cardinal's clerical advisors, Henry Manning and Robert Whitty, had requested that Thomas Grant secure a community of five Mercy sisters from Bermondsey to staff it, preferably those with Crimean nursing experience. As Bishop Grant told Clare, Dr. Manning himself thought "it was very important that the experience of hospital work acquired by your Sisters should not be sacrificed" (BA 1:[308]).

After much consultation, the Bermondsey community decided to undertake this work and found an autonomous community in Westminster. The sisters Clare selected for the new endeavor were Mary Gonzaga Barrie, who was appointed superior, Mary Stanislaus Jones, Mary Helen Ellis, Mary Anastasia Kelly, and Mary Bernard Knight. All but one had served under Florence Nightingale in the Crimea, and at least two of them—Mary Gonzaga and Mary Stanislaus—would correspond with her for many years.

On November 18 they took possession of the large house on Great Ormond Street that was to serve as both convent and dispensary. They discovered on their arrival that "after so much delay & apparent preparation, there was nothing ready for their accommodation, and the house was in such a disordered state that they were engaged until two o'clock the next morning arranging the apartments & fitting up the Chapel for the opening and blessing" (BA 1:[312]). On November 19—the feast day of the young thirteenth-century widow who had exhausted her life feeding, clothing, and nursing the sick poor of Marburg, Germany—Cardinal Wiseman dedicated the convent and hospital under the title of her name, Saint Elizabeth of Hungary (1207–1231). After the ceremony, he gave Mary Gonzaga "a supply of money for the House expenses," and hearing that the sisters wished to put the garden in order, "he went himself to buy some gardening implements which he brought back to them" (BA 1:[312]). (A decade later, after Henry Manning had become Archbishop of Westminster, the poverty of this community and the mistreatment they experienced as he tried to remove them from the hospital will be frequently mentioned in Florence Nightingale's letters to Clare Moore and others.)

As negotiations for the new foundation were concluding, Florence wrote Clare the first of her extant post-Crimea letters, in reply to a request Clare had made on behalf of a soldier she had met during the war. Lord Monteagle was a trustee of the Nightingale Fund and the owner of an estate in Ireland, and Lady Monteagle was on the oversight committee of the Harley Street institution where Florence had worked before the war, but the exact nature of Clare's request on behalf of Corporal Morris is not known:

### 13. To Mary Clare Moore

*October 1/56*

My dearest Revd Mother

I lost no time in writing, the day I received your very kind and welcome letter, to Lord Monteagle (whose son is Second Chief of H.M.'s Customs) on behalf of poor Corpl. Morris. I trust that the application may be successful. I gave his direction at Liverpool.

I have seen Lady Campden who told me that the negotiation about the Hospital which you are to undertake had been completed & that you were about to be installed. I am very glad of it. I can but hope that the beginning will not be too much for you personally.

I fear that you are not getting much more strength. I hope my Cardinal will go on writing to me about you, dearest Revd Mother. You and your goodness are constantly in my thoughts. Will you thank her very much for her letter & tell her that with me, "la reconnaissance n'est qu'un vif sentiment

des bienfaits futurs" & that she must "benefit" *me* by writing again about you.
I would write to her. But I have been & am very busy—my business being, as
you will guess, a modification and reform of the system of Military Hospitals,
so that what took place, in the winter of /54, may never be able to happen
again. Remembering as I do, how I sent in the same plans & suggestions at
the beginning of the War, how they were accepted & yet nothing was done,
I do not feel very sanguine, tho' I seem to be making progress. But God does
everything in His own good time.

    Pray for me. Dearest Revd Mother

ever yours
affectionately & gratefully
F. Nightingale

*Autograph: Archives of the Sisters of Mercy, Bermondsey.*

Three weeks later Mai Smith wrote to Clare, asking her to provide
a statement to Mary Stanley about the conduct of Charlotte Salisbury
in Scutari. In September 1855, Florence had dismissed this lady nurse
from service, on the grounds that she had misappropriated property
from the Free Gifts Store—a supply of materials sent by private donors
to Miss Nightingale in Turkey for distribution at her discretion (Vicinus and Nergaard, eds. 128–30). Miss Salisbury had, on her return to
England and with Mary Stanley's support, attempted to bring a libel
suit against Florence Nightingale (Goldie, ed. 187 n. 20). When this
failed, Mary Stanley—who had her own misgivings about Nightingale's methods of governing during the war—evidently kept the issue
alive, if only privately and unofficially. This circumstance undoubtedly
rankled Florence; hence the request from Aunt Mai:

### 14. To Mary Clare Moore

*Vicar's Cross*
*Chester*
*October 20/56*

Dearest Revd Mother
    Only too full of business as I know you to be, it is not without anxiety &
regret that I take up any of your time & thoughts. I will endeavour to explain
why I feel compelled to do so.
    Among many accusations which have been raised against Miss Nightin-

gale, is that of having dismissed Miss Salisbury harshly & without sufficient reason. You will believe, dear Revd Mother, that she would pursue whatever work our Heavenly Father may set before her with single heart obeying His call, that both herself and her friends would be indifferent to such accusations as far as they *personally* concerned her, but this accusation if uncontradicted may be injurious to her work, and it is therefore my husband's strong opinion that we ought to possess ourselves of the means of contradicting it.

No evidence which can be turned against Miss Nightingale on this subject can be more important than the Revd Mother's, from the undoubting confidence which her word commands, & from her having lived in the Hospital with Miss Salisbury. That Revd Mother's evidence is at present in the hands of Miss Stanley against Miss Nightingale is the reason I venture to trouble her with this letter. Dearest Revd Mother, if you knew how it grieves me to give you any trouble, I am sure you would believe that I do so only for the love of truth, & for the sake of Miss Nightingale's work, both dear to you as to me. Miss Stanley has been told by Revd Mother that Miss Salisbury's fault was "imprudent generosity"; had this been her only fault, Miss Salisbury would have reason to say that she has been harshly & unjustly judged.

I should not presume to offer information on this subject, but that I know how strictly, how devotedly Revd Mother gave her time & thoughts to the work she had undertaken, not inquiring into that which was not hers, & unwillingly hearing evil of those to whom it belonged. I will mention some particulars perhaps never known to her. Miss Salisbury, on joining Miss Nightingale, entered into a written agreement to give away none of the property committed to Miss N. by the people of England or otherwise, without Miss N.'s permission, given under her hand.

That she did give away such property, without Miss N.'s knowledge, Miss Salisbury herself admits. Moreover, in the room of the Maltese servants in Miss N.'s house & concealed about their bed, was found property belonging to the Stores under Miss Salisbury's charge, brought there by her direction, estimated at above £100. For whatever purpose this property was intended, its discovery in those circumstances surely proved that Miss Salisbury was not to be trusted with the care of it. Further, Capt. Keatley informed Miss Nightingale that he had conveyed packets of goods to Constantinople at the request of Miss Salisbury, who told him she had been desired by Miss Nightingale to send them, though Miss N. had no knowledge of their being sent. Miss Salisbury also told the women in the house that she was sending things to Constantinople to a married daughter of Capt. Keatley who was in distress, though Capt. Keatley had no married daughter.

Without entering into other grounds which Miss Nightingale had for withdrawing her trust in Miss Salisbury, I will ask whether on those I have mentioned, all of which are on proof, it does not appear to Revd Mother that Miss Salisbury's fault was a dishonest discharge of the trust committed to her, which rendered her dismissal by Miss N. a necessary duty. One word from Revd Mother in answer to this question is all I ask.

Sorry as I am to write so much at length, because I know not how to ask this question with less explanation, I will conclude at once with the expression of heartfelt respect, & if you permit me to say it, with that of tenderest affection to one whose example will ever be light to my path [[faith?]].

I remain my dear Revd Mother's
sincere & affectionate
M. Smith

When you are kind enough to write, please to direct to me at

Combe Hurst,
Kingston on Thames,
where I shall shortly be.

*Autograph: Archives of the Sisters of Mercy, Bermondsey*

Evidently Clare wrote the requested letter, for later that month Aunt Mai responded:


## 15. To Mary Clare Moore

*Atherstone*
*October 26th/56*

Dearest Revd Mother

I cannot express how much I felt relieved in receiving your answer to my letter. I had so much feared that I might not have well explained why I was giving you the pain of hearing again of this distressing subject, but you have entirely apprehended my motive, & I can quite conceive that on which you remained in ignorance of the facts of that painful case. I am desirous to add that Miss Nightingale herself would never have troubled you on this subject, so unwilling is she to add to your weight of labour or care, & so unwilling also to enter upon self defence. I have only to add that your letter to Miss Stanley contains all the explanation we could desire, & to thank you, dearest Revd Mother, for your kind and prompt answer.

With every best wish to you & yours, I am dear Revd Mother's
grateful & affectionate
M. Smith

*Autograph: Archives of the Sisters of Mercy, Bermondsey*

The Archives of the Sisters of Mercy in Bermondsey contain an un-dated letter to Clare Moore from Mary Stanley. Apparently, it is her response to Clare's explanation:

> You need never apologize for any thing you say to me on any subject.
> With regard to Miss Salisbury, all you told me, exactly accorded with what I had from every quarter with the one exception that you did *not* think it *impossible* that she was given to drink.
> The outside therefore of what I *may* have said, tho' I do not recollect that I did so except at home, is that you thought as others did that she was most imprudent but had not stolen the gifts to sell for her own use.
> It is unnecessary for me to enter into further detail—except to say that my one desire has been throughout to have the case sifted & Miss Salisbury *fully* exposed if guilty.
> It has been *most unfair* to Miss Nightingale that the case has been so hushed up by her friends—if they had the means of answering the document which was litho-graphed & circulated by Miss Salisbury. . . .
> One question I sh'd be glad if you would answer me.
> Did Miss Salisbury express *to you* her desire of becoming a Catholic when she got into trouble, or have you heard this from others?—and if *to you*, at what period of the 3 days previous to her departure? (Autograph: Archives of the Sisters of Mercy, Bermondsey)

Whether Clare responded to this letter is not known, though she certainly may have.

In November 1856, Clare must have told Florence, either in a letter or during a visit of Florence to Bermondsey, that she was searching for the address of a particular soldier's mother. In Florence's letter of December 1, enclosing the address, the reference to Clare's brushing out gutters may be directly related to a claim Florence later made, in a letter to Jowett in 1862: "After we came home [[from the Crimea]] I found her one day cleaning out a gutter with her own hands" (BL Add. MSS 45783, f. 12). Florence now writes:

*16. To Mary Clare Moore*

*30 Old Burlington St.*
*Dec. 1/56*

Dearest Revd Mother

I have made a search for the direction of poor Geo. Wates's mother &
*found it*, in order to save you the trouble of looking.

Please don't brush out any more gutters (like a cat) this cold weather &
with best love to all my Sisters, pray believe me yours

ever affectionately & gratefully
F. Nightingale

*Autograph: Archives of the Sisters of Mercy, Bermondsey*


After New Year's Day, Florence wrote another short note, from
Mai and Sam Smith's home, where she was evidently visiting:


*17. To Mary Clare Moore*

*Combe Hurst*
*Kingston on Thames. S.W.*
*Jan. 5/57*

Does my dearest Revd Mother remember putting into my hands the first winter in Scutari a Cheque for £60, I *think* it was. (But I have not my accounts
by me.)

As she gave not only her money but her words and deeds, which are
above all money's worth, to the suffering soldiers, I hope that she will not
object, at this season of the year when she must have so many claims upon
her, especially with a new foundation, to receiving it again with the stipula-
tion that it is to be at her own disposal only, not at that of any Committee or
authority.

Ever my dearest Revd Mother's
loving & grateful
F. Nightingale

*Autograph: Archives of the Sisters of Mercy, Bermondsey*


The British government having received from His Imperial Majesty The Sultan a monetary gift in gratitude for those who had nursed

the sick and wounded soldiers in Turkey and the Crimea, Sir Benjamin Hawes, the Under Secretary for War, wrote to Bishop Grant in December 1856, inquiring how to distribute portions of this gift to the two parties of Sisters of Mercy—those from Bermondsey, and those, mostly from Ireland, who had gone to the Crimea under the leadership of Mary Francis Bridgeman. On December 10, Grant sent Hawes the names and respective convents of the twenty-three Sisters of Mercy who had served during the war, including the two from Liverpool who had died in the Crimea: Mary Winifred Sprey and Mary Elizabeth Butler. Speaking of the English sisters, Grant told Hawes:

It is pleasing to them to reflect that their desire to undertake the duties assigned to them solely from motives of charity & without any personal remuneration has been admitted & recognized by their country, and they therefore feel that in being permitted to distribute the gift of His I. M. The Sultan amongst the poor & infirm, they will not lose the honour which they so highly prize of having been allowed to devote their services, without the hope of any earthly reward, to the alleviation of the sufferings, & to the care of the sick & dying Soldiers of the Eastern Expeditionary Army. (quoted in BA 1:[314])

From the start all the sisters had insisted on donating their service and had explicitly refused compensation. Their small "earthly reward" from the Sultan's gift—£10 allotted for each sister—certainly did not violate this intention; according to the letter from the War Office, £80 was given "To the Sisterhood of Mercy, Bermondsey," and £150 "To the Sisterhoods of Kinsale, Liverpool, Charleville, Cork, Dublin, Carlow and Chelsea" (quoted in BA 1:[314]). The entire £80 presented to the sisters in Bermondsey was given to the community at St. Elizabeth's Hospital on Great Ormond Street, not only because four of them had served in the Crimea, but because they were poor, having no regular source of income except what was occasionally given to them by Cardinal Wiseman.

In January 1857, Florence Nightingale sent Clare Moore a copy of part of the letter she had received from Lord Panmure, Secretary for War (BA 1:[315]), together with her own formal acknowledgment of the nurses' services:

### 18. To Mary Clare Moore

London
January /57

It is with the sincerest pleasure that I enclose to each of those who rendered such valuable service in the British War Hospitals of the East, the tribute paid by the War Secretary to their services.

I rejoice that this as well as the Sultan's offering have testified how great was the appreciation of their labors.

I may here humbly add my own most grateful acknowledgments for all the assistance which I have received in this work. The devotion to it which I have witnessed both in Catholic and Protestant can never be forgotten by me. It is a remembrance to make glad the memory even of those scenes of suffering, which must also remain with us while life endures.

With every fervent prayer that love can offer for my fellow-workers, I remain their grateful & affectionate friend

Florence Nightingale

To the Revd Mother
of the "Sisters of Mercy"
of Bermondsey.
*Autograph: Archives of the Sisters of Mercy, Bermondsey*

With this formal letter—presumably also sent to other groups of nurses—Florence enclosed a personal note to Clare, promising a visit to Bermondsey:

### 19. To Mary Clare Moore

Dearest Revd Mother
You did not need this—nevertheless I have much pleasure in sending it [[to]] you.

I want to hear how you are and am coming as soon as I can. Also I want to see you *on business.*

Ever yours gratefully
F. Nightingale

30 Old Burlington St. W.
Jan. 26/57
*Autograph: Archives of the Sisters of Mercy, Bermondsey*

Throughout the autumn of 1856, Florence was preparing *State-ments Exhibiting the Voluntary Contributions received by Miss Nightingale for the Use of the British War Hospitals in the East, with the Mode of their Distribution in 1854, 1855, 1856*, a detailed account of the goods and funds she had received from private donors and her disposition of these contributions. During 1857 she continued the urgent work of re-porting to the government on her experiences and observations in the Crimea and of trying to establish some reliable means of instituting the numerous reforms she advocated. The memory of the Crimean dead haunted her. In a private note written in late 1856, she had lamented:

Oh my poor men who endured so patiently. I feel I have been such a bad mother to you to come home & leave you lying in your Crimean grave. 73 per cent in eight regiments during six months from disease alone—who thinks of that now? But if I could carry any one point which would prevent any part of the recurrence of this our colossal calamity . . . then I should have been true to the cause of those brave dead. (Vicinus and Nergaard, eds. 171)

Whether the constant demands of the work she had assumed, or her own physical collapse in August 1857, or the destruction or in-advertent loss of her letters is the reason, there are no further extant letters of Florence to Clare for the rest of 1857 and well into 1858. Clare herself was busy. The Hospital of St. Elizabeth on Great Ormond Street had been founded in November 1856, with five sisters from Bermond-sey, four of whom, including Mary Gonzaga Barrie, had served in the Crimea. Now in 1857, Clare was arranging for a new convent in Wig-ton. The community selected for this foundation, where they would, in time, assume responsibility for an orphanage, included Mary Martha Beste and Mary de Chantal Hudden, two of the Crimean volunteers. Clare went with them to Wigton on September 4 and remained there until October 5. Of the sisters who had gone to the Crimea, only one, Mary Joseph Hawkins, now remained with her in Bermondsey.

It seems unlikely that Florence and Clare did not correspond for over fifteen months; in fact, Florence's May 13, 1858 letter to Lady Herbert suggests that she was well aware of what had been going on in Clare's life: " 'Revd Mother' (of Bermondsey) whose name you will remember has been and is dangerously ill. She has had all her food from here" (BL Add. MSS 43396, f. 59). In mid-April 1858, Clare had come down with pleurisy and inflammation of the lungs. On May 17 Florence wrote to her, offering her own home as a place of rest:

*20. To Mary Clare Moore*

Dear, dear Revd Mother

How very kind of you to write to me yourself.

All I want now to say to trouble you is that I cannot think you will ever regain any strength without some little change.

I need not tell you how happy it would make me to keep you *here*, quite quiet with one Sister—and I do not think you would see much more "of the world" here than at home. But I am afraid you would not go anywhere but to a Convent. Could you not go back with "Mother" Gonzaga, as she would so dearly like, when she is obliged to go? You would find all your own children again so.

Not but that I think that to go quite away to Boulogne or Hastings for a very short time (there is too a Convent at St. Leonard's) would be very desirable, *if* you would consent.

Ever my dearest Revd Mother's
grateful & affectionate
F. Nightingale

May 17/58
*Autograph: Archives of the Sisters of Mercy, Bermondsey*

Though she was still sick in bed, Clare responded by return post, telling Florence that Lord Carnarvon, Under Secretary of State for the Colonies, had on May 12 requested that Mercy Sisters from Bermondsey go to Mauritius to establish female nurses in the public hospitals on the island—a request that Florence herself had privately initiated through Lord Stanley (BA 2:[13–14]):

*21. To Florence Nightingale*

*Convent of our Lady Mercy*
*Bermondsey May 17, 1858*

My dearest Miss Nightingale

I ought to have said what I am now going to write, last week but I wished first to tell you that I was getting strong & well, because I know your thoughtful affection & tenderness too well.

And now our Bishop Dr. Grant wishes me to thank you for so kindly directing the attention of Lord Stanley to the Convent to get Nurses for the

Hospital in Mauritius. The letter came on Ascension Day and the Bishop desired me to write to Lord Carnarvon saying I was then too ill for business and begging leave to defer my answer for a few days. They wish the experiment to be made with only two or three at first—and I very gladly offered myself as one of the number, but Dr. Grant says I must not go—however it is very clear that if the plan be likely to succeed three Sisters would not be enough to manage Hospitals of any extent & it would be but right to make arrangements from the first starting, for the number which might be ultimately required.

Now would it be too unreasonable if I were to ask you to express in a letter, which I might forward to the Colonial Office, the average number of nurses required for a given number of patients, that so the Government authorities may not deem us injudicious in petitioning for a given number of Sisters to be sent out if the plan be found successful—& besides those actually engaged with the Sick, one or two would be required to mind Convent business. The Bishop said that if you were to express an opinion that the whole nursing department ought to be under the Sisters, it would be a means of preventing disquietudes hereafter.

I am troublesome I know in asking all this—but it is part of your own good work & I almost feel I am coming to help you again—I wish I may be able indeed to help with you in any way so many suffering members of Him who will take it all as done for Himself. May He ever bless you—

I will ask Sister Gonzaga to copy the letters I got. I am able to do it myself, only it is so awkward to write in bed—but I was up yesterday, and walked a few steps in the Corridor—so you see you really must not think of me as an invalid any longer. Your kind care has made me well so soon. All the Sisters feel it so much—& indeed I do not know why you are so good to me.

May I beg to be affectionately remembered to our dear Mrs. Smith and to your own dearest Mother & Sister—

May God bless you again and again.

Ever dear Miss Nightingale
Your own devoted & grateful
Sister M. Clare

*Autograph: BL Add. MSS 45797, ff. 13–15*

Florence immediately responded, sending a personal note and enclosing a plan Clare could share with the Colonial Office:

## 22. To Mary Clare Moore

May 18/58

My dearest Revd Mother

I am very sorry that you should have this anxiety now, & almost sorry that I should have been the means of bringing it upon you at all.

I wish you could get strength first. If you could, I think the beautiful climate of the Mauritius might do you good. But I don't know how you are to be spared from home.

I agree in every thing you say. And have written the enclosed, which I will re-write & alter in any way that may put it better, to your thinking.

This is the way I should like to work it myself—viz. with Hindoos under Sisters. But I have no direct acquaintance with the Mauritius & feel quite ignorant on the Hindoo question.

I should think it important that the Sisters who go should understand French.

Ever my dearest Revd Mother's

F.N.

*Autograph: Archives of the Sisters of Mercy, Bermondsey*

With this letter Florence enclosed the following plan for Clare's and the Government's perusal as they contemplated the Mauritius request. Clare must have shared it with the Colonial Office because the copy preserved in the Bermondsey archives is not the original autograph but Clare's fair copy of it:

## 23. To Mary Clare Moore

30 Old Burlington Street. W.
May 18, 1858

1. Average number of nurses required for a given number of patients:

*Patients*

1 Sister
3 Men Nurses        to 28 – 32 Men
(or 2 Men
1 Woman)

| 1 Sister | ⎫ | |
|----------|---|---|
| 3 Female Nurses | ⎬ | to 28 – 32 Women |
| (or 2 Female) | ⎪ | |
| 1 Man) | ⎭ | |

The Sister to be distinctly & solely responsible for the whole charge.

After much anxious thought I should recommend, if it be possible, that the men and women *nurses* (under the Sisters) should be Hindoos, sent from India expressly for the purpose. In our Regimental Hospitals in India, such men nurses are found very useful.

2. I do not think that the plan is likely to be successful if three Sisters alone are sent out at first.

They should be in greater numbers, and the whole nursing department of at least one Hospital should be under them at first (to be extended to more if found desirable).

Besides the Sisters exclusively engaged in nursing, there must be one or two more for general purposes connected with the Sisterhood.

On the whole, I cannot think it desirable, that so small a number should be sent out even at first.

Florence Nightingale

Note:

With regard to the matter of the Hindoo nurses, the Colonial Office would alone be able to judge. I only wish to express an opinion derived from serving in French Hospitals under "Sisters of Charity"—that where Sisters are employed & patients are natives such a system works better, viz. that of having Sisters and attendants under Sisters, than that of having all Sisters or all Nurses.

F. N.

*Fair copy: Archives of the Sisters of Mercy, Bermondsey*

The project came to nothing in the end. Bishop Grant was uneasy about placing the sisters under the authority of the Governor of Mauritius: "as there had been so much ill feeling expressed by different parties on account of his having permitted them to go to the East subject in Hospital work to Government Authority, his Lordship demanded on this occasion that the Sisters should be altogether under the jurisdiction of the Catholic Bishop, even in what regarded the management of the Hospital." The Governor of Mauritius therefore withdrew his request, "deeming it unsafe to bring in the Ecclesiastical Authority in matters which seemed to him to belong solely to the Medical Officers" (BA 2:[14–15]).

When negotiations for the Mauritius project finally ended in November 1858, Clare must have regretted this. For despite all the difficulties of her Scutari sojourn, her letters of that period evince a certain élan and a conviction that what she and the other sisters were doing in the hospitals of Turkey and the Crimea was of the essence of their vocation as Sisters of Mercy. While she was an excellent administrator and teacher, deep down she may have had the heart of a nurse; she was most exhilarated when she was caring for the sick or the truly destitute.

No additional letters from Florence Nightingale to Clare Moore have so far been discovered for the rest of 1858, and none at all for 1859. In fact, as will be seen in the next section of this chapter, Florence's extant letters to Clare do not resume until October 1863, although there are nine extant letters from Clare to Florence in 1862.

## 1860–1862

The long gap between Florence Nightingale's known letters to Clare Moore—from early 1858 to October 1863—is not in itself evidence that she did not correspond with Clare during this five-year period. In fact, references in Clare's letters to Florence in 1862 imply that Florence did write to her that year. Rather, the absence of extant letters may be explained in other, more or less plausible, ways.

Either Florence and Clare wrote to one another infrequently during this time because they were both too busy, which seems unlikely, given the help they were to one another precisely when they were most overloaded with work; or the letters they exchanged simply remain undiscovered, which is plausible at least for Clare's letters to Florence, given the sheer volume and the numerous locations of the Nightingale papers; or, and this possibility seems most likely, their letters to one another were burned, or otherwise destroyed—as Florence, at least, frequently instructed her correspondents. In a postscript on Clare's December 28, 1862 letter to Florence, the last of the nine extant letters Clare wrote to her that year, she says: "I have been careful to burn your letters" (LMA, HI/ST/NC2—V31/62). Evidently Florence had asked her to do this in 1862, and perhaps at other times as well.

After her physical collapse in August 1857, from accumulated exhaustion and self-imposed overwork, Florence was an invalid; in November 1857, she presumed that her death was imminent and so wrote letters to family and friends to be delivered after her death (Vicinus and Nergaard, eds. 191–92). Although she recovered from this view, the pressure of the reform efforts she subsequently undertook, her frustration at the slow pace of governmental action, the departure in March 1860 of Aunt Mai who had been her household companion since September 1857, the evident illness of Sidney Herbert—her one hope for progress in the War Office—his death in August 1861 and the death of her friend Arthur Hugh Clough in November 1861, added to all the meticulous work she was trying to do during these years, left a certain bitterness and even self-pity in her thinking. In her letters these feelings were sometimes translated into harsh accusations or self-exposures that embarrassed her.

Under these circumstances and given her temperament, it would have been logical, especially in 1861 and 1862, for Florence to write "Burn" on some of her letters, including some to Clare. Since there is no reason to suspect a deliberate termination of her correspondence with Clare during these years, the only way to account for the absence of extant letters is to suppose that her letters to Clare during this period were infrequent, that some of these were burned, and that others, if there were any, were somehow lost over the last 140 years. It is also possible that in December 1861, in her deepest despair after the deaths of Sidney Herbert and Arthur Clough, Florence included Clare, too, in her categorical claim that "women have no sympathy." On December 13, in a remarkably long letter to her friend in Paris, Mary Clarke Mohl—a letter partly excusable on the human grounds of her extreme loneliness and desolation in the loss of her personal and governmental supporters—Florence wrote:

> . . . you say, "women are more sympathetic than men." Now if I were to write a book out of my experience, I should begin, *women have no sympathy*.
>
> Yours is the tradition. Mine is the conviction of experience. I have never found one woman who has altered her life one iota for me or my opinions. Now look at my experience of men. A statesman, past middle age, absorbed in politics for a quarter of a century [[Sidney Herbert]], out of 'sympathy' with me, remodels his whole life and policy—learns a science, the driest, the most technical, the most dif-

ficult, that of administration as far as it concerns the lives of men, not, as I learned it, in the field, from the stirring experience, but by writing dry Regulations in a London room by my sofa with me.

This is what I call real sympathy. . . .

Now just look at the degree in which women have sympathy—as far as my experience is concerned. And my experience of women is almost as large as Europe. . . . No Roman Catholic Supérieure has ever had the charge of women of the different creeds that I have had. No woman has excited 'passions' among women more than I have.

Yet I leave no school behind me. My doctrines have taken no hold among women. Not one of my Crimean following learnt anything from me—or gave herself for one moment after she came home to carry out the lesson of that war or of those hospitals.

No woman that I know has ever *appris à apprendre*. And I attribute this to want of sympathy.

You say somewhere that women have no *attention*. Yes. And I attribute this to want of sympathy. (Vicinus and Nergaard, eds. 230)

Were this complaint not so absolute it might constitute a somewhat accurate report on Florence's experience. Much later in the letter she acknowledges that "perhaps I may draw too much from observations in my own family" (231). The most telling, and possibly the most ironic, passage in the letter is her assertion: "Women crave for being loved, not *for loving. They scream at you for sympathy all day long, they are incapable of giving* any in return, for they cannot even remember your affairs long enough to do so" (231). Significantly, it is in this December 1861 letter that Florence declares of Sidney Herbert, who had died four months before, "I am his real widow," and of Arthur Hugh Clough, who had died on November 12, " 'I am his true widow" (232). Clearly, she was at this time suffering a profound grief, and even more, a devastating conviction that, without Herbert's continued advocacy at the War Office, her efforts to right the wrongs of the Crimean calamity were doomed.

Whether Florence ever wrote to Clare Moore in the same vein as in this letter to Clarkey Mohl cannot now be ascertained; however, if she did send her such self-pitying letters, one can imagine Clare's burning them, even as she responded with understanding and sympathy. Moreover, despite all the mutual solicitude of their friendship, one can imagine that Florence harbored, at least in this period, and even if below the surface of her consciousness, a certain resentment that Clare had, after the Crimean tour, returned to her former life and work in

Bermondsey, not to endeavors more obviously related to the Crimean horror. Occasionally in Florence's letters to other correspondents— for example, to Charlotte Canning in November 1856—one notices a simmering annoyance at what she perceived to be excessive Roman Catholic submission to the causes of suffering: "R. Catholics, even the best, are essentially incapacitated (from their inherent Manichaean- ism) from doing the best kind of good. They are to console the suffer- ings which evils have produced. They are not to remove the causes of those evils" (Vicinus and Nergaard, eds. 166). In 1861 she confided to her friend Mary Jones:

[It would take much more time than either you or I have, if I were to tell the mis- chiefs I have seen in R. Catholic orders, arising from a want of acknowledging the principle of individual independence in their dependents. . . .

The absolute helplessness of big girls of 20 & upwards, brought up in their Orphan Asylums. . . . these dependents are *perfectly incapable*, when they leave the Institutions, whether Educational, Penitential, or what not, of governing them- selves, so as to earn a single sixpence even at the very work they have been used to do for the nuns, or so as to keep themselves from falling into the arms of the first man who tempts them. Pardon the crudity of my expressions.] (Vicinus and Nergaard, eds. 248–49)

Whether Florence exempted Clare and her sisters from these analyses (they had no orphanage in Bermondsey!), or simply refrained from writing such things to her, or said them to her privately when they visited, is not known. However, in Clare's letters to Florence in 1862, with which their extant correspondence resumes, one finds Clare, especially in the later letters in this series, trying to relieve Florence's "blacken"-ed thoughts, overburdened as they were with "the knowl- edge of so much misery, vice & degradation."

By early 1862 Florence had recovered from some of her despon- dency and from some of the physical symptoms she had reported to friends. But now she found herself engaged in what Edward Cook calls "one of the heaviest, and most useful, pieces of work which she ever did": research for members of the Royal Commission on the Health of the Army in India (2:17).

Clare, meanwhile, had been extremely busy: founding new con- vents in Abingdon (1859) and Gravesend (1860), tending the dying in her own community, preparing postulants and novices for their recep- tion of the habit and profession of vows, converting a room over the convent laundry into an infants' school (1861), and visiting the struggling Abingdon and Gravesend communities, among other duties. Then, in January 1862, she had the painful responsibility, on the advice of physicians, of committing Mary Francis Middelton, a beloved sister in the Bermondsey community, to a mental hospital run by religious women in Bruges, her illness having been judged not only irreversible but dangerous to her own health and safety. By late May, after preparing numerous materials for Bishop Grant, who had departed for Rome on May 16, Clare was herself worn down, if not outright sick. Evidently Florence sent a letter and parcel to her on May 22. Clare responded the next day:

## 24. To Florence Nightingale

*Convent of Mercy*
*Bermondsey. May 23 [1862]*

Dearest Miss Nightingale

When your messenger came last night I was not able to write or I should not have allowed Sister Stanislaus to thank you for me—but I am better today—and as I am writing a letter of thanks for many many things to dear kind Mrs. Smith I thought I would ask a fresh favour—that she would convey this little note to you—but you know I never can tell you how grateful I feel and when the Sisters see all you send me they can only say—dear Miss Nightingale, how good she is! Shall we not pray for her—and that is truly the only way in which I can thank you—only I would like to be beside you and tell you so—yet that would be but a passing joy—and we must look on beyond this earth. May our dearest Lord grant you to know & do His blessed will. May He love you and make you love Him eternally—

Dearest Miss Nightingale,
Your's most gratefully
Sister M. C. Moore

*The Florence Nightingale Museum Trust, LMA, HI/ST/NC2—V16/62*

In July 1862, Florence wrote to Benjamin Jowett. Although her letter has been quoted earlier, its sentences about Clare, placed in their chronological context, illustrate Nightingale's thinking at this time. In an extended postscript at the end of this long letter about the "Stuff," that is, her religious views, she tells Jowett:

I don't want the "Stuff" to enter anyone's mind without its having for a result to settle what to say to God, and I am sure I cannot do this, at least not for others. I don't want the "Stuff" to enter anyone's mind without improving his life.

I always recur to the *working* religious orders, as being the only people who have said, that is what we think God says to us. We are going *to do it*.

Now the only satisfactory result of this (or of any) "Stuff" wd. be to do something like that. The most religious mind I ever knew was that of a R. Catholic Revd. Mother, who was so good as to go out with me to the Crimea. After we came home I found her one day cleaning out a gutter with her own hands. I know she did it on no theory. I think she had much better have employed a man to do it, but that is what I mean by a true idea of religious life, and she the only R. Catholic too I have ever known who never tried to convert me. (BL Add. MSS 45783, ff. 11–12)

On July 24, Clare wrote again to Florence, thanking her for her recent gifts to the children in the schools at Bermondsey and suggesting that Aunt Mai, "our most kind Grandmother," might visit Mary Gonzaga Barrie and the St. Elizabeth's Hospital community at their temporary home in Brentford. About this time, Sir George Bowyer—a Catholic acquaintance of Florence's brother-in-law, Sir Harry Verney—had become interested in expansion of the hospital, including construction of a larger chapel, and had proposed affiliating it with the Knights Hospitallers of St. John of Jerusalem, which he had re-established in London. The hospital was subsequently renamed The Hospital of St. John and St. Elizabeth. The troubles that would later afflict the hospital community on the death of Cardinal Wiseman were, at this point, far from Clare's mind:

## 25. To Florence Nightingale

*July 24, 1862*

Dearest Miss Nightingale

Accept our loving thanks for all your kindness. The Sisters as well as the children will value the nice pictures and the book of Prints.

I had been wishing to write & tell you that your poor Cardinal [Mary Gonzaga Barrie] has been obliged to go from Ormond Street with Sisters and patients to a house at Brentford where they must remain until the new Convent and Hospital will be ready for them next year. Their present abode is Clifton House—it would be on our most kind Grandmother's way from Richmond if she should have time to call on them. They have besides their sick the charge of the School boys & girls—

May God bless you, ever dear Miss Nightingale. You are in my poor prayers night & day.

Your ever affectionate
Sister M. C. Moore

*The Florence Nightingale Museum Trust, LMA, HI/ST/NC2 — V19/62*

Evidently Florence had written to Clare about a request she had received from Mary Xavier Maguire of the Sisters of Mercy in Melbourne, Australia, asking her to contribute something they might then attach to her name and sell or raffle at a Bazaar to raise money for their works of mercy. Clare's long response offers some suggestions, but it also implies that Florence had shared some of her "black" feelings with her and had invited her to visit:

## 26. To Florence Nightingale

*Convent Bermondsey*
*Sept. 17, 1862*

Dearest Miss Nightingale

We had a letter from the same Sisters, not for the same object, but more interesting, for it tells of other useful works, & says nothing of the Bazaar. I laughed to myself at the thought of your making fancy things! but I feel very puzzled what to recommend. The first idea was articles of clothing for the young women, as I believe in the colonies some things are hard to be got — then I thought that would not be so profitable as something sent by you which could be sold at the Bazaar — and the only inspiration was — prints or lithographs with a few words written by yourself, not on the prints, but a little letter expressing your kind interest.

The little black child must be the same for I remembered since that good Lord Herbert united with Lady Arundel & Surrey in paying the child's pension at Isleworth, for it struck me that she must have been placed in the best school to require two persons of rank to pay for her, whereas the poor School would have done very well I thought.[25]

You are too good to think of the Chapel for me, but unless I had a companion or that I remained a longer time, I think I should prefer hearing Mass in spirit, as I did when I was with you, although I should have been very glad if I could have got to Mass without going out.

You made me feel a little proud because I am to go to you again. I was afraid I had been too stupid & tiresome—for I had had a cold just before, & my teeth were bad. I am so much brighter now, you would be pleased!

I have thought of you so much. Your hardest task seems to me the knowledge of so much misery, vice & degradation. The thought seems to blacken every thing & almost every one—& we begin to forget there is any thing good or any thing pleasing to God in the world, and yet with what love does He look down on the innocence of children, on the hardships of the poor, and above all on the love of so many who seek to preserve that innocence and to bring some remedy to those who are more wretched because they are sinning, than because they are suffering. It is so nice to think that our Lord Himself brings forth the innocent babes as a barrier against His justice—and we know He looks down with delight on our least acts of charity & goodness. But I am sure you do look on the bright side of the picture—only I judge by myself, for it makes me very sad when I hear or k[now] of wicked people—& I know & hear of so little. Our divine Lord's Heart was oppressed with a[nguish?] because our sins were always in His sight. May He help you in your efforts to remove those [these?] evils,—and I humbly pray that He may open His most loving Heart to you, and there make you know His holy will & give you grace to do it faithfully—

Poor Mother Stanislaus was recalled to her own Convent last Sunday—her help was wanting in sitting up with the sick Priest. I have an idea that Sr. Gonzaga will come here today, for she has be[en] a long time absent for her.

We are preparing for a Clothing next Friday, a lay Sister. She had been in our Schools for many years and about five years since we gave her the place of messenger or [illegible word: courière?] because she had lost one hand & was therefore unable to seek employment as a servant. She has been so good & faithful that now the Sisters have admitted her to the Noviceship.

Next Wednesday will be the grand Feast of our Institute, "Our Lady of Mercy". [It] is such a lovely title—our dear [Fou]ndress used to say Mercy is more than charity—it adds forgiveness of even the worst ingratitude to the benefits bestow[ed]. I shall be asking leave to go to you after that day—and then I can tell you how pleased all were with your presents & how grateful I am both to you & your household, & how afraid that I made myself too much at home for their ideas of Nuns who of course ought to walk up in the air! but now I have made too long a letter & I may only beg forgiveness for taking up your time.

May God bless & guide you, dearest Miss Nightingale & may our Mother of Mercy watch over you & shew herself a Mother to you.

I am ever your most loving & grateful

Sister M. Clare

*The Florence Nightingale Museum Trust, LMA, HI/ST/NC2—V23/62*

Nine days later, Clare wrote again, to inquire when she might visit:

*27. To Florence Nightingale*

Convent. Bermondsey
Sep^r 26. 1862

Dearest Miss Nightingale

I am come with my petition to be allowed to go & see you again, if Monday, Tuesday or Wednesday would be convenient days for you, but I shall be free all the following week, if you should be too much engaged next week. It will be a great joy to see you again.

Dearest Miss Nightingale,
your ever grateful & loving
Sister M. Clare

*The Florence Nightingale Museum Trust, LMA, HI/ST/NC 2—V24/62*

Florence was at this time "harassed" with work for her medical collaborators Dr. William Farr and Dr. John Sutherland, who, as members of the Royal Commission on the Health of the Army in India, were depending on and encouraging her research and forwarding her insistent pleas for sanitary reform in India.

Perhaps Clare visited her sometime between September 26 and October 10—if the reference to "the book" in the following letter is to one Clare had left behind when she visited. In any event, Clare wrote again on October 10, sending copies of some of the letters of Catherine McAuley and offering Florence her continued prayer and support:

*28. To Florence Nightingale*

Convent. Bermondsey
Oct^r 10. 1862

Dearest Miss Nightingale

I did not think you would have taken the trouble to send the book—I

hoped to have got it when I went to see you again. I will not now take time
to look at it, but I shall be able to tell you.

I am so glad you are pleased with our dear Revd Mother—as I always
call her, she seems to be living to me—her words & ways come so often before me. One of the Sisters in Baggot Street copied out some of her *poetical*
letters from foundations—they will amuse you & I venture to send them in
their untidy state.

And now for your own dear self—I do indeed pray for you—it is all
I can do—and I trust your desire is the prayer our most loving Lord now
asks from you—you have spent yourself for His sake—you cannot have the
energy of younger days. This is no comfort—as I well know—but there is the
comfort of seeking to do God's will & trusting that He will come to heal and
help us in His own good time. May He bless and guide you ever dear Miss
Nightingale—

Yours most gratefully<br>
Sister M. C. Moore

*The Florence Nightingale Museum Trust, LMA, HI/ST/NC2—V25/62*

Three days later Clare wrote again, to thank Florence for her recent
gifts, to tell her about her own work, and to inquire, however gently,
about when she might visit. Florence had evidently loaned Clare a
book; in commenting on it, Clare talks about their mutual desire to
meditate well:

## 29. To Florence Nightingale

*Convent of Mercy*<br>
*Bermondsey S. E. Oct<sup>r</sup>. 13. 1862*

Dearest Miss Nightingale

May I hope you will forgive me for being so ungrateful as not to thank
you for all your kind presents last Friday. My mind turned to yourself only—
and just at the time I was called to attend to various things—but you know I
do thank you from my heart, although I fear I must seem unthankful. I tried
so much to write, but our good Bishop sent so many papers to be copied that
I could not get a moment. The Sisters all feel your kindness so much—they
would wish me to say a great many fine things for them—but you will accept
our affectionate good wishes & prayers—poor people have nothing better.

I went to St. George's Church this morning to bring home my writing to the Bishop as I wanted his advice about some of our Convent business—on my way back I felt I must go out of my way to see a poor family, the children have been obliged to stay from School on account of small pox—five had it—one died—a dear little child of six—her younger sister greeted me by pulling out from a dreadful piece of rag, a halfpenny for the poor—"for Katie's soul!" I could not well describe their own wretchedness, for the father has been in a dying state for months. We had five shillings to give them—a small fortune—but I could not help feeling it was the dear child's selfdenial & faith which drew me there, for I hesitated to add to my walk—already very long for me.

We then went on to a poor young man in the last stage of consumption, his only child of two years old lying at the foot of his bed in smallpox of the worst kind, his poor wife making sacks, or rather unable to make them on account of the child's illness—poor man, he was very ignorant & inattentive to religion—now full of joy, having received all the Sacraments. It is a great pleasure though a sad one to be devoted to the Service of the Poor.

I do not know when you will allow me to go to you again, dearest Miss Nightingale. I could go this week any day—next week Mr. Collingridge will be in town—he was Priest in this Church for more than twenty years. Lately he was promoted to Winchester, and he would be disappointed if he did not find me at home. The following week I shall be free, if more convenient to you—and I could go very well by the Rail road, for the Terminus is in Fenchurch Street & the Trains for Hampstead Heath are every quarter of an hour—I feel sorry you should have the trouble of sending for me—

I had a little visit from Mother Gonzaga last Monday. She brought me a loan of Mother Stanislaus to help with some work. The Sick Priest went to Ramsgate last week, but to make up for losing that employment they have opened an evening School—poor Sr. Gonzaga did not seem at all well & I heard from her today—she fears she is getting a regular "attack".

I have had little time for reading but I could not resist going over again the story of the poor man's conversion. I do not wonder that the book is not encouraged for it is very exciting. Your way of telling it was so much more real. Still it makes one think how little we value our Blessed Lord's love & goodness and condescension towards us—& the charity of that good Bishop was but a tiny spark from the furnace of His charity. I wish we could meditate as we ought—I might add, I wish I could meditate at all; it is such a confusion to be full of distractions during the brief space one can give to prayer—but it is also a comfort to feel that our poor efforts are joined with the prayers of God's holy ones by our union with them in the Church, to feel still more that our prayer is united with that of our most loving Lord &

that this union with Him becomes stricter and more intimate each time we approach the Sacraments, especially the Holy Communion. I have so often wished you could have that joy—you who are working so much harder than I do for God's sake—& making such great sacrifices—but I do feel that our Blessed Lord will give you that union with Himself which your heart seeks for so sincerely & I do pray for you constantly as well as I can.

I forgot to say that you could keep our dear Revd Mother's life as long as you please, and our Rule—I hoped you had accepted of—if I might be allowed to offer it.

I fear I am taking up too much of your time. The Sisters come in & I forget what I was going to say & then I write more than I ought.

May God bless you dear kind Miss Nightingale. May He reward all your charity.

Ever your's most gratefully
Sister M. Clare

*The Florence Nightingale Museum Trust, LMA, HI/ST/NC2—V26/62*

Interleaved between these letters from Clare were, apparently, letters from Florence to her. Their content can be known only through references in Clare's letters that suggest the other side of the dialogue. Perhaps Florence explained to Clare the same problem she had described to her mother on September 6: "I regret that I have let visitors talk to me to the last moment before a meal, thereby incapacitating me for food & sleep altogether. . . . Alas if they were to see me after eating, they would never wish to see it again. I regret that I have received two visits on the same day—or after 5 o'clock—things which always bring on my spasm, etc." (Wellcome Institute, photocopy, MS 9000/64).

At the end of October, still seeking an opportunity to visit—presumably, in part, on the supposition that her presence might console Florence—Clare wrote again:

## 30. To Florence Nightingale

*Convent. Bermondsey*
*Oct$^r$ 28. 1862*

Dearest Miss Nightingale

I felt uncertain about writing to you, although your last letter seemed to say I might—but I know you have so much to think of & to write about, I feared to add to your work. I have been anxious too, lest this cold weather may not have made you more ill and suffering. I have been longing to hear when I may go to you—while I have been thinking also that this week may be an inconvenient one to you, as you intend to leave Hampstead at the end of it—but in whatever way my thoughts go to you it is always to pray for you, May our most loving Lord bless & keep you.

I rejoiced to think you had the visits of such dear friends, especially your most beloved Mother—I trust you were able to give her nice time with you. She seemed to be so like yourself, full of tender pity for all and seeking to do good to all.

Sr. M. Gonzaga came here last week. She is better, thank God, but she has many anxieties. She offered to be my companion if I should be allowed to go see you again. I was afraid you would not be able to talk to both, besides I hesitated about taking her away from her Community—as she has been in past months a good deal absent. You know how much she loves you, & if you felt any the least wish to see her, she would be more than glad.

Amid various interruptions, I have nearly read "your Bishop" but I will confess with a feeling of fear because the author seems to make himself the judge of all things, without that submission to the Church which is our only security—he almost justifies the evil deeds occasioned by poverty etc. and yet we feel that the holy martyrs did only what they ought to do in laying down their lives in torments rather than offend God in the least. We must have compassion on the poor sinner, but we cannot say that he is not to be condemned for his sin. What is lovely is the good Bishop's character— but above all God's goodness to the poor man & his return to God. When the ways of Providence become clear to us, we shall see how blessed were the hardships we repine at, how they have saved souls who would have lost themselves had they not been so afflicted. I am taking up your time—and now I will only say that I shall be even more free next week, if it would be more convenient to you, dearest Miss Nightingale—I fear I am troublesome.

Your's ever most gratefully & affectionately

Sister M. Clare

*The Florence Nightingale Museum Trust, LMA, HI/ST/NC2—V27/62*

And again in November:

### 31. To Florence Nightingale

*Convent Bermondsey*
*Nov<sup>r</sup> 19. 1862*

My dearest Miss Nightingale

Am I doing wrong in writing to remind you of your promise to allow me a little visit sometime during this month—I got afraid that your guardian angel did not think I was trying to be good enough & so he would not put it into your mind to send for your

Ever loving & grateful
Sister M. Clare

*The Florence Nightingale Museum Trust, LMA, HI/ST/NC2 — V28/62*

In the weeks surrounding this letter, some hurt or misunderstanding evidently occurred, occasioned by some reference or enclosure in one of Clare's letters, probably on the topic of Florence's religious faith or religious affiliation. There is at present no way of reconstructing the precise cause of Florence's pain, though probably Bishop Grant was in some way involved. Perhaps Clare had quoted to Florence, or had enclosed in a letter to her, a letter from him in which he had commented on Florence. Or perhaps Grant had written directly to Florence.

At the end of December 1862, Clare wrote to Florence—to explain the context, insofar as she knew it, of whatever had offended Florence and to ask her pardon:

### 32. To Florence Nightingale

*Convent Bermondsey*
*Dec<sup>r</sup> 28. 1862*

My very dear Miss Nightingale

It grieved me that I should have sent that letter because it pained you, but I have such confidence in your goodness that I feel you have forgiven me, and I am even glad this should have happened—not that our Bishop or Dr. Manning have spoken to me on the opinions they supposed you to hold, but Sr. Gonzaga did, from what authority I know not—and although since I have spoken with yourself I felt that your faith in our Divine Lord's mysteries was the same with mine—yet it was a comfort to me that you should *say so*—& though apparently you are not a member of the Church, your most upright will & heart makes you such, for if you knew of any thing more you could do to please our Heavenly Father, you would do it unhesitatingly—& therefore I have never felt restraint in speaking with you, or rather, you are almost the only one, dearest Miss Nightingale, to whom I can speak freely on religious subjects—I mean my own feelings on them. I know nothing of controversy—we do not want it here—the poor people only want instruction, and the Christian Doctrine seems always new and delightful.

I did not send you that life of St. Teresa's faithful companion only to give you pleasure[26]—and I never speak of you, except among the Sisters to tell of your goodness & especial kindness to us. I asked the Bishop to pray for you for I rely on his prayers very much, he is so good—and now I think our loving Lord permitted him to take up this wrong idea, that your devoted heart might have a fresh offering to make, or maybe it was that I might have this pain of having caused you pain—for it is one to know that people, even good people, form such judgments of us—although we are quite indifferent whether they praise or dispraise. Still dearest Miss Nightingale, you must really give the Catholics credit for loving and revering you very much! and they have good reason to do so.

I do not suppose there is a chance of my seeing Dr. Manning, but I will write your kind message to him—he has never spoken of your religious feelings to me—indeed he never spoke but that once he asked me to see you—but he then shewed such deep interest, that I resolved to ask you if I might tell him I had seen you again.

I have made a long explanation, and I have not said all I wish—yet I hope our Divine Lord will make you know it all, for it is before Him I think about you & that my heart seems to be with yours. In loving & labouring for Him you are far before me, though I have my advantages over you in the grace of the Sacraments & the direction of His holy Church. I think of you so much at Holy Communion & I wonder what is your faith there—but I am not asking nor do I wish you to tell me anything of yourself—it is very clear that our Lord loves you very much & that you love Him with your whole heart & mind & strength—I wish I could say I did, & I am trying with His grace to do better—

Again I must ask you to believe that our good Bishop meant kindly—he is most kind & anxious for the welfare of all—but probably some one said those things which caused him to write so—

I feel ashamed to take up your time and I beg pardon for many failings in your regard, but not for failing in love and gratitude. May God bless you,

dearest Miss Nightingale—may He bring you to Himself—and make you love
& do His Will.

Your most grateful & loving

Sister M. Clare

I have been careful to burn your letters—
*The Florence Nightingale Museum Trust, LMA, HI/ST/NC2 — V31/62*

Unfortunately, no further extant letters from Clare to Florence
have so far been discovered, and Florence's extant letters to Clare
do not resume until October 1863, although she sends produce and
flowers to Bermondsey in May 1863. From the intimate character of
Florence's letters to Clare during the rest of the decade, one can assume that the pain or misunderstanding to which Clare alludes above
was resolved.

Certainly Clare was large-minded enough and sufficiently at
home with herself to accept responsibility for whatever had aggrieved
Florence. Although she was objective as to the facts, she valued peaceful reconciliation. Some years later she wrote to her friend Teresa
Boyce: " 'Blessed are the peace makers for they shall be called the
Children of God'—and nothing makes such peace in a community as
to look on everything in a cheerful way, as you do." The tensions in
Florence's interior life and in her exterior reform work often made
such cheerfulness difficult, if not impossible, for her. Indeed, she might
have called cheerfulness under these circumstances "blindness." Clare
may have understood all this.

# 1863–1864

In early 1863 Clare was involved, among other responsibilities,
in preparing for publication a small volume of Bishop Grant's *Meditations of the Sisters of Mercy before Renewal of Vows*. Although he had
composed them for the community, Grant would not permit his own
name to be put on the title page, feeling that "If the Meditations are
worth anything, it is better they should go down to a future time as of
the *Sisters of Mercy* in the *Diocese of Southwark*, than as written by me"
(BA 2:[61]). Moreover, in June, Mary Joseph O'Hara, a member of the
Bermondsey community, caught typhus, and Clare was much occupied in nursing her.

Meanwhile, Florence was overwhelmed with completing the Report of the India Sanitary Commission. Edward Cook, who studied the document in some detail, claims that "the amount of work which she gave to it during 1862–1863 was enormous" (2:24). The Report, on the dire sanitation problems of India as they affected the mortality and invaliding rates of the British Army stationed there, is, as he points out, no mere pamphlet:

It is a very formidable thing, consisting of two bulky volumes, containing respectively 1069 and 959 pages—in all 2028 pages, mostly in small print. Of this mountainous mass, the greater part bears in one way or another the impress of Miss Nightingale. It was she in the first place . . . who drafted the questions which were sent to every military station in India. The replies, as they came in from India [which "occupy the whole of the second volume"], were sent to her to analyse. There were van-loads of them, she said, which cost her £4.10s. to move whenever she changed houses. . . . It was said at the time that such a complete picture of life in India, both British and native, was contained in no other book in existence. . . . The "Observations by Miss Nightingale," which occupy twenty-three pages of the Report, are among the most remarkable of her Works, and in their results among the most beneficent. They are also extremely readable; and to make them more instructive, she included a number of woodcuts illustrating, not only Indian hospitals and barracks, but native customs in connection with water-supply and drainage. (Cook 2:24–25)

Florence envisioned her "Observations," a summary of the whole Report, as a public document and paid for the printing of it herself, after the full Report was completed in the summer of 1863.

With such a research task before her in 1862–1863, she was often sick, and strictly sequestered from all but those working directly with her. Yet in September 1863, when the Report was done, she wrote to her brother-in-law, hopeful that the recommendations would be enacted: "Unless the Death rate [[60 per 1000, beyond deaths from natural causes]] & Invaliding rate of the Indian Army can be reduced, to hold India by British troops will become impossible. . . . For everything is there to be done, as every thing had to be done in the Crimea. And this makes it the more, *not* the less hopeful. The discovery . . . of the R. Commission is that the cause of ill health in India lies, not in the climate, but in the absence of all works of sanitary civilization" (Vicinus and Nergaard, eds. 243–44).

The Crimea, with the vivid facts of its preventable deaths—for example, among the British, French, and Piedmontese, "18,000 from cholera alone" (Cartwright 159)—must have been on Florence's mind as she recovered from writing the India Report. On October 21 she wrote Clare a letter reminiscent of those early days of their friendship—her first extant letter to her since 1858:

## 33. To Mary Clare Moore

*Oct. 21/63*

Dearest Revd Mother

I began a letter to you some days ago to tell you that one of the bright jewels in your crown will be your conduct in the Crimean War (to use St. Gertrude's phraseology)—that I don't remember what you allude to (about the key) & don't see any harm in it, if it were so—that I always felt you ought to have been the Superior & I the inferior—& it was not my fault that it was not so—that I always felt how magnanimous your spiritual obedience in accepting such a position—& how utter my incapacity in making it tenable for you—& how I should have failed without your help—that I always wondered at your unfailing patience, sweetness, forbearance & courage under many trials peculiar to yourselves, beside what was common to all. If I did not express this more, which I always felt, it was because I wondered so much that you could *put up* with me—that I felt it was no use to say to your face, either then or since, how I admired your ways. As for your having ever shewn "temper" to me, I don't like to write the word. I can't conceive what you are thinking of. I marvelled how you could bear with us. I would gladly have avoided some difficulties which you must have keenly felt. But I could not. And I said less about my inability than I otherwise should, because I always felt, *Our Lord alone* can reward her. It is not for me to speak.

All this & much more I said in my letter—but then when I wrote last to you, I could not leave my bed to find it. And afterwards it did not seem worthwhile to send it.

I am so very sorry for Sister Gonzaga. It is so very uncomfortable to live on in that scramble.

I have to thank you for a dear kind comfort just received. But I write in such haste.

Ever your loving
F.N.

*Autograph: Archives of the Sisters of Mercy, Bermondsey*

Apparently, Clare was ill, though not incapacitated, in the late autumn of 1863. Thus Florence wrote in December—to inquire about her health, to thank her for some books, and to tell her the good news that Sir John Lawrence, sympathetic to the sanitation reforms she had advocated, was now the newly appointed Governor General of India:

## 34. To Mary Clare Moore

*32 South Street*
*Grosvenor Square. W.*
*Dec. 15/63*

Dearest Revd Mother

To hear of your feverish attacks always makes me uneasy. And I must write to know how you are.

I am here, as you see (my brother in law's house—where you were so good as to see me last year—to think of that being more than a year ago) & have been here a good bit. But I have had all your dear letters. And you cannot think how much they have encouraged me. They are almost the only earthly encouragement I have.

I have been so very ill & even the little change of moving here knocks me down for a month. But God is so good as to let me still struggle on with my business. But with so much difficulty that it was quite impossible to me to write even to you. And I only write now, because I hear you are ill.

I have felt so horribly ungrateful for never having thanked you for your books.

S. Jean de la Croix's life I keep thankfully. I am never tired of reading that part where he prays, for the return for all his services, Domine, pati et contemni pro te.[27]

I am afraid I never could ask that. But in return for very little service, I get it. It is quite impossible to describe how harassing, how heart-breaking my work has been since the beginning of July. I have always, with all my heart & soul, offered myself to God for the greatest bitterness on my own part, if His (War Office) work could be done. But lately nothing was done, and always because there was not one man, like Sidney Herbert, to do it.

Just now things look a little better. Perhaps you may have heard that the Governor General in India is dead & that Sir John Lawrence has been appointed Governor Gen'l. He goes out with very bad health & for two years only. But he was so good as to come here before he went—& I had the great joy of receiving his commands to do what I had almost lost the hope of our being allowed to do, (viz. as to sanitary work in India).

The men at home still thwart it in every possible way—& just as much since he went as before. But his appointment is a great thing for our work.

I don't think S. Jean de la Croix need have prayed to be dismissed from superiorships before he died. For as the Mère de Bréchard says, there are more opportunities to humble oneself, to mortify oneself, to throw oneself entirely on God, in them than in anything else.[28]

I return the life of St. Catherine of Genoa. I like it so much. It is a very singular & suggestive life. I am so glad she accepted the being Directress of the Hospital. For I think it was much better for her to make the Hospital servants go right than to receive their *"injures"*, however submissively—much better for the poor Patients, I mean.[29]

I am quite ashamed to keep Ste. Thérèse so long. But there is a good deal of reading in her. And I am only able to read at night—& then not always a large, close-printed book. Pray say if I shall send her back. And I will borrow her again from you perhaps some day.[30]

I am so sorry about poor S. Gonzaga's troubles. I know what those Committees are. I have had to deal with them almost all my life.

My strength has failed more than usually of late. And I don't think I have much more work in me—not, at least, if it is to continue of this harassing sort. God called me to Hospital work, (as I fondly thought, for life)—but since then to Army work—but with a promise that I should go back to Hospital—as I thought, as a Nurse, but as I now think, as a Patient.

If then I am quite sure I can do no more work, I shall go to a Hospital & end my days there in a ward-bed.

But of course you will not mention this, any more than anything else in my letters.

God bless you.
Ever my dearest Revd Mother's loving
F.N.

*Autograph: Archives of the Sisters of Mercy, Bermondsey*

On December 24, Florence wrote again, sending gifts for the school children and reflecting on the similarity she perceived between the reform work and disappointments of Catherine of Siena and her own efforts and experience:

## 35. To Mary Clare Moore

Xmas Eve 1863
32 South St. W.

Dearest Revd Mother

I send my poor little Christmas gift for your children,* and my great Christmas wishes.

May we all believe in Our Lord's "goodwill towards man"—the same today as 1863 years ago.

As S. Catherine of Genoa says, when she thinks that *Dieu s'est fait homme* in order to make *l'homme* into *Dieu*. I like those words so much— that belief in perfection.[31]

It is a sad time to me, Christmas. For Christmas, two years ago, saw all my friends & fellow workers taken away by death or worse than death—& the day before Christmas Day I was taken so very ill that I hoped I should go too. But that was very disobedient. I have never been able to work the same since.

But I do strive to believe that God's "goodwill towards" the 300,000 men, who are like sheep without a shepherd, is the same now, as when He gave them that good friend, Sidney Herbert—now that they have no friend but a poor creature like me—that He will lead them & guide them.

I often say that prayer of St. Catherine of Sienna—

Je vous offre et vous recommande mes enfans très aymez, car ils sont mon âme. . . . A vous, père éternel, moy misérable offre de nouveau ma propre vie pour eux . . . que toutes fois et quantes qu'il plaira à vostre bonté, vous me retiriez du corps et me rendiez au corps tousiours avec plus grande peine une fois que l'autre, pourveu que je voye la réformation de la saincte Eglise. . . . etc. etc. etc.[32]

St. Catherine did not see the reformation she desired. And I shall not see the reformation of the Army.

But I can truly say that, whatever I have known our Lord to desire of me, I have never refused Him (knowingly) anything. And I can feel the same now.

Pray for us then, dearest Revd Mother, that we may know of God's *goodwill* towards us.

In reply to the Bishop's kind message about the (Colonial Statistics) little Report—

The Colonial Office sent out copies to all the Governors & other officials of all our Colonies—whether they had sent returns or not & told them, I believe, to keep better Statistics.

But no copies were sent, I believe, to any private bodies.

The Benedictines of New Norcia have not therefore received copies, altho' they were so good as to furnish us with excellent returns.

It was therefore, no doubt, that I was commissioned to ask the Bishop whether he thought well, & if so, whether he would be so good, as, to send out copies to Catholics in the Colonies.

And the Benedictines (of New Norcia) were mentioned as an example, as having successfully introduced physical training among the Aborigines & having stated it to be indispensable.

I will furnish the Bishop with as many copies as he may please to send.

The Colonial Office, I am happy to say, (this is confidential) has taken up the subject of its Hospitals, & is busy collecting information & advising upon reformation for them.

But I am so busy about India & the Army that I cannot do anything for the Colonials [[Colonies?]].

What I did was at the request of the Governor of New Zealand, the only Colonial Governor who really treats the Aborigines as fellow creatures. And I am so sorry for his war, for now people will say—this is what comes of it.

It would be leaving my own proper business to take up that of others, if I were now to put my foot in the Colonial Hospital dish.

So, dearest Revd Mother, if at your convenience you would tell me what number of copies the Bishop is likely to wish to send, I will send them.

But I know you are so busy—& the Bishop also.

I have always heard of his life of poverty & mortification.

> Ever my dearest Revd Mother's
> grateful & loving
> F.N.

[[*Footnote on the autograph]] The honey is taken from the back of the island of Malta, opposite to where St. Paul is supposed to have been wrecked—where the bees feed on the thyme & other aromatic plants. When I was in the East the first time, I was often reminded of our Lord's repast on the "broiled fish & piece of an honey comb" by seeing & sharing such a meal with the poor people. It is just the same now as in His time. A little child, tasting this honey, said, 'If I were a bee, I would live at Malta.'

*Autograph: Archives of the Sisters of Mercy, Bermondsey*

Clare must have written to Florence immediately, requesting six copies of the Report on Colonial Statistics for Bishop Grant. She may also have inquired about a visit to Florence. As Florence explains in her response, she had not sent for Clare over the holidays because she was overburdened with work—advancing the recommendations contained in the India Report and proposing solutions to the bureaucratic lack of coordination between the relevant departments of the British government. Her annoyance at the sluggishness of various governmental offices was, as ever—since the death of Sidney Herbert in 1861—at white heat, yet she drew spiritual support from the words of Catherine of Siena and the life of Francis Xavier:

## 36. To Mary Clare Moore

*32 South St.*
*Park Lane. W.*
*Jan. 3/64*

Dearest Revd Mother
    I send thankfully the six copies of my little Report on Colonial Statistics which you are so good as to ask for for the Bishop. And I will try & have some copies sent to the good Benedictines & other Catholics.
    Dearest Revd Mother, if I did not ask you to be so good as to come to see me, if you could—it was not because I see other people at Christmas time, but because I am so busy. We are always very busy for two months before the meeting of Parl't [[Parliament]] (in February). But this time much more than usual, because of the India business. And I will tell you how I spent my Christmas Day & the Sunday after—those being two holidays—in preparing a scheme, by desire of Lord de Grey, for employing soldiers in trades—to keep them from that horrid vice.
    You are busy too at these seasons—but then you are busy in business directly for God. However, I try to remember what St. M. Magdalen de Pazzi says, that she finds God even more in the most distracting business than in prayer.[33] Alas! the time I find him *least* is, when I am quite exhausted with His business & can neither read nor pray. That is the hard part of my lot, I think. Because that *kind* of exhaustion does not follow active Hospital work. But my life now is as unlike my Hospital life, when I was concerned directly about the souls & bodies of men, as reading a Cookery book is unlike eating a good dinner.

I send my dearest Revd Mother a little sketch of mine about India. And we are working hard to bring it to pass. You wonder our labour is so ineffective. But you would scarcely believe what Gov't offices are—it is a curious fate which ever made me run my head into them.

When Sir John Lawrence sailed for India, he left certain things for me to do with Lord de Grey. Ld. de G. is quite willing. But I soon found that *he* had never considered what the respective jurisdictions of War Office & India Office are—tho' he has served in both Offices—that *they* have never considered what the respective jurisdictions are—that it has now occurred for the first time to both that these had better be settled—and that

> India Office
> War Office
> Commander in Chief at home
> Commander in Chief in India
> Governor General in India

are as much in chaos as to their *respective* powers & duties as if India were the Sandwich Islands.

This is what we are trying to settle now. But I never, never should have chosen this sort of work.

Because they don't *want* to settle anything. Except Sidney Herbert & Sir John Lawrence, who never wanted anything but a good reason to do any good, they want a great deal besides a good reason to induce them to move.

Please burn.

. . . But St. Catherine of Sienna says: En toutesfois je permets cela luy advenir, afin qu'il soit plus soigneux de fuyr soi mesme, et de venir et recourir à moy . . . et qu'il considere que par amour je luy donne le moyen de tirer hors le chef de la vraye humilité, se reputant indigne de la paix et repos de pensée, comme mes autres serviteurs—et au contraire se reputant digne des peines qu'il souffre. . . .[34]

My sister & her family come to spend here two or three nights occasionally to see friends. But I was only able to see her for 10 minutes; & my good brother in law, who is one of the best & kindest of men, not at all—nor his children.

They are all now at my father's house for the Christmas-time & New Year.

My Uncle Sam Smith after whom you kindly inquire suffers much from Rheumatic gout in knee & shoulder, but his health as good as ever. This my Aunt tells me. She, I am sorry to say, has been lately quite a cripple from Sciatica. But her health is good & her pain better. And they are soon coming to London. I have not seen either of them for months & months.

I am glad you are going to Sister M. Gonzaga. It will be a great comfort to her. What a comfort it would be to me.

I sent you back St. Francis de Sales, with many thanks. I liked him in his old dress. I like that story where the man loses his crown of martyrdom, because he will not be reconciled with his enemy. It is a sound lesson.[35]

I am going to send you back S. Francis Xavier. His is a life I always like to study as well as those of all the early Jesuit fathers.

But how much they did—& how little I do.

You see I keep St. Teresa still.

Pray remember me to Sister M. Gonzaga & Sister Anastasia & all of them.

Ever my dearest Revd Mother's

loving & grateful

F.N.

*Autograph: Archives of the Sisters of Mercy, Bermondsey*

On January 10, 1864, Mary Walburga Law, Clare's elected Assistant at the Bermondsey convent, was diagnosed with typhus. She had been ill since New Year's Day, but the characteristic symptoms of the disease were now evident (BA 2:[66]). Apparently, Clare wrote to Florence twice in January about this second outbreak of typhus in the community in six months. Florence responded on January 20, after Walburga's delirium had passed:

## 37. To Mary Clare Moore

Jan. 20/64

Dearest Revd Mother

I was so very anxious to hear about your dear Sister & also how you were—tho' I really was unable to write & ask you.

Now you are the best of Revd Mothers to have known that I wanted to know without my asking.

May I send you 6 bottles of Port Wine for her recovery? If I don't hear from you to the contrary, I shall.

You see I cannot help writing just to thank you for telling me how she is.

Ever my dearest Revd Mother's

F.N.

I meant to have written you a long letter about St. Teresa (of whom I have still the first Vol.) & St. Francis Xavier.[36] But I really cannot.

The books I returned looked as if I had been reading them through the back, as those impostors of clairvoyants pretend to do. But I assure you I did not make those nibblings in the backs—nor the cats!

God bless & reward you always!

*Autograph: Archives of the Sisters of Mercy, Bermondsey*

Evidently Clare wrote to say that Walburga's physician had prescribed brandy rather than port wine. Florence, ever prompt to help and still anxious to know how Clare herself was faring, immediately responded:

## 38. To Mary Clare Moore

Dearest Revd Mother

A thousand thanks for your letter.

I sent the Port Wine before I received it. But if you would let me send you some Brandy, I should be so very glad.

I am afraid you have only too much opportunity of disposing of ten times that quantity of Port Wine among your poor Patients, whether your Sister is allowed to take it by her Doctor or not.

Ever my dearest Revd Mother's<br>
F.N.

I wish I knew how *you* were.

Jan 23/64

*Autograph: Archives of the Sisters of Mercy, Bermondsey*

Since November 1856, three months after she returned from the Crimea, Florence had lived in London, with rare business or health-related trips in the early years and only occasional visits to her family's homes in Derbyshire and Hampshire or to Aunt Mai's in Kingston on Thames. But she had changed houses in London many times, each move taking a toll on her energy and concentration.

In November 1856, she had settled in the Burlington Hotel at 30 Old Burlington Street, where she remained until the death of Sidney Herbert in August 1861; unable to continue at the Burlington, a place filled with bittersweet memories of the work she had done there with Lord Herbert, her "chief," she then took lodgings in Hampstead for three months. In November 1861, she moved into a house of her brother-in-law, Sir Harry Verney, at 32 South Street, and lived there, or at a hotel on Dover Street, or in a rented house on Chesterfield Street, until August 1862 (Cook 2:24); she then moved to Oak Hill Park in Hampstead for two months. During 1863 she alternated her time between 32 South Street, a house in Hampstead, and a rented house on Cleveland Row. In 1864–1865, she lived in four places: in the Verneys' house on South Street, in new lodgings at 115 Park Street, in Hampstead, and finally at 27 Norfolk Street, Park Lane, where she resided from November 1864 to May 1865. For the remainder of 1865 she divided her time between a house at 34 South Street and Hampstead (Cook 2:84). Finally, in 1866, her father took a long-term lease on a house for her at 35 South Street (number 10, when the street was later renumbered), and here she remained until her death in 1910, except for visits to Malvern, Lea Hurst, Embley, and Claydon (Cook 2:84). It was a long decade of moves and of the disruptions attendant upon them—the various houses usually selected for quieter working conditions, or for closer proximity to the homes of her co-workers or the government offices of those she was trying to influence.

Now, in February 1864, Florence was at 115 Park Street—her sister Parthenope, her husband, and his four children having taken up residence at 32 South Street. Writing to Clare about this latest move, she was remarkably detached. So long as she was surrounded by the materials she needed for her work, and so long as she could focus without interruption on the causes to which she was committed, she was at home:

## 39. To Mary Clare Moore

*115 Park St. W.*
*Feb. 3/64*

Dearest Revd Mother

It was very good of you to write to your child & tell her that your Sister was getting better—God be thanked for it—& that you yourself were not too much knocked up.

As my brother in law & his family are come to London, I am here, as you see, but as it is only a lodging house, I was unfixed at first as to how long I should stay. Moving does however so put me off my work that I think it is most likely I shall not move again, as long as I am able to work—"Foxes have holes", you know the rest.[37] And I ought to esteem it a great honor to be like my Master in this. Else I think no one ever was such a root as I, or so little fitted to be an adventurer as I have been. I would gladly have spent my life as a Village Schoolmistress or Hospital Nurse. But I shall get back to the Hospital, I believe.

Ever yours<br>F.N.

*Autograph: Archives of the Sisters of Mercy, Bermondsey*

Although the precise issue is unclear, Florence had evidently received an inquiry from a Jesuit priest about something related to Eleonora Cordero, a Sister of Charity who had attended the sick and wounded Sardinian soldiers in the Crimea. After the war Florence had called her "one of the most remarkable women it has ever been my good fortune to know" (Vicinus and Nergaard, eds. 166). Now in May 1864, Florence writes to ask Clare's advice about how to respond to this inquiry; in the same letter she also discusses Garibaldi's visit and her annoyance at being asked to "burn my fingers" for the British government:

## 40. To Mary Clare Moore

*115 Park Street. W.*<br>*May 12/64*

Dearest Revd Mother

I knew you would be so good as to write to me. And it was very kind to write so soon. All that the Messenger was charged to say was, that I begged you would not trouble yourself to write *by him*. [I know what it is to have people coming & stopping to carry back "an answer by Bearer", just when one is busy.] Thank you for your dear letter.

Since I wrote, I have had a note from that Jesuit Father I mentioned to you. And what I write for now is to ask you whether I should leave it unanswered, or whether I should write & tell him it is all a mistake of S. Cordero'. He evidently does not know her, tho' he quotes her.

I really lose all confidence in my own judgement as to the routine of life. I am always in scrapes. Poor Ld. Herbert used to laugh at me & tell me I was so over-civil, that I was always in scrapes from over-civility. But really the scrapes I get into are those of a person always going about doing insulting, rude, coarse things.

My impulse was *not* to answer this Father's note. But I remember Dr. Manning was, or pretended to be, hurt that I did not answer one of his, which really required no answer. So I trouble you to know what you think I had better do—& if to answer, what I had better say?

I really feel quite ashamed of troubling you.

Yes, I saw Garibaldi. And the whole world seems to have known it. It was from no curtisy I saw him, & after refusing twice, I consented at last, because I was told to say something it was a duty to say to him, (*not* with reference to his going away, but) which it was thought might possibly save a future disturbance in Italy being stirred up by him.

All my life I have been the cat employed by the monkey to burn my fingers in getting out his chesnuts. Sometimes I have been more silly than the cat. For I have offered my paws to be burnt.

Our poor Govt. has been abused by the Italian Govt. for letting Garibaldi be received. It has been abused by its own people for letting Garibaldi go. But it is quite strong enough to take care of itself & to laugh—while I, poor silly wretch, can't laugh but cry. I think I had 300 letters come to me in consequence of that visit of Garibaldi.[38]

Don't forget, dearest Revd Mother, to tell me what book you would like from Paris.

I ventured to send those five little books, tho' I am quite sure you have more complete copies of all that are worth it, because there seemed to me little bits not commonly put in. The *Combattimento* is a great favourite with me.[39] It was all to pieces—& I had had it bound.

Ever, dearest Revd Mother,
your loving & grateful
F.N.

How sorry I am to hear of poor S. Gonzaga's troubles & especially of her eye-sight. If I were to lose my eyes, as I am losing the use of my hands, I should be able to do nothing for God's service.

I seem to me to be always writing about myself. I am so glad to hear that there is a little money coming in to the Convent. Thank you for telling me. I almost wish it could stay & do good in some good works under your own eye.

*Autograph: Archives of the Sisters of Mercy, Bermondsey*

The money coming into the Bermondsey convent resulted from final settlement of the considerable estate of Lady Barbara Eyre, daughter of the late and sister of the present Earl of Newburgh, who had

entered the Bermondsey community in 1839, taking the name Mary de
Sales. She had died in 1849, but a lawsuit contesting her disposition of
her inheritance delayed settlement of her will until April 1864. The Bermondsey Annals report that "Of the Legacy thus secured to the Convent a sum of £600 was given, at the desire of the Bishop, to our Sisters
of Abingdon, £200 to Gravesend, and some years before £600 had been
advanced to the [Mercy] Community at Blandford Square, London [in
accord with Mary de Sales's earlier wish]" (2:[67]). The money retained
by the Bermondsey community was used to pay for construction of an
infants' schoolroom and a middle school. Obviously Florence wished
that more of this money could have remained under Clare's "own eye."

Florence was still suffering from her stomach complaint. In June
she told her mother: "In the morning . . . everything but Grapes excites
my vomiting—even a cup of tea" (Wellcome Institute, photocopy, MS
9001/40). When she wrote to Clare on June 21, to thank her for a loan
of books, she briefly acknowledged her sickness:

*41. To Mary Clare Moore*

*115 Park Street. W.*
*June 21/64*

Dearest Revd Mother
    I send back your two books with a great parcel of thanks.
    Boudon's P. [[Père]] Seurin is indeed as full of demons' tricks as a pan-
tomime. But I like very much certain parts of it, particularly the chapter on
*pureté de coeur*, Chap. 2, Book 3—& all that he says about P. Seurin's not
only submitting but offering himself to the humiliation of madness, (if the
will of God,) is so striking, it puts it quite in a new light. There is so much
that is morbid in a solitary imprisonment like mine, with sickness into the
bargain—so much that is quite unavoidable—that I am glad to look upon it,
as P. Seurin, as a humiliation to which one should offer oneself willingly, if it
presents itself clearly in the path of God's will.
    But I like the other book of P. [[Père]] Lallemant's better still. How curi-
ous is the absolute brief compressed precept of the part by P. Seurin, when
compared with Boudon's flowery pantomime. I think it far more striking. Indeed I think P. Lallemant & all that we have of P. P. [[Pères]] Rigoleu & Surin
so singularly sublime—in this—that there is not an effort to dress up their
high & noble doctrine or to make it attractive with flowers of rhetoric. It is as

brief & dry as it is possible to have it. And I should never be tired of reading P. Lallemant. I am so much obliged to you for letting me keep them so long.[40]

No: dearest Revd Mother, you can't think that your letters would ever "trouble" me. And I know how little time you have to write which makes me all the more grateful. On the contrary, they are the greatest refreshment I have. But answering is often beyond me.

I am not gone to Hampstead. I have not been there this year. May be, I shall not be able to go till late in the autumn. And sometimes I think God may do something else with me before that.

I am so sorry about poor S. Gonzaga's troubles.

Pray tell her that she never said a truer word than when she called her "Pope" "soft." Everybody always tells me so in more or less civil language. And there never was any thing so true.

> Ever dearest Revd M.,
> your grateful & loving
> F.N.

*Autograph: Archives of the Sisters of Mercy, Bermondsey*

Over the summer, while she was working to secure implementation of the India Sanitation Report, Florence received an invitation to propose a plan for nursing the sick poor in the Liverpool Workhouse. Having long abhorred the way the English Poor Law was administered, including the mismanagement of the sick in its workhouses, she seized this opportunity to institute change and named Agnes Jones, a nurse trained in the Nightingale School she had founded in 1860 at St. Thomas Hospital, to be the superintendent of nursing at Liverpool. From Hampstead, in September, she wrote to Clare—to tell her this good news and to invite her to visit:

## 42. To Mary Clare Moore

> *Oak Hill*
> *Hampstead. N.W.*
> *Sept. 3/64*

My dearest Revd Mother

This is the first day, the very first day that I have felt I was getting ahead of my business, instead of my business getting ahead of me, miles, miles ahead, over my head & ears.

You see I am come down here. And would you come & see me? This next week I have less to do. Would you come on Monday, 5th? or would you come on Friday, 9th? I know well how much you have to do—& that it is always difficult, sometimes impossible, for you to find even one hour. And should that be the case next week, I will ask you to name your own time any day these next two months. And I will say sincerely if *I* can't manage it.

I would send a carriage for you, whatever time you said. And I could give my dearest Revd Mother a bedroom, & one for a Sister, if more convenient to bring one, & if you really can arrange to sleep.

And I would ask you in that case to have the carriage to fetch you so as to be here that I might see you a little before your dinner, which I think is 4 o'clock—& that I might see you the next morning, before you started, if you *can* sleep.

I know that it is a great favour for a Revd Mother to grant. But it is not the first time *my* Revd Mother has granted me favours.

I am sure you will be glad to hear that we are going to undertake the Liverpool Workhouse to nurse 1000 pauper sick in it—with 15 Head Nurses & a Supt. whom we have trained, 15 Assistant Nurses—& 52 women chosen out of the Workhouse paupers but separated from them entirely, & paid, so that we hope to train these paupers to get an honest living. We undertake only 600 Patients at first. A Liverpool man actually gives £1200 a year to do this.

I have always felt that workhouse patients were the most neglected of the human race—far more so than in Hospitals.

And I am so glad to make even this beginning—tho' there has been more than usual vexation & vacillation to overcome, I think, to give these poor creatures a little comfort.

I hope London workhouses will follow—& Manchester. I remember years & years ago when I used to visit at Marylebone Workhouse feeling how hopeless those depths of misery were to comfort—& that visiting did nothing but break the visitor's heart.

I wish we could have gone in to Liverpool Workhouse first, & made our plans afterwards, as we did in the Crimea. But they insisted on our making a plan first. And there has been as much diplomacy, & as many treaties, & as much of people working against each other, as if we had been going to occupy a kingdom, instead of a workhouse.

Ever my dearest Revd Mother's loving<br>F.N.

I know you have been very poorly all this summer, tho' you did not say so. Perhaps a drive into the country would do you good.

You see I always count upon your sympathy & tell you our doings—tho'

I think you are the only Revd Mother in the world who would, or could, hear them with indulgence. They must all seem to you so futile and imperfect.
*Autograph: Archives of the Sisters of Mercy, Bermondsey*

Presumably Clare visited Florence at Hampstead in September or October; she would gladly have made time for such a visit. While she was there, or in a letter before or after her visit, she apparently asked to borrow copies of the recipes Alexis Soyer had used in the Crimea. In late September, when Florence found them, she immediately wrote to her:

### 43. To Mary Clare Moore

Dearest Revd Mother
You will have been surprised not to hear from me & my Soyer. But the truth is: I was never able till yesterday to hunt in my stacks of papers for these things.
The three copies of Soyer's Receipts are pretty much alike. But I am not able to look them through to see which is most complete. So I send them all.
Warriner's Receipts, p.p. 67-72 and 72-74, *may* be useful (in the Report on Cooking Apparatus) so I send that too.
I do not think any of these receipts appear in Soyer's Books.[41]
I am afraid I must ask to have all four reports back, as I have no other copies. But your friends may keep them as long as they like. And pray do not *you* trouble yourself with them.

In great haste,
ever my dearest Revd Mother's
loving & grateful
F.N.

Sept. 24/64
*Autograph: Archives of the Sisters of Mercy, Bermondsey*

After her visit in September or October, Clare evidently wrote to Florence, offering to nurse her, either personally or by sending another sister. When Florence responded at the end of October, she was overwhelmed by Clare's offer. Though she would not accept it, she reminded Clare of her wish to go one day to St. Thomas Hospital as a ward patient—as she had informed Selina Bracebridge in January (Vicinus and Nergaard, eds. 261). But for the present she would "scrat on."

October also brought Florence a new request for help: Sir Henry Storks, Commander of the British installations in Turkey during the Crimean War, was now appointed Governor of Malta and wanted Florence's assistance in implementing sanitary improvements on the island. Florence found in his request a fresh reason to hope that her previous work on army sanitation had not been for nought:

## 44. To Mary Clare Moore

Dearest, very dearest Revd Mother

I never can forget your kindness. To think of your being willing to leave your most important post to come & nurse only me, or to send me one of my dear Sisters. I feel as if I never could, God only can, tell you how grateful I am.

But I must not take advantage. I am not looking out for a Nurse, as you heard. I shall "scrat on" as well as I can, as long as I can work at all. And then I shall go, please God, to where I mentioned to you.

I am obliged to go to London tomorrow for the "season".

27 Norfolk Street. W.

will be my address. And mind you write to me, dearest Revd Mother, for your letters are nearly the only comforts earthly I have.

But I have great support. You remember Genl. Storks. You know he had the Ionian Islands afterwards. Now he is appointed to the Government of Malta. He has written to me to ask to see me, in order to carry into effect some of the improvements we had suggested. He sails this week. Do you remember my shewing you the plans for a Workhouse (of 1000 beds) and a Workhouse Incurable Hospital (of 600) for Malta?

It is a great exertion to me to get up & dress & sit up to see these gentlemen. But I feel as if I never could be thankful enough to Almighty God. I feel always a kind of wonder that He should employ so miserable an instrument as I—to give me such chances as He does. It has always been so. The Army work hung fire, till Sidney Herbert worked it. The Indian work the same, till Sir John Lawrence of his own accord came to ask to do it when he was appointed Viceroy. The Malta work the same—& now Genl. Storks takes it up of his own accord. I forget whether I told you that one of the last things I made poor Sidney Herbert do was to send a Commission to the Mediterranean Stations. For 3 years all they recommended has been overlooked. Now, as far as Malta is concerned, Genl. Storks, whom I have not seen since 1857, will do it.

I suppose I *am* much worse (this is in answer to your kind enquiry). But I shall struggle on till I can work no longer.

All thanks to you, dearest Revd Mother, on the very knees of my heart.

I found accidentally (in packing up) Soyer's receipts which he made in the Crimea. Those I sent you were what he made for us after we came home. I don't know whether these will be any use to your people. If so, they may keep them as long as they like. But I should like to have them back at last, as I have no copies. I wish, however, *you* were not troubled with sending them.

I am so sorry to think of all poor Sister M. Gonzaga's many troubles.

It was such a great pleasure to hear of the Irish Workhouse Nursing.

I can write no more but am ever, my dearest Revd Mother,

yours overflowingly<br>F. Nightingale

Oct 31/64
*Autograph: Archives of the Sisters of Mercy, Bermondsey*

In various places in Ireland, Sisters of Mercy were now engaged in workhouse nursing or visiting, and Clare had evidently sought copies of Soyer's recipes for some of them. Meanwhile, in the Bermondsey community, Mary Teresa Holden, a young sister who suffered from "asthmatic cough," became seriously ill in November; and at St. Elizabeth's Hospital in December Mary Gonzaga Barrie discovered to her sorrow—for she was his personal friend—that Cardinal Wiseman's health was in severe decline.

# 1865–1866

Mary Teresa Holden, whom Clare had nursed for several weeks, died in the Bermondsey community on December 10, 1864. In early January 1865, Florence wrote to Clare, full of sympathy for her loss:

## 45. To Mary Clare Moore

*27 Norfolk Street*
*Park Lane. W.*
*9/1/65*

Dearest Revd Mother

I am sure you are so good that not only out of your goodness you wrote to me about the loss of your "Sister", but out of your goodness you would know how much I felt for you. Tho' one cannot but rejoice when God takes those peaceful, useful souls to Himself, yet they are a great loss—there are so few of them. And it seems as if they already made this the better world, & did not need to go.

But God knows best.

I am quite ashamed of keeping S. John of the Cross so long. But I kept St. Teresa much longer. I feel like a child who excuses itself for being naughty by telling how much naughtier it is sometimes. I hope to send back the 2nd Vol. soon. I am often afraid that I have not so much as entered into the first Obscure Night. Yet that Obscure Night does seem so applicable to me.[42]

I have never found S. John of the Cross mystical or fanciful. On the contrary, he seems to have had the most wonderful practical knowledge of the ways of God in the heart of man.

You are a very dear Revd Mother to write to me, and I *know* you *know* how much I thank you for it, even tho' I can't write. I am afraid I must not now, or this will never go. For I have so much less strength than I had.

We are getting on pretty well. I mean about India matters.

I don't know whether you have heard of a dreadful Case of a poor man who died from bedsores contracted in the Holborn Union Infirmary by manifest neglect. But I trust good will come out of evil—& out of the enquiry which is being now made—& that the whole system of workhouse nursing will be altered in consequence.[43]

Ever my dearest Revd Mother's
grateful & affectionate
F. Nightingale

*Autograph: Archives of the Sisters of Mercy, Bermondsey*

On January 12, Cardinal Wiseman—who had been largely an invalid since late December—was diagnosed with erysipelas, a potentially fatal infectious disease affecting the skin and subcutaneous tissue, often of the face. Those who attended him realized on January 15 that his death was near, and he was anointed. At the Cardinal's request, Mary Gonzaga Barrie had become his private nurse and personal secretary at his residence at 8 York Place, and she or another Sister of Mercy from St. Elizabeth's Hospital was constantly at his bedside. However, he rallied after a few days and lingered for another month (Carroll, *Leaves* 2:227–30).

Years before, on January 23, 1832, Clare Moore had been clothed in the habit of the Sisters of Mercy, and on January 24, 1833, she had professed her religious vows of poverty, chastity, and obedience—in the first such ceremonies in the first convent of the Mercy congregation, on Baggot Street, Dublin. In 1865 Florence Nightingale noted the anniversary of these events so important to Clare:

## 46. To Mary Clare Moore

*27 Norfolk Street. W.*
*January 23/65*

Dearest Revd Mother

I must send you my tenderest good wishes on the day of the anniversary of your first taking the habit.

I am sure that *you* not only renew your vows, as St. Francis Xavier tells us, with as much fervour as the first time, but with more fervour every time.

What a good servant you have been to our Almighty Father! I am sure *He* thinks so, though you will not allow it.

May He preserve you many years in life yet for His service—which is a wish more for our sakes than for yours. I was quite afraid you were ill, I don't quite know why.

The greatest blessing is to know & *feel*, as you say, that one is doing His will.

I never am in full possession of this *feeling* tho' I have nothing left at all in this world, except to do His will. But I have not deserved that He should give me this feeling which is the greatest strength of all.

I think it was a compensation for poor Sister M. Gonzaga's many troubles to be called in to assist at Cardinal Wiseman's death bed. It is a great privilege. And tho' I am thankful that it has pleased God it should not be his death bed, for indeed it is a very valuable life, still it was alike a reward for Sister Gonzaga to be present at what St. Catherine of Sienna calls God's withdrawing from the body & restoring to the body the soul "tousiours avec plus grande peine une fois que l'autre".[44]

Dearest Revd Mother, I thank you always "tousiours une fois plus que l'autre" for your goodness in writing to me & am ever

my dearest Revd Mother's
grateful & affectionate child
F.N.

*Autograph: Archives of the Sisters of Mercy, Bermondsey*

In this letter Florence evidently enclosed another short note:

## 47. To Mary Clare Moore

*27 Norfolk St.*
*Park Lane. W.*
*January 23/65.*

Dearest Revd Mother

If you want a copy of the (English) S. John of the Cross, which you were so good as to lend me, for your own uses, & would let me get you a copy for your birth-day, as I dare say you call this day, I should be so proud—or any other book you would name.

F.N.

*Autograph: Archives of the Sisters of Mercy, Bermondsey*

Cardinal Wiseman still lay severely ill. Mary Gonzaga's frequent letters to Bermondsey, written as Wiseman slept, recorded the slow progress of the disease. On January 25 she wrote: "The Cardinal has rallied a little; there are no good signs medically, but he feels himself better, and you know a sick person's expecting to recover is always a great help. I don't like the carbuncle at all. . . . The great anxiety is a spot on the temple, in a place where it can't be operated on with any hope of success, even if he had the strength." However, a few days later the boil over the eye was lanced, and Mary Gonzaga wrote: "He is extremely prostrate and exhausted. He bore the cutting in the most beautiful manner; it was terrible pain, but he never moved or groaned" (Carroll, *Leaves* 2:231–32).[45]

Clare kept Florence apprised of Wiseman's condition, and Florence, who had developed considerable respect for the cardinal, in part through her knowledge of Gonzaga's affection for him, responded with sympathy:

## 48. To Mary Clare Moore

*27 Norfolk Street*
*Park Lane. W.*
*3/2/65*

Dearest Revd Mother

It is very, very good of you to write me accounts of Cardinal Wiseman. I have prayed, & do pray earnestly that it will please Almighty God to spare his valuable life yet a few years longer to this earth—especially that the Sisters may yet find a father in him—for it would be to them the loss of a father indeed. Though our Almighty Father knows what is best about that, as well as about all other things.

I trust that now it appears, as if his life *is* likely to be prolonged. And I think Sister Gonzaga must have found this time a great gain—tho' I doubt[46] she is bodily very weary. I had such a very touching & interesting note from her about a week ago. May God Almighty give His best blessings to this & all her concerns.

I hope you will keep the Manual of the Sisters of Charity. I sent three other manuals, tho' not, I am afraid, of much use to you. If you like to keep them for anybody, pray let me have them put up in plain, strong bindings, as well as their dilapidated state will allow. [I am very much ashamed of the untidy state of all my books.] Or if *you* would, have them put up in the way you like, & charge the bindings to me, & oblige

my dearest Revd Mother's
ever grateful & loving child
F.N.

I did not tell you that there is much in Dr. Faber's book which you were so good as to lend me, that I like very much indeed—tho' it is impossible not to laugh when he says so quaintly, "Religious people are an unkind lot."[47] I like his Conference on "Sensitiveness".

*Autograph: Archives of the Sisters of Mercy, Bermondsey*

Several months later, after his appointment as Archbishop of Westminster, Henry Manning sought to advance his plan to replace the Sisters of Mercy at the hospital on Great Ormond Street with Sisters of Charity from France. Perhaps inklings of this future possibility had reached Bermondsey much earlier, and Clare had asked Florence for a copy of the Manual of the Sisters of Charity so that she might discover the reasons for Dr. Manning's preference.

Nicholas Wiseman died on Wednesday morning, February 15, 1865, at half-past eight. Mary Gonzaga was with him, and after his death she cut a lock of his hair to keep as a memento of the one person, beyond Clare Moore and perhaps Florence Nightingale, who understood her impatient temperament as well as her good will. However, the lock of hair was taken away from her by a man who presumed he had the authority to do so, a person whom Mary Austin Carroll's transcript of Mary Gonzaga's subsequent letter to one of the cardinal's relatives in Ireland—this particular autograph has not been discovered—identifies only as "G_____":

I dare not think of the cardinal; it is all like a horrid dream. Not but I have been made to know it is true by annoyance about _____. G_____ could not wait for the funeral to be over before he began again the annoyances by which he teased the cardinal for the last six months; but I must not think of him or I shall fail in charity. I never believed a Catholic could have spoken of his bishop and of religious as he has done of the cardinal and of us. I don't believe, if half were known, any Catholic constituency would let him represent them. . . .

. . . I had a note from Mrs. Chapman [a cousin of the cardinal's, *née* Strange]. I fear she has been hurt by _____'s letters. You must not mind him—he knows no better. He thinks it all zeal, and that it proves what a good business man he is. The worst for us is that he has locked up my hair [some of the cardinal's hair she had cut off], and I am rather despairing of ever getting it back; but you shall have some if I do. (qtd., with square brackets, in Carroll, *Leaves* 2:235)

The "G_____" in Carroll's transcript of Mary Gonzaga's letter may be a substitute for the name, Sir George Bowyer. Although this is only speculation, there are some grounds for it. Sir George was a barrister, and perhaps currently engaged with Wiseman in legal matters. Certainly there is enough documentary evidence to suggest that he had earlier pressed Wiseman about the affiliation of the hospital with the Knights of Saint John (Knights of Malta) and about the construction and operation of the Church of Saint John of Jerusalem annexed to the hospital, and that he had found Mary Gonzaga Barrie troublesome to his proprietary attitudes about the church.

Sentences in Wiseman's letters to Gonzaga suggest further that, at least in 1864, Wiseman himself found Sir George hard to deal with.

For example, "But Sir G. likes making his own arrangements" (undated); "While Mgr. Talbot was in the Hospital, Sir G. invited him to say Mass there, on Sunday at 9! He accepted. So much for rules etc.!" (July 8, 1864); "I send the enclosed for you to read [evidently a letter from Wiseman to Sir George requesting that the door from the Church to the convent and hospital be locked from the inside, "the key being in the hands of the Community"]. Has Sir G. returned the key?" (August 19, 1864); and "I have written to Sir George to thank for some game, and expressed a hope that the Church may now be put right, on a true ecclesiastical footing. But I doubt if he will ever act reasonably on the subject. I believe that all the worry about it has had no little to do with this indisposition of mine. However, I am better; and I certainly will keep myself out of all scrapes with Sir George" (September 7, 1864) (Carroll, *Leaves* 2:235).[48] Gonzaga's grief at Wiseman's death, and at the way the sisters who had nursed him were treated afterward, took a long time to heal. On February 16, Florence received Clare's letter telling her that Cardinal Wiseman had died and that Gonzaga had gone to the Mercy convent in Brighton to rest. Florence responded immediately, noting also the death of a young postulant in the St. Elizabeth's Hospital community and expressing her long-felt concern and affection for Gonzaga:

### 49. To Mary Clare Moore

Dearest Revd Mother

I had not heard of the death of Card. Wiseman (I hear so little) till your letter was just now put into my hand. I feel for the poor Sisters as if they had lost a father. And the death of that good man will be felt in many other ways also. But *he* is glad. I had hoped too that Sister Gonzaga would have spent her rest with you. I am sure she would have found it a much greater rest to be with you, even tho' the seaside is healthier than Bermondsey. But I trust that she will have found it a permanent rest to her spirit to have been with the Cardinal at his death. It seems to place all the difficulties of doing God's will in such shadow, under the great light & peace of doing His will, when one is by a death bed such as that.

Indeed, the poor Sisters' troubles are very great. I could not but be glad that the poor Postulant Sister was dead, especially as there was peace at the last. If it was insanity as well as delirium, there could be no hope of permanent recovery—and tho' great Saints have been able to wish for a state of insanity as a state of humiliation & utter dependence upon God,[49] yet one cannot but be thankful when a state has been spared which is one of utter uselessness & of constant troublesomeness to others.

And I feel so for you too, dearest Revd Mother, who have given your oldest friends among the Sisters (tho' I well know that you make no partialities among them) & your most intimate, to this work—and to see them now so laden with cares & troubles that it must almost seem as if they had better never have undertaken it.

But we know that is not so.

Pray, when you write to Sister Gonzaga, tell her that I would, if I were worthy, pray her to take heart—& that I do in my heart wish her joy for her presence at the Cardinal's death bed. I am glad his bodily pains are over, as it did not please Almighty God to bring him back to earth. But, as you say, we know not who his successer [sic] may be.

May God Almighty give us all, the peace which passeth understanding— not selfishly, but in order to enable us to do His will thoroughly.

And how can I thank you, dearest Revd Mother, for having written to me in the midst of all your own labours, to tell me of what you know is of such deep interest to me.

Pray for me, dearest Revd Mother, and believe me

ever your grateful & affectionate child

F.N.

27 Norfolk Street. W.

Feb 16/65

What a dreadful long dark winter for the poor people. And fever all about.

I wonder whether you remember Miss Morton (of Scutari). She is just dead of Typhus Fever, contracted in attending her district in London. She was not a wise but a very good motherly woman.

I am hoping so to do something with the Poor Law Board for the dreadful state of the Workhouse Infirmaries. They are really willing. But there is much to overcome, with the Guardians.

We have got 7 millions for improving the Soldiers' Stations in India. Sir John Lawrence says it should be 10 millions—and Mr. Massey (whom I have seen, & who goes out to India as Finance Minister next week) says it shall be 10 millions.

And the soldiers' wives & children will come in too for a measure of reform Sir J. Lawrence has in his head.

I know you are so good that it cheers you to hear these things.

F.N.

*Autograph: Archives of the Sisters of Mercy, Bermondsey*


Anne Morton was a nurse in the Barrack Hospital in Scutari during the Crimean War. When Clare was seriously ill in March and April 1856, Anne replaced her as manager of the Linen Stores.

Writing to Clare again at the end of the month, Florence was still caught up in the death of Nicholas Wiseman. She also described to Clare the physical ailments she had been experiencing through the long winter:


## 50. To Mary Clare Moore

*27 Norfolk Street*
*Park Lane. W.*
*28/2/65*
*Shrove Tuesday*

My dearest Revd Mother

I am so sorry to hear about your eyes. I am afraid, like many other ailments, they will not get quite well till this interminable long winter has passed.

I have never thanked you for that beautiful prayer of Card. Wiseman's which you were so good as to copy for me. I am sure I want it much more than Sister Gonzaga. I think the verses of the Cardinal deeply touching—particularly the last, the VI th Section.[50] I always thought him an able, honest, devoted man—but such deep simplicity & humility in so great a man is more than touching, it is sublime.

Faber's *Conferences* I think very interesting—especially "Wounded Feelings".[51]

I am very much obliged to you for sending M. Olier's life. I shall read it with the greatest interest.[52]

I am not able to write much, for I have had rheumatism in the spine all the winter, which made me more helpless than usual—& then it seemed to fix itself in my right elbow, of all places, which is the only sound place I have in my body. But it disappeared from there almost as suddenly as it came, and I was most thankful to God. For as all my business is writing, I might almost as well have lost my head. I could hardly wash my face, or crook my finger &

thumb to hold my pen. However, I never did intermit my writing for a single day—for, if I did, my arrears would be quite hopeless—in business.

Ever my dearest Revd Mother's own most loving child & grateful

F.N.

I pray God heartily that we may pass a good Lent. I wish Sister Gonzaga may be coming to you. Pray for me, my own good Revd Mother.

*Autograph: Archives of the Sisters of Mercy, Bermondsey*

On March 3, 1865, Charles Newdigate Newdegate, a longstanding critic of Catholic convents, introduced into the House of Commons once again a motion to establish a Select Committee "to inquire into the existence, character, and increase of Monastic or Conventual Establishments, or societies, in Great Britain" (Arnstein 66). While his motion failed in 1865 (it subsequently succeeded in 1870), the debate in the press and in Commons raised once again all the hair-raising stories, whether true or fictional, about the oppression that allegedly occurred in Catholic convents. Undoubtedly, Florence is referring to Newdegate in her letter of March 11, and to Sir George Grey, the Home Secretary. Frederick Faber, whose *Spiritual Conferences* Florence was then reading, had died in 1863, so he was not among the Fathers of the Oratory who witnessed the debate in the Commons:

## 51. To Mary Clare Moore

*27 Norfolk Street*
*Park Lane. W.*
*March 11/65*

Dearest Revd Mother

I don't suppose you are very uneasy about being killed or turned out of your houses.

I knew that a man makes in the House of Commons every year a "motion" for an enquiry into "monastic or conventual societies". But that was all I knew. However, when I had your letter, I thought I would enquire how long you had to live. But I understand that the only feeling of the House of Commons was:—to bear with the annual "Mover", (because he is an old & respectable man,) to get rid of it as soon as possible, & to negative the man's "motion" by a majority. A frantic Protestant got up, & raked up all the stories he could get hold of—& behaved like a "mad bull". This, I was told. But the

House of Commons only laughed at him, & "pooh-poohed" him. And the quietest of all men, the Home Secretary, made a joke (for the first time in his life) at him. I heard that some of the Fathers of the Oratory were sitting under the Gallery of the House of Commons. And they certainly could not have been impressed with the weight and importance of frantic Protestant Members with the House of Commons.[53]

I am afraid you are far from well, my dearest Revd Mother. I was very glad to read the discourse you were so good as to send me, on the touching & sublime life & death of the Cardinal. I wish S. Gonzaga could come & stay with you.

Ever my own dearest Revd Mother's<br>
affectionate & grateful<br>
F. Nightingale

*Autograph: Archives of the Sisters of Mercy, Bermondsey*

Charles Newdigate Newdegate was the "Mover" in the House of Commons to whom Nightingale refers, and the "frantic Protestant" may have been George H. Whalley, M.P. for Peterborough, who supported Newdegate and who, under the pseudonym "Patrick Murphy," published *Popery in Ireland; or, Confessionals, Abductions, Nunneries, Fenians and Orangemen: A Narrative of Facts* (Arnstein 67). On this occasion, Newdegate's motion was "defeated . . . by a vote of 106 to 79" (Arnstein 69).

Meanwhile, in accord with custom, the Catholic cathedral chapter of Westminster had recommended to Pius IX three names of bishops to succeed Nicholas Wiseman as Archbishop of Westminster: William Clifford, Bishop of Clifton; George Errington, Wiseman's former co-adjutor, now Archbishop of Trebizond; and Thomas Grant, Bishop of Southwark. Both Clifford and Grant withdrew their names in favor of Errington. However, on April 30, 1865, Pius IX appointed Henry Edward Manning, a confidant of Wiseman and a man who Pius assumed would see things English from the perspective of Rome (Norman, *The English Catholic Church* 251–62).

Shortly after his installation as Archbishop of Westminster on June 8, 1865, Henry Manning began his move to replace the Sisters of Mercy at the Hospital of Saint John and Saint Elizabeth by a group of French Sisters of Charity, a religious order he evidently regarded as more Roman in its outlook. The sisters at the Hospital and Clare Moore did not become aware of the Archbishop's plan until November 1865.

Florence's first extant letter to Clare after Archbishop Manning's installation does not refer to the Hospital situation in these terms. Her letter expresses her gratitude for Clare's letters and her usual solicitude about Clare's health. Her reference to "poor S. Gonzaga's affairs" may simply be to the ongoing difficulties Gonzaga had with the hospital's lay committee and, since the affiliation of the hospital with the Knights of Saint John of Jerusalem, with Sir George Bowyer.[54] But it is also possible that the phrase, "S. Gonzaga's affairs," refers to the government's inquiry into her role in transporting a mentally ill Sister of Mercy from London to an asylum in Bruges, at the request of the superior of the Sisters of Mercy on Commercial Road, London (a separate Mercy community founded directly from Tullamore, Ireland, in 1859, and unaffiliated with either the Bermondsey or the hospital community).

In the House of Commons debate on "nunneries" in 1865, Charles Newdigate Newdegate cited, as one of his examples of the personal harm perpetrated by convents, "the case of Mary Ryan, an English nun who had been transferred against her will to a Belgian lunatic asylum" (Arnstein 67). In an undated letter written to her sister Juey (probably in 1864 or 1863, because Cardinal Wiseman was still alive and she had consulted him about the letter), Mary Gonzaga recounts that she had, indeed, with the assistance of a Protestant nurse and another Sister of Mercy, taken "S. Theresa," that is, "Mary Ryan," to St. Julian's in Bruges on September 7–8 (Mary Gonzaga does not give the year, but it was probably 1864 or 1863). She describes the difficult journey, and the resistance and sometimes violent behavior of the patient.

According to Arnstein (who cites *Hansard*, the official record of the proceedings in Parliament), by 1865:

The home secretary, Sir George Grey, had inquired into the case. The British consul and minister in Belgium had visited the asylum, had found it well conducted, and had concluded that Mary Ryan truly was insane. A member of the British Lunacy Commission had reached the same conclusion. Although the Belgian authorities had expressed their willingness to return the lady to English soil, the British government decided not to make such a request. Nor did it prosecute those who had taken her to Belgium. The commission did suggest that Roman Catholics might find it useful to set up their own insane asylum within the United Kingdom. (Arnstein 234 n. 15)

Gonzaga Barrie's letter to her sister is a factual account of the journey to Bruges and of the circumstances by which, as a nurse, she had become involved, but it does not lack salty comments on the anonymous observers who asked her no questions and offered her no help along the route, but did not hesitate afterward to slander her in "penny papers": she says, "why even Land Transport Corps men would be ashamed of such foul ideas," coming from "cowards that didn't dare face a woman, but would take away her character behind her back." Florence Nightingale understood this "trying" affair, whether or not she is referring specifically to it in the following letter:

## 52. To Mary Clare Moore

*July 3/65*
*34 South Street*
*Park Lane*
*London. W.*

Dearest, very dearest Revd Mother

I only write one word to thank you for your St. Gertrude, which I read with the greater pleasure because it comes from my dear Revd Mother. I hope I shall be able to profit by it. For indeed it contains great lessons.

We are in all the misery of winding up our unfinished business, which means: leaving it unfinished.

I fear we shall not do much for the Workhouse Infirmaries this year. But I hope the wedge is in. And God will carry it, whether we are here or not.

Our India business has been very trying. Sir John Lawrence has sent home a man to try & get more out of the home Govt. I believe in Sir John Lawrence—& that great things will be done. Did I tell you that we have got 10 millions for the Soldiers' Stations?

When Parliament is up, then you know we begin to think of such trifles as men's lives. And the work comes very heavy then.

Poor Hilary Carter, whom perhaps you remember, is dying of internal tumour.[55]

Beatrice Smith, whose mother you remember,[56] is married to a Mr. Lushington, a very good youth.

I am afraid my dearest Revd Mother has had but a poor summer in health.

I do so wish to hear that poor S. Gonzaga's affairs are happily settled. It is very trying to her.

I know how trying it is to have to deal thro' other people—you know my life is made up of nothing else.

I prize my dearest Revd Mother's letters & prayers more than any thing else—more than I can say.

I would ask her: to offer me to God when she speaks to God. And it will do me good to think of that, when I am too ill to do it myself as I ought.

> Ever my dearest Revd Mother's
> loving & grateful
> F. Nightingale

*Autograph: Archives of the Sisters of Mercy, Bermondsey*


Three weeks later, Florence wrote again, referring to letters about Clare's recent illness that she had received from Mary Gonzaga Barrie (the Bermondsey Annals for 1865 do not indicate the nature of this illness):


## 53. To Mary Clare Moore

> *July 22/65*
> *34 South Street*
> *Park Lane*
> *London. W.*

Dearest Revd Mother

I have thought of you constantly during your illness. And I thought it so very kind of Sister Gonzaga to write to me twice to tell me how my dearest Revd Mother was going on. And she must have thought me so ungrateful not to answer. I do hope you are now pretty much as usual—tho' I am afraid that "usual" has been a poor one this year. I was so glad Sister Gonzaga was at home (I call yours her home) to keep you in order. I wish she were always there.

She told me of all the crosses of what she called the field day with the S.S. [[Sisters]] from Brighton.

But really I do think men are as bad as women about such confusions. What do you think I had? The Director of the Assistance Publique at Paris—a man I never saw—telegraphs to me to get him introductions to all the Workhouses & other places in 24 hours when he is to arrive in London—& that on a Sunday—& when every soul on the Poor Law Board is out of town at the Elections for the first time for 6 years. And they the only people who can give some introductions. And I in bed, as usual, & overdone with business. And he with no particular reason for coming then rather than any time these 6 years.

This is the sort of way men always serve me. And I am not like my dear Revd Mother who is never ruffled —

whose loving & grateful<br>F.N.

I *always* am, even when I cannot write. *Pray for me.*
Autograph: *Archives of the Sisters of Mercy, Bermondsey*

A small fragment of a letter from Florence, written on December 4, 1865 and preserved in the Bermondsey archives, says only: "Many thanks for the Advent Meditations. . . .she says . . . the truth. . . .But I would she could be silent." Conceivably this fragment, probably written to Clare, refers to Mary Gonzaga Barrie's tendency to say directly what she thought. This characteristic had, long before Cardinal Wiseman's death, not endeared her to the Catholic lay committee who, with the Cardinal, oversaw the hospital—among its members were the Duke of Norfolk, the Viscount Campden, Lord Herries, Lord Petre, and Sir George Bowyer. According to Mary Austin Carroll, Gonzaga's American contemporary:

It was even reported to the cardinal that . . . she could easily be provoked to use the strongest condemnatory expressions and other naughty words. Once when some "things" got in her way she consigned them, in the fewest possible words, to perdition. This was told to the cardinal, who regarded it as rather a vulgarity than a sin. "Things cannot be damned," corrected his eminence when he heard that his protégée had cursed. (*Leaves* 2:240)

Cardinal Wiseman's many extant letters to Gonzaga are full of kindness and affection, invariably cheering her when she was contrite about something or other she had done. In view of these letters, one cannot imagine that he was overly upset about an occasional "damn it."

But now Cardinal Wiseman was gone. On November 10, 1865, Clare Moore wrote to Bishop Grant to apprise him, apparently for the second time, of what was happening at the hospital, although as the Bishop of Southwark he could do nothing directly. In this letter Clare indicates that Archbishop Manning's desire to remove the Sisters of

Mercy from the hospital and install the French Sisters of Charity was made known to the Mercy community at the hospital the week before:

I heard from Miss Nightingale last night, and she must have had the intelligence through Lady Herbert, that Dr. Manning "cannot or will not draw back, in his plan about our Sisters"; he says it is by the "unanimous advice of the Council [the lay committee], including Lord Petre and others"—that as to the future "he (Dr. Manning) would provide, in fact had already done so." Miss Nightingale is as much grieved and astonished as we are. I would not trouble your Lordship on the subject only I thought perhaps there might be some means of helping them—and I would venture to ask your advice. I have ascertained that they have had no communication at the Hospital from Dr. Manning since he first intimated his intention of placing the French Sisters there—that was last Wednesday week.

Our poor Sisters are ready to submit to any arrangement & they can see God's goodness in it, but we do not know whether we ought to represent the unfairness. Card. Wiseman executed a Deed by which he thought he had secured them the possession of that Convent.

Since the Mercy community at the Hospital of Saint John and Saint Elizabeth was autonomous and situated in a separate diocese from her own, Clare had no jurisdiction in relation to it—only the more profound bonds of affection and concern for the sisters' well being. It was she, after all, who had founded the hospital community in 1856, with five sisters from her own Bermondsey community, all of whom were her friends and spiritual daughters.

Thomas Grant responded on the same day, in two separate letters. In the first, he advised: "It is best to leave St. Elizabeth's to prayer & to avoid dealing with the subject since if you appear in it, it will favour the idea that the Rule of the Sisters of Mercy supposes the return of Sisters to their original houses. It will be right therefore to be silent as it will only make their case weaker if it seems to be urged by persons out of the Community"; in a postscript he noted, "I fear the Card. spoiled the effect of the Deed, as it was, I believe, the same one which has resisted in Sir George Bowyer's case." (Grant is referring, no doubt, to some discussion of the deed in relation to Sir George's construction of the hospital church dedicated to Saint John of Jerusalem.) In his second letter to Clare on November 10, Grant said: "I have been thinking again about the Hospital of which I know nothing save what you have written, and I remain still of the same opinion that it is your only course to remain quiet, as any representation made by you would make their position more anxious than it is at present by leaving it to be supposed that they still had a claim upon Bermondsey."

About this time Florence Nightingale wrote a note marked "Private" to her Uncle Sam Smith. (The British Library estimates that this undated note was written during the period "June–November 1865", but it was probably written in November.) In the note Florence says:

> Dr. Manning turns Sister Gonzaga and Co. out of house & home, bestowed on them by a Deed of Gift by Card. Wiseman. I have had a terrible collision (terrible to me) with Dr. Manning about it. It is just the old story of the Jesuits & the Jansenists.
> You must not mention this at all—least of all to them, the Sisters. But if Aunt Mai, or Bertha, could call, or send garden produce—either to Revd Mother at Bermondsey or to Sister Gonzaga in Great Ormond St. (they are not ousted yet)—I think it would gratify & soothe. Revd. Mother is broken-hearted about it. (BL Add. MSS 45793, f. 68)

Evidently, Nightingale had written to Archbishop Manning, or had had some other contact with him, about the hospital community. Two years later, on August 5, 1867, she tells Clare that "It would only do them harm for me to appeal to him again. The last time I did so he only wrote a nasty letter . . . with insinuations against people."[57]

On November 18, 1865, Clare wrote again to Bishop Grant:

> A special Committee was summoned yesterday by the Archbishop to decide the fate of our Sisters at the Hospital, but that decision has been postponed until next Wednesday. Sir George Bowyer wrote to me the enclosed letter, but I told him that I had now no controul [sic], and that I felt sure Sr. Gonzaga was ready to give up her office [as the superior of the hospital community] if obedience required it. This is a very painful time of suspense.

Writing directly on Clare's letter, Grant repeated his earlier advice: "silence with all parties, although you are free to give any advice you deem proper to the Sisters."

Two days later, Dr. Manning offered a slight modification of his original plan. On November 20, 1865, Clare wrote to Bishop Grant: "As I presumed to trouble you with our anxieties, I venture now to tell your Lordship that the Hospital business seems to be taking a favourable turn. Dr. Manning told S. Gonzaga that he found so many averse to his plan of sending them away he doubted whether he could carry it out—for the present no change can be made & if he makes any he will do it as kindly as he can." On Clare's letter, Grant wrote: "In this case, could she [Mary Gonzaga] say, 'allow me to resign and let another be chosen whom I am quite willing to obey'? And add: 'if you wish to use the Church for a Mission [a church open to the public], settle it and we will use it as the Sisters at Bermondsey use that [parish] Church'?"[58]

However, the problem at the hospital was far from resolved. In the course of the next year Archbishop Manning would remove the Mercy sisters from the hospital and close it, turning away the patients (who at that time probably numbered about thirty incurable cases). The sisters would be allowed to remain in the convent attached to the hospital, but as they would have no income in relation to the hospital, they would have to sell needlework in a local shop to help support themselves.

Florence Nightingale was well aware of these proceedings as they unfolded. In fact, she was a principal source of Clare Moore's information as it related to the lay committee involved with the hospital. In May 1866, she wrote to Clare:

## 54. To Mary Clare Moore

*May 11/66*
*35 South Street*
*Park Lane*
*London. W.*

Dearest Revd Mother
Only one word to say that, last night in the House of Commons, Sir G. Bowyer spoke to my brother-in-law, Sir Harry Verney, about S. Gonzaga. [*I have not talked about her. I was only afraid of doing her more mischief. But Dr. Manning must not suppose that other people have held their tongues— Catholics least of all—about his injustice.*]

Sir G. Bowyer had met my sister & her husband at S. Gonzaga's—
So he began:—

"Dr. Manning is treating her & the Sisters there very ill. He does not know how to treat them. He does not appreciate their merit. He wants to turn them out & replace them by French nuns—*but he won't succeed.* I have as much influence at Rome as he has. The question is submitted to the Propaganda,[59] where are cautious thoughtful men, who will not permit such injustice & want of consideration. Cardinal Wiseman would never have allowed it, but Manning is not half the man that Wiseman was."

A little more passed in the same strain—& then Sir G. Bowyer added:—
"You may depend upon it that *we shall be finally victorious.*"

My brother-in-law wrote me this this morning. (My sister is not in London.)

Pray for me, dearest, dearest Revd Mother & offer me to God.

Ever my dearest Revd Mother's
faithful & grateful
F. Nightingale

Holy Thursday/66[60]

You are very, very good, dearest Revd Mother, in writing to me.

*Autograph: Archives of the Sisters of Mercy, Bermondsey*

On November 7, 1866, Nightingale wrote a long letter to her close friend Mary Jones, the superior of St. John's House, an Anglican religious community who undertook the nursing at King's College Hospital, London. In this ardent letter, labeled "Private" and "Burn," in which she advises Jones to persevere in her efforts to remove, or at least to limit the interference of, an Anglican chaplain, she offers, as support for her views and as encouragement to Jones, the experience of Roman Catholic sisterhoods, and in particular, that of "my nuns"—the Mercy sisters at the hospital on Great Ormond Street:

If indeed a Chaplain *were* a spiritual physician, if he really had insight into our moral diseases, & could help us to find the strength & the remedy, we lack—how gladly would we run to him—

But who is there now, in *any* Church, who answers to this description?—

I should be afraid that you would think me almost irreligious—at least, not alive to the religious wants of women—especially of women living a religious life in community—were it not that the view I have just mentioned is that of all the real, old, hard-working female orders of the R. Catholic Church.

You know I have lived among them, sleeping under their roofs, working among them—not as the R. Cath. female laity work among them but as they work among themselves—And I believe scarcely any one knows them as I do—[at least I am always astonished at the ignorance of such persons as Lady G. Fullerton, Dr. Manning, Lady Herbert etc. etc. about their real principles & practices. Of course *they* think it is *I* who am ignorant. But I hold my tongue]. I speak now of the real, genuine good Saints—not of the new-fangled devotees which Dr. Manning is introducing. [He says he is inaugurating "a new era" for the Church—a "new era" with a vengeance. You know that he turned my nuns—the nuns who worked so well in the Crimea—out of their Hospital in Gt. Ormond St, closed the Hospital, turned the Patients out into the street—one of whom died before she could reach home. He said "he would provide for them," of course. And, of course, he never did. And all this to bring the ultramontanes, the "Sisters" of S. Vincent de Paule into the Hospital. But in this he has not yet succeeded. We are still fighting the battle for the old nuns. But we shall fail.] (LMA, HI/ST/NC1—V66/17)

Thus, by November 1866, the patients in the hospital on Great Ormond Street had been removed and the hospital closed, though the Sisters of Mercy remained in the convent attached to the hospital.

On December 7, in keeping with her annual practice, Florence asked her mother to send "four splendid hampers of Christmassings on either Saturday or Monday—for Revd Mother, who has been ill again,—for Miss Jones, who is in great trouble,—for Mrs. Wardroper [[at St. Thomas Hospital]] & others" (Wellcome Institute, photocopy, MS 9002/81). In an apparently related list of directions for delivery of "Christmas greeneries," she lists, in addition to the three friends mentioned above: "Mrs. Barrie, St. Elizabeth's Hospital, 47 Great Ormond Street, Bloomsbury W.C." (Wellcome Institute, photocopy, MS 9002/83). Though she continued to live in the hospital community, Mary Gonzaga Barrie was by this time no longer their superior, having served ten years in that office.

When Florence writes to Clare a week before Christmas, she is grateful for Clare's several letters and, as always, concerned about the welfare of the hospital community. Once again she resorts, in her own troubles, to the writings of John of the Cross:

## 55. To Mary Clare Moore

*Dec 17/66*
*35 South Street*
*Park Lane*
*London. W.*

Dearest, very dearest Revd Mother

I cannot tell you how deeply I was touched by your welcoming letter to my "little cell" many weeks ago. And then I had another. And this afternoon I have another. And I have never thanked you. But you know how grateful I am. It is almost the greatest earthly support I have. I am going to write again. This is only to say how very anxious I feel about your health. Might I not send you a little more Wine & Ale? You know you ought to have gone away for a little. But you would not.

Indeed, about the poor Sisters at Ormond Street, I am always hoping it will come right at last—tho' I know not that I have much earthly reason for that hope. I am sure they are right in not asking to go away.

I think my troubles are always greater at Christmas than at any other time, tho' I do desire humbly to follow in the footsteps of S. John of the Cross. And I constantly read over the Life & some Extracts I made from what my dearest Revd Mother sent me. And I thank her from the bottom of my heart for offering me to God on the day of S. John of the Cross.[61]

Pray for me—ever yours

F. Nightingale

I am always quite alone at Christmas, even more so than at other times in London.

*Autograph: Archives of the Sisters of Mercy, Bermondsey*

Three days later, Nightingale wrote again to Mary Jones, urging her to press her case with the Anglican Bishop of London and noting that "Priest craft (in the Ch. of Rome) is held at bay only in religious 'Sisterhoods.' In these *alone* has the priest no personal power. . . . A Pusey, a Liddon, a Close, a Spurgeon, a Manning is *worshipped* in families as they never are in 'Sisterhoods.'" In this letter, Nightingale offered to intervene with the Bishop of London, but claimed: "No one dislikes more than I do this kind of private meddling—[tho' I did it for the sake of St. Elizabeth's Hospital]" (LMA, HI/ST/NC1—V66/25).

In a similar vein, on Christmas Day she wrote a "Private" letter to her brother-in-law, Sir Harry Verney:

I am sure that, after all you have done for the (Gonzaga) nuns at Gr. Ormond St, you will be sorry to hear that Dr. Manning sent for the Superioress on Saturday & told her that he had powers from Rome (which I believe to be a lie) to remove them, & that he would let them know his decision in a week. Nothing more can be done. Priestcraft is the same in all countries—it *cannot* allow independent action & good administration to any under its power—whether that power is Anglican or Roman. (Wellcome Institute, photocopy, MS 9002/87)

Archbishop Manning's desire to remove the Mercy sisters from the convent on Great Ormond Street was never implemented, but the issue dragged on for another year, and the hospital itself was not re-opened until 1868. The entire situation remained a constant source of distress for Clare Moore, affecting her already fragile health, although she tended to underplay this personal effect. And, as will be apparent in the letters of 1867–1868, Florence Nightingale continued to share Clare's suffering.

# 1867–1868

In early 1867, Florence Nightingale was deeply involved in efforts to bring about reform of the nursing provided in the London work-house infirmaries, trying to salvage key elements of a scheme whose support had died in June 1866, when the Whig government fell from power. By spring she had secured sufficient Tory support to have a bill introduced in Parliament. Though the bill provided less than what she had been advocating, its passage on March 29, 1867, represented, in her mind, some necessary first steps to securing proper nursing care for sick paupers (Cook 2:130–39).

Meanwhile, in Lent 1867, Clare Moore had become severely ill. Her doctor having ordered her to rest away from her duties, she went for two weeks to the convent attached to the now closed hospital. Evidently Mary Gonzaga Barrie kept Florence Nightingale informed of Clare's condition, for in the midst of her own ailments and her "up-hill fight about the Workhouses," Florence wrote to Clare:

## 56. To Mary Clare Moore

*March 1, [[1867]]*

Dearest Revd Mother

I don't know how you are. I had a letter from S. Gonzaga a little while ago, for which I was very grateful to her—but it did not give a very good account of you.

Neither, I am afraid, is there any good news about their own prospects.

I have had such a very bad month—(with an attack on my Chest, so that for 17 nights I could not lie down)—that I could scarcely get on with my work.

And I am afraid you are not much better.

I read over & over again your little S. John of the Cross—& many Extracts which I made from your books.

We are having a very up-hill fight about the Workhouses. We have got to bring a Bill thro' Parliament. We *have* obtained some things—but I am very doubtful myself whether, unless we obtain a great deal more, it will do much good. But we know God will take care of His own work, if it *is* His work.

The things we have obtained are:

the removal of 2000 Lunatics, 800 Fever and Smallpox cases & all the remaining children out of the Workhouses—(& the providing for them out of a Common Fund, in order to relieve the rates); the paying all salaries of Medical Officers, Matrons, Nurses, etc., etc., out of a Metropolitan (not Parochial) rate. But, as the Guardians are still to appoint them, I am afraid this will do but little good except relieving the rates, for there will be so much jobbery.

Also:—the removing all other sick into separate buildings which are to be improved—& constituting fresh boards of Guardians for these sick, with nominees from the Poor Law Board. I don't think this will answer— the sick ought to be entirely provided for (as they are in Paris by the "Assistance Publique") by the Poor Law Board out of the Consolidated Fund.

We hope however that this is a beginning—& that we shall get more in time—when our own friends come back to Office.

I send you a few little things, which I *insist* upon Sr. Gonzaga's making you eat yourself. May I send you some wine?

Pray for me, dearest, very dearest Revd Mother & believe me

ever your loving & grateful

F. Nightingale

*Autograph: Archives of the Sisters of Mercy, Bermondsey*

On Good Friday, April 19, Florence wrote her father a letter expressing her estimate of the Passion of Christ and her longstanding conviction about the significance of human suffering in general—a conviction she shared, no doubt, with Clare and, as she claims, with Teresa of Avila:

This day reminds me that I think religion immensely fallen since the days of the (so called) Mystics—

Of all the sermons that will be preached to-day in all sects & churches, of all countries, called Christian—not one will get beyond the wounds, the "Passion" of Christ.

Now I find St. Teresa saying, in her strong picturesque language:—

"Notre Seigneur me dit: *que ce n'était pas ces blessures qui me devaient affliger mais celles qu'on lui faisait presentement.*"[62]

So I think.

If instead of dwelling upon those few hours of Passion, interesting as they are, as if they were the only point of interest in God's scheme of Government—why not look at the Passion which God is undergoing, rather undertaking, every hour, every day, in every part of the world? (BL Add. MSS 45790, ff. 348–49)

By August matters at the hospital and convent on Great Ormond Street had heated up again. Apparently Dr. Manning was now proposing a division of the premises into two hospitals—a hospital for male patients to be run by the Sisters of Mercy and a hospital for female patients to be assigned to the Sisters of Charity. Florence's next extant letter to Clare records both her exasperation with the situation and her own failed efforts to resolve it:

*57. To Mary Clare Moore*

*August 5/67*
*35 South Street*
*Park Lane*
*London. W.*

Dearest Revd Mother

Indeed nothing that you can say to me ever "troubles" me, except with the feeling how impotent I am. All your "news" I beg to hear, "bad" as well as "good". But the worst is, that I can do nothing.

I have cried to all the authorities on earth & all the Saints in heaven against Dr. Manning. The fact is—that he is, as the Catholics themselves call him, a "deucedly clever fellow", & "somehow or other, by foul more than by fair means, gets all things his own way." [I know you don't like me to say these things. But it is not *I* who say them, dear Revd. Mother.]

You know he has such a convenient bad memory. And he always falls back upon this.

If this is the final "offer of the Trustees", I really don't see that anything can be done.

But I think that Sir G. B. may show "that the fault is" *not* "on his side."

As I understood, the Trustees or Committee first appealed to the Archbishop.

He decides.

He communicates the decision to Sir G. Bowyer—calling it the "offer of the Trustees".

It is obviously impossible for him, Sir G. B., to comply with it.

Sir G. B. should call a meeting of these "Trustees" or Committee (or whoever the administration is,) state the case to them, *shew* them that he *cannot* comply with the decision or "offer."

Then the Trustees would either try another "offer" (or negociation)—or at least "blame" would not fall on Sir G. Bowyer for not doing the impossible.

Probably this has been done already.

In that case, I really do not see how anything but newspaper publicity remains to be tried.

Funds are wanted. And the *Trustees* should, by such a Meeting as I describe, (if not already tried & done with,) clear the way for a successful appeal to Catholics (& Protestants too).

Somehow or other, I am told, the Archbishop has got the game in his own hands.

Some of the proposals he makes would not stand in law.

But then, you see, the complication of the whole matter is that the Sisters obviously could only, must only, "abide by the decisions of their Superiors".

The only advantage which I can see of a Meeting would be that Sir G. B. could lay anew before the Trustees all the facts and let *them* take the responsibility of discontinuance. They might start at this—& some better arrangement might be come to. [I understand that Catholics themselves believe it to be quite impossible, if Dr. Manning insists on two Hospitals, that two can be supported, (even with Protestant help), and therefore believe the "offer of the Trustees" an impossible one.]

I assure you, dearest Revd Mother, excepting you yourself, I don't believe any one can have thought more of this matter than I have, night & day, day & night. If there were only any thing I could do? But I did try Lord Clarendon & Lord Stanley & Dr. Manning himself. Lord Stanley says he can do nothing more—& advises an appeal to the newspapers. Sir G. B. says *he* won't do this (tho' I don't see exactly why) & that *I* must. I don't think, & no one else thinks, that I ought. And, even if I ought, I don't see what good can come of it. Because the Sisters must obey the Archbp. It seems to me that the only thing for them is to consult him. It would only do them harm for *me* to appeal to him again. The last time I did so he only wrote a nasty letter (for which I never can forgive him) with insinuations against people & a fine flourish in my honour to poor Mrs. Herbert.

I have turned the thing over & over again in every possible way these 18 months in my head & also in writing.

My belief is that, from the very moment Dr. M. became Archbp., he determined to have the "Soeurs de Charité". He never considers that it was he himself who put the Sisters into the Hospital.

What was the "decision" on "the appeal to Rome" in "December last"?— referred to by the Archbp.

From my dearest Revd Mother's
ever grateful & loving (tho' it seems only words to say so now)
F. Nightingale

*Autograph: Archives of the Sisters of Mercy, Bermondsey*

In the above letter, Florence may have inserted the following "Private" letter, or else she wrote Clare a second letter on the same day:

## 58. To Mary Clare Moore

*Aug 5/67*
*35 South Street*
*Park Lane*
*London. W.*

*Private*
Dearest Revd Mother
If S. Gonzaga is wishing to leave the Order for a "holier life", I have only suspected it. I do not know it.

I wish it may not be so. From the most worldly, as well as from the most spiritual motives, it is so important that they, the Sisters, should keep together, & give no ground of offence—under such a man as Manning who does say the most unwarrantable things—& then says, he forgets what he has said.

S. Gonzaga only said to me: that she was waiting every day to see Dr. M. I thought this implied what you say. [How I wish she could come back to you. But that is impossible.]

I felt such a mind to write to S. Gonzaga. But I refrained. I thought I should only do harm.

I wish I could think you were better.

It is 6 years last Friday since Sidney Herbert's death. And things, according to our poor human thinking, have gone so wrong since.

God bless you, dearest, very dearest Revd Mother. Words seem so vain when I can give nothing but words.

If anything comes to me, I will write before Saturday.

Ever your loving
F.N.

*Autograph: Archives of the Sisters of Mercy, Bermondsey*

No documentary evidence has been discovered to confirm or support any wish on Mary Gonzaga Barrie's part to "leave the Order."

Florence may have alluded to such a wish in an earlier letter to Clare, or Clare may have heard something to this effect elsewhere. Perhaps Clare then wrote to Florence (inquiring about Florence's source, or asking her if she had heard anything about such a wish), and Florence was now responding. Certainly, Mary Gonzaga was in a difficult situation at the still-closed hospital, and perhaps she was already contemplating her permanent return to the Bermondsey community, for which both Dr. Manning's and Bishop Grant's permissions would have been needed. Florence may have misinterpreted or overinterpreted the intention behind Gonzaga's "waiting every day to see" Dr. Manning. When on November 18, 1867, Mary Gonzaga left the hospital community for good, she returned to the Bermondsey community for the rest of her life.[63]

Florence had earlier enlisted her brother-in-law, Sir Harry Verney, to write a letter to the *Times* exposing the situation of the Sisters of Mercy at the hospital, but now she thought better of it. In a letter to him on August 24, 1867, she says:

> I have been so occupied that I have not been able even to tell you why I did not send your kind letter to the "Times".
> They (Manning & Co.) are so crafty that they will always turn one's flank.
> They would answer:—
> "We are not going to turn out the Crimean Nuns. We are going to make the charity more efficient. We are going to divide the Hospital into two—leaving men & boys under the Crimean nuns & putting women & girls under the French nuns."
> I have tried in vain to alter your wording by a word or two in order to put the thing so that it cannot be contradicted.
> At one time I thought of asking you to consult Sir G. Bowyer. But, you see, *he* does not speak the truth, any more than the others. He wrote me 3 letters, asking me to collect subscriptions, as if the Hospital were to be re-opened on its old footing!!!
> Of course *we* know that it is utterly impossible to support two R.C. Hospitals, instead of one—
> that Manning *has* turned away & *will* turn away the subscriptions from the Crimean nuns—
> & that his object is to centralize the subscriptions in the hands of the ultramontane nuns, *without* appearing to "turn out" ours.
> But I don't know how to tell this story in a newspaper, in such a way as that Manning would not come out of it triumphantly. That is the worst of having no better counsellor than Sir G. Bowyer.
> A great wrong has been done to the poor (by closing the *Hospital*.) A great wrong has been done to the Crimean nuns by depriving them of their occupation.
> [And I believe a great wrong has been done to Sir G. B.]
> But Manning is aware that he cannot legally turn the nuns out of their *Convent*,

& will say he has no intention of doing so. He wants to persuade them to *ask* to be sent away to Walthamstow ("to beg" (*sic*) i.e.—to live on begging!) (Wellcome Institute, photocopy, MS 9002/172)[64]

In 1867, some of the sisters originally in the hospital community moved, at the request of Archbishop Manning, to a convent in Walthamstow, a suburb of London, where they served young girls in an orphanage (industrial school) attached to a workhouse.

In mid-November 1867, in a personal effort to alleviate in part the conflict between Archbishop Manning and the Sisters of Mercy in the hospital community, Mary Gonzaga Barrie departed from Saint Elizabeth's convent. The Bermondsey Annals for that year simply say: "On November 18th Sister Mary Gonzaga Barrie returned to this Community after having spent eleven years at the Hospital of Saint Elizabeth which she had been sent to found in 1856, and where she had held the office of Mother Superior for ten years" (2: [127]). Gonzaga had resigned her office in 1866. She now left the Saint Elizabeth's community and returned to Bermondsey—a gesture aimed at removing from the site any personal reasons for Dr. Manning's or the lay committee's antagonism. Mary Stanislaus Jones, who had served in the Crimea, had already become the superior of the hospital community. However, the hospital itself was still closed. A year and a half later, on May 26, 1869, Clare will write to Mary Angela Graham, the former superior of the Mercy community in Brighton:

You know already that Mother Gonzaga in order to induce that perverse Committee to open the Hospital begged to come back to us, because they, I mean those Gentlemen, said things against her. Dr. Manning and Dr. Grant gave leave, but she begged to return only as the youngest professed—however, as the Sisters at the last Election [May 13, 1869] chose to have her for Assistant, the words of our Blessed Lord are verified: he who takes the last place shall be told to go up higher.

Similarly, in an undated letter transcribed in Carroll's *Leaves from the Annals of the Sisters of Mercy*, with three discreet blanks where names obviously appeared in the original, Clare is reported to have written:

The late Cardinal Wiseman loved darling Sister M. Gonzaga as his own child. When he died her great trials began. The *[Archbishop]* wished to put S*[isters of Charity]* in place of our Sisters, which was against the agreement made and signed by all parties. Then the hospital was closed and the patients heartlessly sent out, some in a dying state. For nearly two years this trouble went on. The hospital re-opened November, 1868, but the funds were withdrawn and everything done to hinder.

However, one good was attained—there was no L[ay] Committee to quarrel or lay down laws. The Sisters have to seek funds for their patients, but they are free from lay control. (*Leaves* 2:246–47)

Florence Nightingale, who had been consumed by this issue, was greatly relieved by Gonzaga's decision to return to the Bermondsey community. She wrote immediately to Clare:

*59. To Mary Clare Moore*

> *20 Nov. /67*
> *35 South Street*
> *Park Lane*
> *London. W.*

Oh dearest Revd Mother, it is such a relief to me that dear S. Gonzaga is come back to you. I always felt, humanly, that that was the best & indeed the only way out of it. It is the greatest joy that I have had for many a year. And I have also a reason of my own, which is that I think S. Gonzaga makes you look a little after your health—& that she will sometimes give me news of it.

I am very sorry for poor Mother Stanislaus. I think she is worn by long anxieties. Otherwise I do hope she might see that there is a better prospect of the Hospital being re-opened. Tho' I never believe a word that Dr. Manning says, I think he has been a little deterred by the general "row" that has been made. If the Hospital could but be re-opened under fairly favourable circumstances, I should hope that matters might go on more smoothly than they have done ever since Cardinal Wiseman was taken away.

And what a good Revd Mother you are to write to me.

I have been trying to find a minute to write to you—& have only just time to say how much I am ever my dearest Revd Mother's faithful and grateful

F. Nightingale

*Autograph: Archives of the Sisters of Mercy, Bermondsey*

The next day Florence wrote to her sister Parthenope:

In haste, for I really have not time to "bless myself"—as Irish say. . . .

The only good news I have I send for Aunt Mai. Manning's persecution of the nuns had passed all bounds. *But Sister Gonzaga has been got back to Bermondsey under Revd Mother*. The relief is quite beyond description. [Latterly I had been contributing to buy *food* for the Ormond St. Sisters!!]

Of course you will burn this. (Wellcome Institute, photocopy, MS 9002/187)

In December she wrote a similar letter to her mother. By now, Florence had involved the entire Nightingale and Verney families in concern for the well-being of the sisters in Bermondsey and on Great Ormond Street—a solicitude they expressed, in part, by frequent gifts of food.

But in early 1868 Florence experienced a fresh and severe personal and professional loss: the death from fever on February 19, at age thirty-six, of Agnes Jones, the superintendent of nursing in the Liverpool Workhouse Infirmary. Florence herself had approved the choice of Miss Jones to inaugurate the reform of workhouse nursing in Liverpool, when the opportunity presented itself in 1864. The day after Agnes's death Florence wrote to Clare:

*60. To Mary Clare Moore*

> *Feb. 20 [[1868]]*
> *35 South Street*
> *Park Lane*
> *London. W.*

Dearest, very dearest Revd Mother

My darling, the Matron of the Liverpool Workhouse, is dead. Her life was trembling in the balance till yesterday. But still we hoped. Yesterday she died.

With her, we believe, it is "well". But for us it is terrible.

All the Head Nurses have behaved nobly.

As to what is to come next, we are in the hands of the Vestry.

Of course a good many arrangements fall upon me.

God will take care of His own work.

That is my only hope.

I should be so very glad to know that you were better.

Let me hear, please, by Sister Gonzaga.

Pray for us—

> Ever my dearest Revd Mother's
> F. Nightingale

*Autograph: Archives of the Sisters of Mercy, Bermondsey*

In Liverpool, Agnes Jones had demonstrated many of the positive effects of the reforms Florence still hoped to achieve in the London workhouses, but she had unwisely overworked, taking little sleep.

Florence was deeply affected by her death—as by the deaths of all those whose work she counted on. She was consulted to find a suitable successor, under considerable pressure from the Liverpool authorities. But in 1870, after one new matron proved unequal to the demanding work of organizing the nursing care of over 1000 sick poor, and a second was dismissed for intoxication, Florence acknowledged to her friend Sir John McNeill: "I look upon Agnes Jones' work as completely wrecked. In a few days she will have been dead 2 years. And as these days come round, I cannot even think of her without tears which I have not time to shed. . . . It has been one of the great misfortunes of my life" (Vicinus and Nergaard, eds. 305–6).

But now, in early 1868, Florence was not only grief-stricken over Agnes Jones's death, but still incensed over the protracted chaplaincy crisis at St. John's House. The simultaneous difficulties of the Great Ormond Street community and of Mary Jones and the women at St. John's House further fueled her chagrin at "ecclesiastics." In her complex attitude toward the roles of women, the intricate dimensions of which have yet to be fully explored, Florence resented every situation in which women were denied their proper jurisdiction or were not negotiated with truthfully, as equals. She saw the medical, clerical, and governmental professions—with notable exceptions—as occupationally prone to these injustices. With such instances fresh in her mind, she wrote to her Uncle Sam Smith on April 16, 1868:

Aunt Mai will be sorry to hear that Revd. Mother, after ailing for many months, has been very ill. She is now, however, thank God, better.

The affairs of the Ormond St. Sisters still in the same unsatisfactory state.

Rome has written to Manning (an event to which I believe we contributed) to know why the Hospital is not re-opened. And Manning replied that he did not know before what their (the Sisters') rights were. However, he has done nothing.

But the Bishop of London has played just the same trick to the Sisters of St. John's House (Miss Jones').

All ecclesiastics are alike. (BL Add. MSS 45793, ff. 71–72)

Clare Moore's illness in early 1868 is not recorded in the Bermondsey Annals. It was evidently her recurrent pleurisy, complicated by fistula, as Florence Nightingale claims in a letter to Parthenope (see below). As Clare's own sister in Dublin (Mary Clare Augustine Moore) commented years later, after Clare's death, "How she lived so long is wonderful for her lungs were diseased when she was fourteen & continued so for many years after I know, perhaps to the last. The beauty of which she once thought so much left her very early, even before she entered the Convent." [65]

Repeated evidence of Florence's affection for Clare is found in the inventiveness and persistence with which she provided, over many years, foods, and even delicacies, that might restore Clare's energy. In this, of course, she was greatly dependent on her family's generosity. Thus, on April 25, 1868, Florence wrote to her mother:

Revd Mother, of Bermondsey, has been very ill—& tho', thank God, she is better— yet she does not at all recover her strength or appetite. She liked some Orange Jelly which was sent me from Embley two or three weeks ago better than anything else. And, since then, I have been supplying her with Orange Jelly & other things from Gunter's.

If, by Tuesday's box, Mrs. Watson could send some more *Orange* Jelly for her— & also, are there not nourishing things like *Arrowroot Blancmange* or *Rice Blanc-mange?*—we should be very much obliged.

She was delighted with some flowers I sent her from Embley. (BL Add. MSS 45790, f. 365)

Just before Whitsunday that year she sent a similar message to Parthenope:

Revd Mother of Bermondsey has been dangerously ill with Pleurisy & Fistula. [Mrs. Bracebridge says Manning will kill her.] All my Embley things, including flowers, have recently passed on to her—besides Gunter's Turtle Soup. She understands that I shall never forgive her, unless she becomes as fat as a Lord Mayor with time & soup. (Wellcome Institute, photocopy, MS 9003/21)

On August 1, the eve of the anniversary of Sidney Herbert's death in 1861—"the loss, now more terrible to me year by year"—Florence wrote to Elizabeth Herbert, his widow, who had become a Roman Catholic in 1865 and had recently returned from a stay in Rome. In this letter Florence noted:

The order has come from Rome to re-open the Hospital of the nuns who served your husband (in Great Ormond St.) Perhaps we are indebted to you for this. But it is not yet, re-opened. They are still haggling about money with the nuns—wanting to cut them down, after having invited them there as a Community, from being a Community. A word from you would set this right.

Revd. Mother at Bermondsey is very suffering—. . . .

I never see the beautiful sunset light on the trees without remembering how *he* noticed it on that last evening this day 7 years. (Typescript, BL Add. MSS 43396, f. 214)

Whether Lady Herbert directly intervened on behalf of the hospital community, and if so, when and how and to whom she represented their case or the case of the patients once served in the hospital on Ormond Street, remain questions whose answers are not yet clearly known. Edward Cook claims that she interceded with Archbishop Manning in 1867, with the result that the case was referred to Rome, where she may also have intervened (1:487 n. 1).

Later in August 1868, while she was reading the writings of John of Avila that Clare had loaned her, Florence wrote to Mary Gonzaga Barrie. She was still anxious about Clare's health and still trying, not always successfully, to "hold [her] tongue" about "men":

*61. To Mary Gonzaga Barrie*

*Aug 20/68*
*35 South Street*
*Park Lane*
*London. W.*

Dearest Sister Gonzaga

Indeed I *was* "expecting a letter"—not because you are bad to me (in writing) but because you are very good to me.

I wish I could hear that Revd Mother was better—but indeed I don't expect it. I believe nothing but a complete change & rest would do her any good. I wish she would go away somewhere (as a duty) with you. I had some faint hopes that she might be better for the Retreat. But I suppose that, really (to a Revd Mother), that is only another charge added to her many others.[66]

I never believe Revd Mother about herself, but only you. I wish she could go to Walthamstow where Sister Helen is, if there is accommodation there.

I feel sick of expecting the re-opening of the Hospital in Gr. Ormond St. It is a dreadful trial to Mo[[ther]] Stanislaus—but as B. Jean d'Avila says, how are we to prove the "modération et tranquillité de notre esprit" except under "contrariétés"?

I think men are the same all over the world—of every profession & condition—War Office Ministers, Poor Law Ministers, Boards of Guardians, Archbishops, Bishops & Generals. But this is a sentiment which will not meet Revd M.'s approval, so I will hold my tongue.

Men don't think first of the good of the poor or the sick—& frame their business, first & foremost, to meet it. But the poor are there to make them an Office—*not*, their Office is there for the poor.

Here has the War Office given me something to do for the Military Hospitals, which it ought to have given me a full year's notice of it,—& now when every soul of a man of business is out of London & one is gone away ill, it gives it to be done at once.

However, this kind of thing is so frequent in my business that I really don't complain of it—but am very thankful that God allows me to do His work at all. But I *can* sympathize with Mo[[ther]] Stanislaus, altho' very unworthy.

I am sure Revd M. prays for me. And so do you. May God's best blessings be always hers & yours. And they *will* be.

Ever yours
F. Nightingale

*Autograph: Archives of the Sisters of Mercy, Bermondsey*

It was perhaps in this letter to Gonzaga, or in some other letter written to Gonzaga or Clare in 1867 or 1868, that Florence enclosed the following brief note:

I am sure dear Revd Mother's kind heart will be glad to hear that we are getting on at last with the Workhouses.

We have an official application from one of the largest Workhouses in London— from the great Divinities themselves, the Board of Guardians.

Think of that!! But don't speak!![67]

Despite Florence Nightingale's many references to Clare Moore's poor health in 1868, the Bermondsey Annals narrate numerous activities and decisions that engaged Clare's time and energy that year: agreeing in January to part permanently with a sister who was needed for work in Abingdon, where a death had occurred; receiving a sickly novice from Abingdon into the Bermondsey community; undertaking repairs of the convent infirmary when a donation was given for this purpose; preparing children for the sacrament of Confirmation in June; exchanging a sister with one from the Gravesend community in July; coping with the severe illness of Bishop Grant, the onset of the cancer that would later claim his life; directing the spiritual retreat of the community in August; arranging to have the large day school repainted before the children returned to classes in September; preparing the first publication of the *Sayings* of Catherine McAuley and communicating with other Sisters of Mercy in Ireland, England, and Australia about this; securing care and instruction, eventually in France, for a little girl who was deaf and mute and had been forsaken by her parents; carrying on all the supervisory duties associated with an infants' school, a middle school, a day school, and the visitation of the sick poor in their homes and in hospitals; and, with all this, bearing, as a painful undercurrent, continual worry about the community on Great Ormond Street.

How often Clare wrote to Florence during these months is not known. Her letters were probably infrequent. Certainly when Florence wrote to her in September, she was grateful to see her handwriting again. The atypical salutation of this letter may be, in part, playful, although it may also reflect the respect, even deference, Florence always had for Clare, going back to their days in the Crimea:

### 62. To Mary Clare Moore

*Sept. 8/68*
*35 South Street*
*Park Lane*
*London. W.*

Your dear Reverence

is very good to me. I was so thankful to see your handwriting again. But there is one point on which I never believe your Reverence. And that is: your own health. I am afraid you are not so much better as you say you are. I wish you would go, if it were only for one week, to Gr. Ormond St. That is a very little move. And the most mortified person could not call it a dissipation. I know so well how you can never take the least rest, but must always lead all the Exercises, & every thing else, your own dear self.

I am very sorry to hear of the Bishop's illness—but I think he ought to look after you better.

Alas! dear Revd Mother, you ask after me. I feel as if I was only quite in the infancy of serving God. I am so careful & troubled & have such a want of calmness about His work & His poor—as if they were *my* work & *my* poor instead of His. I have not learnt yet the first lesson of His service. "Je m'en vais à Dieu: cela seul doit m'occuper," as B. Jean d'Avila says—meaning, of course, in serving Him. I know you pray for me. *Offer me* to Him, that His will may be done in me & by me. I feel, you know, that, if I really believed what I say I believe, I should be in a "rapture" (as St. Teresa calls it) instead of being so disquieted. And therefore I suppose I don't believe what I say I believe.

I *think* I seek first the kingdom of God & His righteousness. But I am sure I don't succeed in being filled with His righteousness. And so I suppose that I regard too little Himself & too much myself. I should like to try to listen *only* to His voice as to what He wishes me to do, among all His poor.

It is 12 years last August 7 (do you remember?) since we came to you at Bermondsey, returning from the Crimea.

It is 11 years last August since I have been a prisoner more or less to my room.

It is 7 years last August since Sidney Herbert died. You know what a terrible break up that was to what we were doing in the War Office. Still God has pleased to raise up the India work & the Poor Law work since that. And I ought to be very thankful.

But it does me good, I assure you it does, (tho' I can't bear myself,) if I think that your dear Reverence is offering me to God, that whatever He wills may be carried out in me.

I have so little of the only true patience.

I feel very anxious about Mo[[ther]] Stanislaus' Hospital. I think of it every day. And yet I scarcely ever write to her. I think she *must* think, tho' she is far too delicate ever to say so to me, that I might do something more to promote its opening, after all she & you did for us. But indeed I would, if I could. But this makes me shy of writing to her.

May God bless her—she has been sorely tried. And may He protect this Hospital.

Ever your dear Reverence's<br>most grateful & affectionate<br>F. Nightingale

I send a little offering for your poor (on the other side).

I often pray God that He would give me the opportunity of being able to show you the gratitude I feel to you. But you see He does not.

*Autograph: Archives of the Sisters of Mercy, Bermondsey*

The hospital on Great Ormond Street was reopened in late 1868. The Sisters of Mercy resumed their nursing without receiving any regular funding, except for whatever donations or subscriptions succeeded in reaching them. This arrangement infuriated Florence. On

November 24, she wrote to her brother-in-law: "I have followed exactly your advice—sending it to the poor Sisters of Ormond St. With the gigantic, I had almost said diabolical, power wielded by the Confessional, Manning is equally able & willing to deprive them of Subscriptions. And I know of at least one instance where he has done so. It would be madness for *them* to undertake to raise funds. And they are so simple-minded" (Wellcome Institute, photocopy, MS 9003/57). Ten days later she complained to Sir Harry again: "With regard to Sir G. Bowyer, I will ask leave from the 'Revd Mother' of Bermondsey to tell you what the Sisters of Ormond St. are suffering, while he thinks he is 'supporting them entirely' " (Wellcome Institute, photocopy, MS 9003/58).

Perhaps the sisters at the Hospital of Saints John and Elizabeth were "simple-minded" about fund-raising, as Florence Nightingale claimed. But they evidently had some wisdom and skill about how to survive on the support of friends, and some unusual capacity to make do with what they had. Mary Stanislaus Jones, the superior in 1868, remained at the hospital for many years, except for a period of service in the 1880s at the orphanage in Walthamstow. In September 1897, after the death of Mary Helen Ellis, she returned to Walthamstow as superior. She continued to correspond with Florence Nightingale until at least 1906. The hospital itself gradually outgrew the site on Great Ormond Street, and at the end of the century was relocated to St. John's Wood in northwest London. There it still flourishes—but now as a private hospital and, since 1991, no longer staffed by the Sisters of Mercy who had founded it to serve the poor (*Trees of Mercy* 22–24).

Thus the close of 1868 brought a workable resolution of the hospital issue that had figured so passionately in Florence Nightingale's letters to Clare Moore and others in the preceding three years. While the funding arrangements remained unjust, at least the wards of the hospital were re-opened, and those who were poor and sick had recourse to the nursing care of women who had long suffered for their sakes.

# 1869–1874

In the five years preceding Clare Moore's death on December 14, 1874, no extant letters from Florence to Clare, or from Clare to Florence, have so far been discovered. However, references in Florence's letters to other correspondents indicate that Clare and she continued to correspond and that their friendship endured, with all its previous depth and affection. The period ends with Florence's heartbroken letter to a sister at Bermondsey, on December 12, 1874, as Clare lay dying.

These years were eventful ones for both Florence and Clare, so one can imagine that their letters and visits were less frequent than before. The specific projects in which they were engaged and the illness and death of some who were especially dear to them took their time and energies in new directions that evidently did not permit their usual correspondence—or else numerous letters are lost or undiscovered.

In early 1869, Clare was involved, not directly but in a supportive way, in the famous lawsuit brought against the former superior of the Convent of Mercy in Hull by a former member of the community. The case, *Saurin v. Star*, was tried in Westminster Hall, and London newspapers excited their readers with accounts of the "horrors" alleged to have been committed or sanctioned by the defendant and her assistant superior. The jury "found in favor of the defendants on the counts of assault and imprisonment and for the plaintiff on the counts of libel and conspiracy [to remove the plaintiff from the convent]" (Arnstein 120). The seeming "pettiness" of some of the Convent's rules, the theatrical descriptions presented by the counsel for the plaintiff, and the mocking prose and cartoons in *Punch* could not have failed to grieve Clare Moore. The Bermondsey Annals for this year say only that "many persons felt anxious about the consequences of such unprincipled misrepresentation of Religious Rules and Customs," and note that "through prudential motives all conversation on the subject was carefully avoided, but when the appeal was made to obtain money for Costs, etc., a collection" among the school children and their parents, "in addition to the small offering of the Community, produced a sum of about £13.10" (2:[145–46]). The trial ended in March, but its transcript appeared to give Charles Newdigate Newdegate the grounds he needed to press for "a parliamentary statute authorizing the periodic inspection of convents by a duly appointed commission" (Arnstein 122). Thomas Grant commented: "It is so hard to furnish explanations of a thousand trifling details to a prejudiced audience" (BA 2:[146]).[68]

In May 1869, Clare was reelected superior of the Bermondsey community, and Mary Gonzaga Barrie was elected her assistant. Clare continued her secretarial work for Bishop Grant, now increased by his preparations for the Vatican Council to be convened on December 8,

1869. Prior to his departure for Rome, Grant gave Clare his penknife, telling her, "I will come back and use it in Bermondsey." On November 13, the evening before he left, he said to her: "Well, all these years we have worked together and never had any quarrel" (BA 2:[156–57]). When he departed the next day, Clare little realized that his internal cancer was so advanced that he would die in Rome, and she would never see him again.

The year 1869 also brought changes in Florence's life—some more significant than others. In January she was chagrined to discover that one of her servants at South Street had "constantly been taking rum all the time." Asking her brother-in-law for advice about letting the man go, but fearing the harm his dismissal would cause his wife and children, she admitted: "I must tell you that Sister Gonzaga, in her outspoken way, wrote to me: 'if you are fool enough to keep that man' etc. etc." (Wellcome Institute, photocopy, MS 9003/71).

By April, Florence was heavily engaged in new research: gathering statistics on death rates in lying-in hospitals, including those at workhouses, and on the high rates of puerperal fever among lying-in women in these and other institutions. The Poor Law remained an object of her scorn. In penciled notes written during this month, she says:

The principle of the P[[oor]] Law has been, to drive the helpless to help themselves.

And signal has been the failure.

They *have* helped themselves indeed—but it has been out of others' earnings.

The principle of a true Pol[[itical]] Eco[[nomy]] is to help the helpless to help themselves.

Not that I would not drive, if it answered. But it does not. . . .

That those who do not produce ought not to eat up the earnings of those who do produce is a truism in these days (tho' not in St. Teresa's days).

But the P. Law goes on to say—not, we will teach them how to produce but—we will offer them the Workh[[ouse]] Test—or let them starve—That will teach them how to produce.

Surely no greater error in understanding human nature could have been committed than this—since the Workhouse (& still less starvation) is no teacher of production—no teacher of physical, still less of moral or intellectual energy.

What a want of power of applying Pol. Eco. to education this is!

Perhaps there has scarcely been a greater religious genius than Ign[[atius]] Loyola—his object was to reduce Religious training to a method—to Rules. Just as we say that Moral Science is as much subject to laws as Physical Science (we have scarcely made the first step even in discovering a method to discover these laws)

so Ign. Loyola thought that he would reduce Practical Religion—the method of becoming religious or spiritual–to Rules.
[And much of his Spiritual Exercises *is* the right method.]

But, just because of that very want of knowledge of human nature, of Moral
Science, which you see reigning in the Poor Law, Ign. Loyola did not see (& St.
Teresa did not see) that a great proportion of their Rules & of their Method actually led human nature directly down to its lowest depths—just as the Poor Law
form of Political Economy does—by bringing up, or rather by bringing down, men
& women to be either lazy beggars or to be slaves without a will, without independence, without freedom of thought, without a wish of their own to enquire after
the truth.

Ign. Loyola & St. Teresa, just like the Workhouses, destroyed in man & woman
the power of production—because they did not see, just as Political Economy does
not see, that you supply no one motive for production to man (his chief end), you
teach him in no sense to produce by these methods. (BL Add. MSS 45801, ff. 222–23).

If Clare saw these notes or similar ones, she has left no record suggesting that she would have accepted Florence's interpretations of Ignatius's and Teresa's teachings. Though she agreed, in general, that in-
culcating passivity is destructive of human potential, she was a more
compassionate realist about the prospects of those whose motivation
and productivity were already severely damaged. She also made a dis-
tinction between the energy that can arise from obedient surrender to
God and the listlessness that can be engendered by passive obedience
to Poor Law Guardians.

Florence's many years of intense work for the War Office came to
a close in 1869, when her last friend and ally there, Captain Douglas
Galton, retired. But the work on Indian sanitation continued, and with
the outbreak of the Franco-Prussian War (1870–1871) she was again
involved in efforts to secure proper care for "sick & wounded soldiers as such, irrespective of nationality" (Vicinus and Nergaard, eds.
309). Her focus during these years also turned more explicitly to the
Nightingale Training School at St. Thomas Hospital and, in particular,
to the probationers and nurses. She mentored these from a distance,
through correspondence with them or through messages sent to her
cousin Henry Bonham Carter, Secretary of the Nightingale Council,
which supported probationers in the School, or to Mrs. Wardroper, the
Matron of the Hospital.

Meanwhile, on June 1, 1870, Bishop Thomas Grant of Southwark
died in Rome. Clare Moore was in Brighton at the time. Earlier that

year she had settled arrangements for a community of Bermondsey sisters to move into the convent in Clifford that had been vacated a decade before by the Sisters of Mercy in Hull. In April, by a margin of two, Parliament set up "a Select Committee to enquire into the existence, character and increase of the Conventual and Monastic Institutions of Great Britain" (BA 2:[181]). Mr. Newdegate had at last succeeded, and the Committee began its sittings on May 24.[69] Arnstein suggests that the Hull case of 1869 (*Saurin v. Star*) may "have whetted the public appetite for further convent horror stories," but that among more fundamental reasons for Parliament's passage of the 1870 bill, "by a vote of 131 to 129," was distress at the "audacity" of the Vatican Council's declaration of papal infallibility, as well as deep-seated belief in individual freedom and in the scope and supremacy of English law, from which no institutions should be exempt (129, 132–35).

Throughout the winter months of 1869–1870, Clare's health had been "rather failing." During Lent it declined further, and on Palm Sunday (April 10) she was diagnosed with fever. The Bermondsey Annals note, in Clare's own hand, that

As soon as Miss Nightingale heard of her illness, she took upon herself the charge of providing everything required. Besides sending regularly Wines, Jellies, & all kinds of nourishment, she gave £30 that nothing might be wanting, and also, that when [Clare was] sufficiently recovered, the expense attending any change required might be defrayed. As soon as this kind benefactress knew that the patient would be allowed to leave her bed she sent an Invalid Chair;[70] nothing was forgotten; no parent could have been more tenderly solicitous. (BA 2:[182])

Slowly Clare began to recover, and on May 25, heeding her doctor's recommendation, she went to the Mercy convent in Brighton to recuperate further. She was there when word of Bishop Grant's death reached Bermondsey at midday on June 1. Mary Gonzaga Barrie, fearful of any possible effect of this sad news on Clare's health, went that afternoon to Brighton to tell her in person. Clare had known that Grant had been seriously ill for some months, but she had hung on to glimmers of hope, like his cheery letter to Bermondsey on May 6.

Since Grant's body would not be returned to London for some weeks, Clare remained in Brighton until June 10. No extant letter or Annals entry records her personal sorrow at this time, but her grief must have been great. She and Thomas Grant, who was two years her junior, had worked together for nineteen years, without "any quarrel."

He had relied on her judgment, and she had relied on his advice. One of her last practical gifts to him, before he left for Rome, was to sew "another pocket" into his waistcoat. Now all that mutual support was gone. By his own design, in deference to the convenience of others, attendance at his Requiem Mass on June 23 was restricted to the clergy of St. George's Cathedral, his brother, and two or three other men, so Clare was denied this liturgical farewell to her longtime ecclesiastical partner.

When an opportunity for obtaining a freehold reversion occurred in 1870, Clare purchased for £222 the remaining parcel of land on which the Bermondsey Convent and Schools had been erected and for which the community had been paying yearly rent—in order to obviate any future difficulties about the premises. And in July of that year the community responded favorably to a request to send additional sisters to join a Mercy convent in Wellington, New Zealand. However, by September the plan was abandoned. The Bishop of Wellington wanted sisters "possessed of accomplishments suited for the education of the wealthier classes and was unwilling to take any over the age of thirty." Evidently, of those who could be spared from Bermondsey, few met his specifications. The year ended sadly for the community, with the clandestine departure—on November 19, the anniversary of the founding of the Bermondsey convent in 1839—of a sister who had been a professed member of the community for over eleven years (BA 2:[192–94]).

In 1871, Clare was occupied with the usual work of her office: overseeing the life of the Bermondsey community; responding to requests from the new Bishop of Southwark, James Danell; making clothes for poor children; arranging, at Bishop Danell's suggestion, for government examination of the three schools on the premises (the day, middle, and infants' schools); dealing with the inspector's unofficial recommendation that "more special attention" be paid "to the subject of Arithmetic"; fixing frozen water pipes; and partially resuming the charge (relinquished in 1856) of supplying altar breads to the churches in London. By the end of the year, she was again severely ill. Writing to Mary Angela Graham in Brighton on November 13, 1871, she says:

I have been under the Doctor's care for several weeks—he begged me to go to the Hospital for a fortnight, that I might be exempt from all duties as he considered complete rest quite essential. Well, I obtained the Bishop's leave for that, but I was worse at the end of the time, and I came home only on condition that I would stay in our [i.e., my] cell & attend to no duties whatever. Last Saturday he gave leave for me to come down to the Parlour & to go to a few of the observances—here are symptoms of old age & infirmity! I feel very ashamed to be so taken care of. . . .

We are all rather good for nothing this month, yet no serious illness, thank God. I did not find time to finish this stupid letter yesterday—and today [November 14] is the anniversary of our late dear Bishop's departure for Rome—his memory is ever coming before us.

On Christmas Day 1871, Clare wrote again to Angela: "my days are made very short—rising late—going to rest early—taking food ever so often—& above all sitting in an Easy Chair to which the Doctor has taken a fancy—for whatever change he allows, he is sure to add, & the Easy Chair is to go down, or go up. He inquires too, if I sit in it, which is rather a hard task now I am downstairs, for I must work after my long idleness."

Meanwhile, in 1871–1872, Florence Nightingale was occupied with writing: publishing her *Introductory Notes on Lying-in Institutions*; drawing up, with Dr. John Sutherland, and in response to numerous requests for advice, a Code for Workhouse Infirmary Nursing (Cook 2:186); sketching sermon notes and whole sermons for Benjamin Jowett at Balliol College, Oxford; and working on her projected anthology of excerpts from the spiritual writings of medieval and Renaissance authors. Her correspondence with Jowett increased appreciably after her long career of work for the War Office had ended. She was, as she said, "out of office," and in 1871 Jowett encouraged her to use her new leisure to write, telling her:

I think you are quite right in not propounding schemes of Army Reform at the present time. But there remain a great many subjects on which you have thought & had experience. . . .

You will find writing troublesome at first. The great point is to be moderate & consecutive. . . .

I am glad that you have given up drudging for the public offices. The occupation was too servile & also too hazardous. (Quinn and Prest, eds. 206)

In many ways, Jowett's encouraging and nurturing role in Nightingale's life was similar to Clare Moore's, but with the added benefits that, beyond theology, his intellectual interests were more akin to Nightingale's than Clare's were, and he was a man. Nightingale seems to have had a greater affinity for relationships with men than with women. In the heyday of her reform work, she had depended on and directed many of them, in pursuit of her goals. Perhaps Jowett was the one man, certainly in her later years, whom she regarded as in some sense, her intellectual and moral equal. Since her first contact with him in 1860, Nightingale had found a kindred spirit in his reforming posture at Oxford. They also shared a personal commitment to Broad Church principles. While her knowledge of philosophy was not as extensive or as disciplined as his, she was extremely well read, thanks to the education her father had provided, and was at home debating Jowett. If Nightingale's dependence on and correspondence with Clare Moore slackened in the early 1870s, this may have been because she now drew greater comfort, or a different sort of comfort, from her associations with Benjamin Jowett.

Florence Nightingale's life had changed in still other ways. Her parents were now aging and in need of her help. Fanny Nightingale was eighty-three in 1871 and losing her memory. In October, Nightingale wrote to Jowett from Lea Hurst: "I was due in London to-day—but have been kept here for the last 6 weeks & shall be for a few days more by doing some most harassing & painful business (looking into things which had gone *very* wrong) for my father & mother—(which has taken more out of me than 2 years of real Crimean work). Do not mention this, please" (BL Add. MSS 45785, f.1). Whether she was arranging for domestic help or nursing care at Lea Hurst or Embley or in London, Florence found, in the following years, renewed energy to respond to her parents' needs.

In mid-January 1872, Clare learned that her old friend Mary de Pazzi Delany had just died at Baggot Street in Dublin. For Clare this personal loss presaged the end of an era, even as it brought vivid recollections of Catherine McAuley and the first Sisters of Mercy. Although she had been away from Ireland for thirty years, she still corresponded with sisters at Baggot Street and in Carlow and Belfast, as well as with her own sister, Mary Clare Augustine Moore, now working at Goldenbridge Refuge in Dublin, and she still treasured detailed memories of Catherine McAuley. She wrote immediately to the Baggot Street community to console them on the death of their senior member and to inquire about Catherine's thimble and sewing basket, which de Pazzi had safeguarded all these years.

But 1872 and 1873 brought other sorrows and challenges to Clare: the death of Bishop William Morris, a Benedictine and the retired Bishop of Mauritius, who had been confessor to the community for eighteen years; the need to raise funds for legal counsel, in face of the governmental inquiry into convents instigated by Charles Newdegate; Archbishop Manning's complaint that the altar breads the community baked were "too thin" and that "doubt was raised, as to whether there remained sufficient 'gluten' after the process of making was finished" (BA 2:[216]); the aloofness of Canon Bamber, the parish priest and now the community's confessor; and all the other daily obligations of her role as superior, to which she was reelected in the spring of 1872.

However, Clare's greatest human loss in these two years was the death in April 1873 of Mary Gonzaga Barrie, at age forty-seven. In the elections in 1872, Gonzaga had asked to be relieved of the role of assistant to the superior so that she might devote her full energies to teaching in the schools and visiting the sick poor in their homes. The Bermondsey Annals note that with the sick "she was so kind & gentle, never sparing herself." Clare "could ask her to go out in all weathers, & when out in the early part of the day, she would gladly go again in the afternoon." The winter of 1872–1873 had seen a severe outbreak of typhus among the poor. On the day Gonzaga became ill she had been visiting a family of nine persons, every one of whom had typhus:

The poor Mother on whose work all depended had it very badly. She had no religion, was living unmarried, & altogether her state was most pitiable. Dear Sr. Gonzaga tried all she could to prepare her [for] the Sacraments, & as the fever caused deafness, she was obliged to lean over her & so caught the disease herself. The very day her illness manifested itself, she had been out in the morning to see this poor creature & a dying man. After twelve she had a large division of children for primary lessons in Arithmetic. . . . Later on in the afternoon she came quite cheerfully to tell her Superior that she felt ill. In a week's time it proved to be a severe attack of Typhus fever. (BA 2:[218–19])

Gonzaga was stricken on March 19, and she "lay in acute sufferings for four weeks, without a murmur or complaint." Besides the effects of typhus, congestion of the lungs developed, so recovery was hopeless. Clare and two other sisters took turns nursing her, and Clare and Mary Camillus Dempsey were with her when she died at three in the morning on Easter Wednesday—April 16, 1873. Clare later wrote: "Her death was full of consolation, yet it was a heavy trial and a very serious loss in many ways; but I could not wish it otherwise, even if I were allowed to choose. God's will is always the best for us" (Carroll, *Leaves* 2:247). In June, still grieving the absence of her vivacious companion and co-worker, Clare went to Clifford in Yorkshire, at the request of the new Mercy community, and remained there some time.

Florence Nightingale's "Cardinal" was now dead. Clare must have written to Florence immediately, and she to Clare, but neither letter appears extant. However, on May 9, Florence wrote a long letter to Mary Jones. In the second paragraph she says:

A very dear friend of mine who went thro' the Crimea with me died at Bermondsey, after 4 weeks' struggle with Typhoid fever,[71] at Easter tide. And tho' I could not wish her back, O no,—yet 19 years of troublous recollections pass away for me with her. She was a nun. (LMA, HI/ST/NC1—73/2)

Florence's affection for Gonzaga, a woman who shared her penchant for outspokenness, had remained unabated all these years, even when she could see, at least in Gonzaga's case, the political disadvantages of this habit. Moreover, her practical sympathy for Gonzaga and the community during their troubles at the hospital had been, after Clare's own help, the only steady support they had, even to the food she put on their table.

But Florence's life was also being stripped of other emotional and intellectual supports. Charles Holte Bracebridge, who with his wife Selina had accompanied her to the Crimea in October 1854, died in August 1872. John Stuart Mill, whom she regarded as the greatest living British philosopher, died in May 1873, having never fully convinced her of the proper right of women to enter all professional fields, including medicine.

Throughout 1873, she evidently intensified her correspondence with Benjamin Jowett who had become seriously ill (Quinn and Prest, eds. xxviii). His published letters to her sometimes occur at weekly intervals and indicate a nearly constant, perhaps even excessive, solicitude on her part—for his health, his work, his overwork (Quinn and Prest, eds. 235–50). Jowett apparently sought this solicitude, and Nightingale, ever the nurse, was always most alive when giving such advice, whether to him or to others. In some sense, she found a new identity in letter writing and a way of recovering from the loss of public power and the absence of the government work she had complained about, but thrived on, in the 1860s. For on August 9, 1872, she had drafted a letter to Jowett, in deep uncertainty about the worth of her life:

You tell me to look back on the good that has been done. It is not in me. I am just as much stripped of my past life, "stand naked there" on the brink of the grave, as if it had really been done in another life. . . . I cannot remember, still less "think of" my life in the Crimea, or my 5 years incessant work with S.H.[72] or my 9 years Indian work, more than if it had been really the life of others. . . .

If I am forgotten it is no more than I have forgotten myself. If I am like a dead man, out of mind, it is not more than a dead man is out of his own mind.

And F.N. is not less stripped out of anyone else's mind than she is out of her own. (Quinn and Prest, eds. 231–32)

Jowett encouraged her to write, and in 1873 she published two articles in *Fraser's Magazine*. He also urged her to draft a Preface for her projected anthology of excerpts from religious authors, telling her, "The subject . . . should be the use of the ideal, & especially the spiritual ideal. I do not say what may be the case with great saints themselves, but for us I think it is clear that this mystic state ought to be an occasional & not a permanent feeling—a taste of heaven in daily life. Do you think it would be possible to write a mystical book, which would also be the essence of common sense?" (Quinn and Prest, eds. 238–39). Whether Florence shared any of these writings with Clare is not known.

The year 1874 brought still further personal losses to Florence, most notably the sudden death of her father, William Edward Nightingale, on January 5 at Embley and the death of Selina Bracebridge on January 31. Florence had spent a great deal of time with her parents in 1873. Her father's death was not only an emotional shock but a vivid reversal of her long-held expectation that she would die before her parents. On January 6 she wrote from London to her sister Parthenope and her husband: "I am glad that my mother has been told: I shall come exactly as is thought best for her—by you. It was quite a new idea to me that I should survive her. The idea that I should survive him never once (really) crossed my mind. I thought he had 10 years of life: I not one" (Wellcome Institute, photocopy, MS 9006/64). Writing to Elizabeth Herbert from Embley on February 3, she admits: "For me: the place 'all withered since my Father died.'" Of Selina Bracebridge she says:

She was more than mother to me: and oh that I could not be a daughter to her in her latter times; what should I have been without her? And what would many have been without her?

To one living with her as I have, she was unlike any other being here below: hers *was* faith: real sympathy with God: as unlike others as a picture of a sunny scene is to the real light & warmth of sunshine. (BL Add. MSS 43396, f. 223)

Florence spent two months at Embley in early 1874. By July the family had moved her mother to the Verney estate in Claydon. Writing to Elizabeth Herbert from South Street, Florence is exhausted: "The seeing our Matrons & Nurses forms a great addition to my present fatigues. And we have had to remove my poor mother from her home of 56 years. . . . I am full of Indian business: overweighted" (BL Add. MSS 43396, f. 225). In November and December she is worrying about arranging servants for the house she wishes to hire for her mother and herself in Hampstead in January, and complaining that, in choosing instead a house on Berkeley Square in London, the Verneys had not consulted her. Her mother was now eighty-six years old and spending fifteen to sixteen hours a day in bed (Wellcome Institute, photocopy, MS 9006/138). In Nightingale's extant letters to her family and friends in 1874—at least in the hundreds of such letters reviewed for this study—there is no mention of Clare Moore or of her last illness and death.

The Bermondsey Annals for 1874, written sometime later, are so preoccupied with events in the last months of Clare's life that they do not narrate activities occurring earlier that year. However, the ten extant letters Clare wrote in 1874 are evidence of both her vitality and her peaceful awareness of death. Writing to Teresa Boyce in Brighton in April, she recalls how few remain of those who were present at the first profession ceremony in Bermondsey on April 22, 1841:

Two who made their Vows with you have passed to their eternal rest, and so many who on that day stood around you at the Altar of God are gone from us. You & little Sister M. Joseph [Hawkins] remain—and here I am too—how soon may the summons come for any of us, we know not, but we must try to be quite ready— Lamps trimmed, good works packed up and we joyfully looking out for a glimpse of His Divine Face who is to make us happy for ever. It is worth while suffering anything to have a happy death.

Writing to a new novice in August, she reassures her: "the first days are very blank, but if we seek God alone we are certain to find him in all things. Yes, indeed, He is near us in every place and ready to help us in every duty, or to do it for us when our weakness renders us, as it were, unable for the task. All He desires from us is our good will." To Mary Angela Graham, she says, of a woman who had just died: "She was truly good—no nonsense of piety—but reality—yet, we know not how God sees us—I trust we shall be ready when He calls us." Of the feast day of Saint Clare (August 12), which was Clare's own patronal feast, occurring during their annual retreat, she writes: "The Sisters have transferred St. Clare to [the] 22nd. Some Chelsea Sisters are to come & help to make noise!!!"

But the great work of the last months of Clare's life involved young girls in rags. In September, Bishop Danell asked the Bermondsey community to assume charge of a run-down and mismanaged industrial school, called Torrington Lodge, in Eltham, a few miles southeast of London. On September 24, the feast of Our Lady of Mercy, Clare wrote to Angela Graham:

> I never know what my day will bring me! On Monday I was just stepping into the Chapel to say the *De profundis* [Psalm 130] before Dinner when Sr. de Sanctis told me Can[on] Wenham wanted me—he said, the Bishop wished me to go to St. George's next morning at 11 1/2—this was to know if we could undertake the Girls' Reformatory or Industrial School at Eltham, as the Superintendent, Sr. Dominica, was absolutely obliged to go on the 1st Oct. A Community had offered to supply, but that Community could not keep the engagement, and if we could take the work?

Clare further explained that the present staff at Bermondsey, afflicted with sickness, "has not many working hands—but we must do what we can, and give our Bursar & a Lay Sister for the present."

The situation at Eltham was desperate. In the same letter, Clare says they "will find only bare walls," as the superintendent "carries off every scrap of furniture except what the children have in use, & that seems scanty enough, so that I have to bestir myself to buy a few chairs, tables, bedsteads—and we can share our beds & blankets." Moreover, the departing lay superintendent "requires . . . a high remuneration for her services & she claims the October Government payments for the children's maintenance—therefore we have to help in every way." But, nonetheless, "the work comes from Our Lady of Mercy, a work of obedience," so "we must make the best of it."

Mary Camillus Dempsey and Francis, a lay sister, moved into Torrington Lodge on September 30. Clare accompanied them, staying at least a week, and then made several additional trips to Eltham during October and November. On arrival, they found twenty-five young girls, all in a state of neglect, with "hardly a change of clothing." Besides having to purchase food and other supplies on credit at shops in Eltham, Clare had to promise, from Bermondsey funds, £75 toward the £200 to be paid to the former superintendent in installments over the next two years (BA 2:[224–25]). In a few weeks the number of girls assigned to the school increased to sixty.

Clare's letters of October and November reveal her enthusiasm for this work of mercy, her quick grasp of the government regulations for industrial schools, and, most of all, her compassion and affection for the girls. She had evidently written to Florence Nightingale about the venture, for on October 20 Clare wrote from Bermondsey to Camillus Dempsey in Eltham: "I had a very kind letter from Miss Nightingale this morning. She wrote to Rev. Sydney Turner in favour of her old companions & he has replied most graciously, of course to her, but you may be at rest for your visit—he says, 'I shall hope to visit the School at Eltham in 3 or 4 weeks'—so that we shall have time to make the house untidy & to tidy it again." Apparently, Sydney Turner was a government inspector of industrial schools.[73]

But Clare's involvement with Eltham, added to her other work, took its toll. In a long letter to Mary Camillus on November 30, in which she describes how to make cocoa for the girls out of "cocoa nibs"—"they will *stew* as they are, only they require a much longer time . . . always on the fire the day before for some hours"—she acknowledges, in speaking of the sick sisters at Bermondsey: "I have a very bad cold—nearly had to go to bed myself." By December 2, Clare was indeed confined to bed in the convent infirmary, the "bad cold" having turned out to be a severe attack of her lifelong weakness, pleurisy. When news of her illness spread, there was "universal lamentation in the parish. Masses & prayers were offered in abundance for her recovery, but it soon became evident that it was not the will of God to prolong her life & labours in this world" (BA 2:[236]).

Florence Nightingale was surely contacted in early December, but there is no extant letter from her until two days before Clare's death. Meanwhile Clare gradually lost strength. On Saturday, December 12, the anniversary of the founding of the Sisters of Mercy in 1831, she realized that her death was near:

. . . she asked if the Sisters were taking recreation at breakfast according to our custom on that day & being told that they were too full of grief to talk, she sent word they were to try & take the same cheerful recreation as usual, & afterwards [she] would like to see them.[74] They soon gathered round her & looking at them with great tenderness she with great difficulty said, "I am so grateful, oh! so grateful for all your kindness to me, for all you have done for me, for all you have done for the poor. Dear Sisters, I have nothing new to say to you, but I repeat what I have so often said to you: 'Keep the Rule, & be united.' All our turns must come. It may please God to raise me up again, but it is not likely. Keep the Rule—that is everything. Be united & do not mind the difficulties which must come—only go on faithfully. I will pray for you that God may bless you & make you all so good." (BA 2:[236–37])

On the same day, Florence Nightingale, who obviously knew that Clare was dying, wrote a penciled note to an unidentified sister in Bermondsey:

## 63. To a Sister of Mercy at the Bermondsey Convent

*12/12/74*

Dear Sister

I know not what to write.

Perhaps she is at this moment with God.

But this we know: She could scarcely be more with God than she was habitually here: & therefore all things are well with her, whether she be there or still here:

It is we who are left motherless when she goes.

But she will not forget us:

I cannot say more.

I send 2 or 3 Eggs for the chance.

And I have got a little game which I send: for I think you, & perhaps others, must be so worn out with watching & sorrow that perhaps you can- not eat.

And you know she would wish you to eat.

We pray with our whole hearts to God.

Ever yours
F.N.

*Autograph: Archives of the Sisters of Mercy, Bermondsey*

Later that day Clare "received the Sisters one by one & gave them each a few last loving words of advice & consolation." When Mary Camillus Dempsey arrived from Eltham, where she was now fully re- sponsible for the industrial school, Clare, with great effort, said to her: "My poor child, my poor child, I will help you all I can." The next morning she asked Camillus to call at the Great Ormond Street community and at Bishop Danell's residence, to let them know how she was, and then to go back to Eltham where she was urgently needed. James Danell had visited Clare every day toward the end of her illness. He had left with her "his pectoral cross . . . which formerly had belonged to the revered Bishop Grant" (BA 2:[237–38]).

By Monday morning December 14, it was clear that Clare would live only a few more hours. As many of the sisters "as could be spared from the schools, etc., gathered round her bed to recite the prayers for the agonizing." At noon, while the Angelus was ringing, and the sisters were repeating for her the name of Jesus—as she herself had done in 1847 for the dying Bishop Griffiths, and as he had promised to do, one day, for her[75]—Clare died, at the age of sixty. Earlier that day she had said: "We must give an account of our talents" (Carroll, *Leaves* 2:270–71). Her Requiem Mass was celebrated on Friday, December 18, with Bishop Danell presiding, and her body was buried that afternoon in St. Mary's Cemetery, Kensal Green, London.[76]

According to custom, notices of Mary Clare Moore's death had been sent immediately to all the early foundations of the Sisters of Mercy and to those communities with whom Clare had corresponded. On December 17, Mary Catherine Maher wrote from St. Leo's Convent, Carlow, Ireland:

It is a little over thirty-five years since I first saw her here, and even then, tho' I was but a giddy postulant, the charming sweetness, polished manner, and humble religious bearing took my fancy so much, that I could never forget her. Two years later I had again the great pleasure of seeing her, and renewing the first impression her beautiful character had made on me. . . . She seemed perfectly unconscious of the possession of such noble, simply winning attractions, or if she knew them, it was only to bless God in His gifts. May her precious soul now enjoy the glory and brightness from which her great humility made her shrink in this passing world.

I had some occasion to write to Bermondsey within the last few months & each of my scribbles got such kind, elegant notes in reply, so brim full of charity & mercy. . . .

. . . Her piety was so deep and sincere that she knew nothing of ostentation. God knew the chosen soul, and blessed it, and will for ever gladden her with the clear vision of His presence for all eternity.[77]

On the Sunday following Clare's burial, Canon William Murnane preached in Holy Trinity Church, Bermondsey. His sermon focused on her life: "A humble, unobtrusive life, yet full of sublime self-sacrifice & painful labour in the cause of God, doing far more for Him & suffering humanity than the accumulated acts of many others, who with much noise & stir win the applause & glory of the world—a life from which many indeed shrink because of its supposed monotony & weariness, yet having in it the germ of a glorious eternity, which is assuredly the reward of a life so passed, & a fulfillment of those words of Our Lord: 'I am the Resurrection & the Life.' " (BA 2:[240]).

Although Florence Nightingale had anticipated being "left motherless when she goes," no extant letters from her to sisters in Bermondsey in the days immediately following Clare's death have so far been discovered. However, in a long letter written on December 30 to her nursing protégée Rachel Williams—a letter mostly about other nurses she was mentoring—Florence lists the deaths she suffered in 1874 and describes her own situation:

My year is ending in sorrows as it began; it began with my Father's death, & Mrs. Bracebridge's, who had been the Angel of my life: it ends with the death of the last of my friends & fellow-workers of the Crimean War after a few days of Bronchitis: & my poor mother is failing, & failing painfully, craving after home & *him* & me: & I cannot be with her. I have been so ill & busied with other than Indian cares that I have been obliged to give up finishing some voluminous Indian work asked for by the middle of January: a trial which I do not bear as I ought: for after all we have a higher & a better hope than from anything we can do or not do: namely, whether we live to see it or not, He who is Perfect Wisdom will complete His work, even thro' our failures & disappointments. (LMA, HI/ST/NC3—SU180/23)[78]

In early January, Florence wrote to Mary Aloysius Booker, Clare's assistant and now acting superior of the Bermondsey community until elections could be held:

## 64. To Mary Aloysius Booker

*35 South St.*
*Park Lane*
*Jan. 5, 1875*

Dear Mother Aloysius,

I don't know if I should have the heart to wish you a blessed New Year, but that I have a duty to fulfil. My Aunt, Mrs. Smyth, whom you may remember at Bermondsey, & who was with dear Revd Mother at Scutari, has written to me, sending £5, which she wishes me to lay out in any manner that would be most satisfactory to dear Reverend Mother. I thought of it as a contribution to her Monument at Kensal Green. Then I thought her heart was very full of the children at Eltham, & that a contribution to them would be most satisfactory to her. I don't think she cared about monuments, you are all her monuments. But you will know best; please tell me—

May "God bless you all," as she said—

Yours ever in Him,<br>F. Nightingale

*Transcribed copy, Bermondsey Annals 2:[241–42]*[79]

After a delay of some months—"out of consideration for the feelings of the Sisters, who still mourned the loss of their beloved Revd. Mother Clare Moore"—elections were held in the Bermondsey community on March 13, 1875, and Mary Camillus Dempsey was chosen superior. In August "a stone cross was erected to the memory of Reverend M. M. Clare Moore" in the cemetery at Kensal Green, and during the year, the oil portrait of Clare, which had been painted in 1854 "at the express desire of the Bishop & to her own confusion & mortification," was returned to the Bermondsey community by the sisters on Great Ormond Street, to whom it had been loaned many years before (BA 2:[242–43, 246]).[80]

Florence Nightingale was now fifty-four, and her "dearest Reverend Mother" was gone—except in memory. Writing on April 17, 1875, to an unidentified friend whose sister had just died, Florence betrayed not only her own feeling of loss in Clare's death, but also her dark estimate of the world around her:

> I grieve indeed at your loss in your dear and noble Sister—but this world seems to me so terrible that when I think of what she has gone from & what she is gone to, life appears to me death & death life, as I am sure it does to you.
>
> I lost this winter the last faithful friend of my Crimean days: the dear Revd Mother of Bermondsey, the purest soul I ever knew. But I could not mourn.
>
> To be able to say: It is finished: into Thy hands, Father, I commend my spirit. What blessedness like that? (LMA, HI/ST/NC1-75/2)

In 1875, Florence Nightingale little realized that the "blessedness" she ascribed to Mary Clare Moore, and sought for herself, would not be hers for thirty-five more years—until her own death on August 13, 1910, when "she fell asleep at noon, and did not wake again" (Cook 2:422).

# Epilogue

IN THE YEARS FOLLOWING Clare Moore's death, Florence Nightingale's most faithful correspondent among the Sisters of Mercy was Mary Stanislaus Jones, her old Crimean colleague. Although some of their letters have no doubt been lost, five from Mary Stanislaus (1889–1906), and six from Florence (1885–1899), have been preserved.[1] These letters begin when Florence is sixty-five and Mary Stanislaus is sixty-three. They are testimony to the bonds of friendship formed in the Crimea and then sustained through five decades.

On December 30, 1885, Florence writes: "Life is too busy for both of us to look back upon the Crimea much. But when I think of it, I always look back upon you, dearest Sister, in the little General Hospital at Balaclava." On December 30, 1886, she says: "Pray for me that the child Jesus may be born anew in my heart. How long it is since I have heard from you. But Christmas evergreens have carried to you a little bit of my heart every year." In the same letter, she asks: "Did you ever tell me whether I should send back any of those books dear Revd Mother lent or gave me—& which I so valued?" In five of her extant letters to Mary Stanislaus, Florence encloses money—for the poor, for Mary Anastasia Kelly's jubilee as a Sister of Mercy, and on March 7, 1899, for Mary Stanislaus's own fiftieth anniversary of profession: "Your 'Golden Jubilee' is past, but our love & gratitude to you can never pass." This is Florence's last extant letter to Mary Stanislaus; she acknowledges that her letter "has been delayed, because I could not find anywhere your address in London[2]—& also by my own increased illness."

Florence was now almost seventy-nine, still living at 10 (formerly number 35) South Street, London, but experiencing the further diminishments of age and rarely leaving her room. Her mother had died on February 2, 1880, and her sister Parthenope on May 12, 1890. Benjamin

Jowett had died on October 1, 1893, and her brother-in-law Sir Harry Verney in February 1894.[3] There were no more visits to Lea Hurst, Embley, or Claydon. Her eyesight failed gradually, and then her handwriting. According to Sir Edward Cook, from "about 1901 or 1902 onwards she could neither read nor write except with the greatest difficulty"—she who, for almost half a century, had lived chiefly in and by reading and writing. Yet in these last years the "abiding impression made upon all who served her was of an unfailing kindness and consideration." By 1907, when she received the Order of Merit from King Edward, her memory and understanding were greatly weakened, and she could respond to this honor only with a gentle "Too kind, too kind" (Cook 2:416–18).

In the extant letters Florence Nightingale wrote to Mary Stanislaus Jones before her capacity to write was taken from her, she speaks three times of "dear, dear Revd Mother . . . now a Saint in Heaven"—on December 30, 1885; on December 30, 1886; and again on October 21, 1896. And on April 26, 1897, she writes: "You & dear Revd Mother are always in my grateful heart & often in my mind."

The correspondence presented in this volume has illustrated Florence Nightingale's enduring gratitude and affection for Clare Moore, as well as Clare's lifelong solicitude and gratitude for Florence. The central reason for their twenty-year friendship is straightforward and specific: their mutual, and mutually recognized, dedication to life-affirming work undertaken and pursued in fidelity to what they perceived to be God's will.

Neither Florence Nightingale nor Clare Moore ever gave birth to her own biological children. At the age of nineteen, Clare had taken a vow of celibacy as a Sister of Mercy, and she persevered in this way of life until her death. Florence chose never to marry, although before 1849 she certainly could have accepted Richard Monckton Milnes's oft-repeated proposal, had she been willing to settle for domestic life.[4] But, as she wrote in 1872, she felt no regret about not marrying, and she found the idea of raising one's own children "immeasurably awful":

There is but one regret in *all* my life that I *never* have. And that is: that I never married. Yet, fortunately for those who desire the continuance of this world, probably I am the only person in the world of this persuasion. Except those who *are* married, there is perhaps not one who does not wish or did not at some time wish to marry—or who does not regret not having married.

But to me the idea of bringing children in the world—not at random we know—God takes care of that—but of performing an act so entirely beyond our own control (i.e., of modifying the children's natures) has always appeared too immeasurably awful to perform. And this whether marriage was or was not for my own happiness. (BL Add. MSS 45793, f. 222)

Yet both Florence Nightingale and Mary Clare Moore dedicated their lives to the "maternal work" of "preservative love, nurturance, and training"—to borrow Sara Ruddick's helpful concepts.[5] While Clare was addressed as "Reverend Mother" and Florence was sometimes called the "Mother of the British Army," their maternity resided not in these titles, but in the workaday actions and passions of their lives—their defense of the vulnerable, their empowerment of the weak, and their formation of daughters and sons trained to perform with discipline the work to which they themselves had been so steadfastly committed.

In a remarkable note written sometime in 1870–1872, Florence asks:

Who are those who have had the most influence over us? over the world?
Who have been our real spiritual fathers & mothers? the real fathers & mothers of the world?
Virgin Mothers?
Virgin Fathers?
Christ to the world?
St. Paul to the world?
St. Teresa?
Mrs. Fry?[6]
J.S. Mill?
& let each one consult his or her own experience.
These Virgin Fathers & Mothers have sometimes been married—sometimes not been childless.
But it is not over their own children that they have had influence. It is over others. They have brought many to perfection—out of darkness into light. (BL Add. MSS 45843, f. 306)

Evidently Florence saw this kind of dedication and influence in Clare, and Clare in Florence. Their encouragement of one another was, more precisely, encouragement of one another's "maternal work"—work which each, in her own way, saw as the preservative, nurturant, and educative work of God in this world, that is, as God's will.

That Clare's motivation was religious is perhaps obvious, but

Florence's was no less so. As one reads her letters to Clare and the hundreds of penciled notes in the various manuscript collections of her writings, one is struck by her enduring sense of her own God-given "calling" to a mission, and by her prayer that she might surrender herself to the will of God with purity of heart. Writing to Mary Jones in November 1866, in the midst of re-doing all the work on reform for the London workhouse infirmaries that she had completed before the Whigs were removed from power in July, she nonetheless says:

> But I still feel that it is *such* a blessing to have been *called*, however unworthy, to be the "handmaid of the Lord"—as St. Teresa says, "O mon Dieu, une si grande faveur doit elle être si peu estimée?"[7] I see women, so far better & cleverer than I, wasting their whole lives, not in improving but in deteriorating their own families—I feel so ungrateful & so wicked not to give the return I ought to God, the return of wishing for absolutely nothing but the accomplishment of His holy Will. . . . I have never felt tempted to *refuse God any thing*. However unworthy, I have always felt, I could live 1000 lives to prove to Him how inestimable the blessing I think it to be "called." (LMA, HI/ST/NC1—V66/17)

The essence of the work of Florence and Clare was to relieve misery and address its causes. For each of them the historical epitome of such work was what Florence called the "practice" of "Christ on the Cross." She had no use for what she regarded as inadequate theologies of Atonement (the one dies for the many in a transaction that is completed in the first century). Rather, like Clare, she had a compelling sense of the present reality of Christ's dying in the world, and of her personal calling to embrace that work, that practice, with her entire energy. Writing to her father in 1863, in a letter critical of Ernest Renan's *Vie de Jésus*, just published, she explains her own understanding of the significance of the Cross of Christ in relation to God's providence:

> I do think that "Christ on the Cross" is the highest expression hitherto of God—not in the vulgar meaning of the Atonement—but *God* does hang on the Cross *every day* in *every one* of us.
> The whole meaning of God's "providence," i.e. His laws, is the Cross.
> When Christ preaches the Cross, when all mystical theology preaches the Cross, I go along with them entirely. It is the self-same thing as what I mean when I say, that God educates the world by His laws, i.e. *by sin*—that man must create mankind—that all this *evil*, i.e. the Cross, is the proof of God's goodness, is the *only* way by which God could work out man's salvation, without a contradiction.
> You say, but there is too much evil. I say there is just enough, (not a millionth

part of a grain more, than is *necessary*) to teach man by his own mistakes, by his *sins*, if you will—to shew man the way to *perfection in eternity*—to perfection which is the only happiness.

The doctrine of the Cross is exactly the same thing.

And in this sense, I do believe Christ is "the way." And, if Renan means *this* by Christ "being the founder of pure sentiment,"—in that Christ was the first who voluntarily, eagerly, in his own person, embraced the Cross, & taught us all to embrace it, I agree entirely. For the *feeling* of the Cross, the "sentiment," the *practice* of the Cross is better than the doctrine of the Cross.

But I believe a practical life of "embracing" "the Cross" oneself is necessary to make one apprehend this. When you say that it requires "imagination" to take in such expressions as St. Paul's "I die daily—yet I live"—"yet not I, but Christ liveth in me"—I think, it requires not "imagination" but *practice*. I feel, not only that I can understand them, but that every day, every night of my life for six years, they are the true expression of my daily, nightly practice. (BL Add. MSS 45790, ff. 313–15)

To the end, Florence evidently retained her conviction that Roman Catholic doctrine was beset with error—particularly as to the "character" of God and of God's relation to the history and social condition of the world. But she apparently found in Clare Moore, and certainly in the so-called "Catholic" saints, a truth, a pure and affectionate devotion to the loving will of God, with which she wholeheartedly identified. In a penciled draft written sometime in 1870–1872, she says:

That the R. Catholic practice better than we do "Blessed are the poor in spirit, for theirs is the kingdom of heaven" is the reason why, if they are, they are more serene in affliction & under provocation—not because they hold some peculiar doctrine or other of faith in a Church; in other words, it is their truth & not their falsehood which is their strength.

Suppose we believed in & practised that beatitude, as they do, do you not think, with the measure of doctrinal truth that we have over theirs, we should be stronger than they are.

St. Teresa's strength lay, not in her doctrine of a God who was a wretched God— she was so much better than her God—but in her absolute purity of intention—her absolute sinking of herself in her God—& that with a strength of affection (which was in her, not in him), not with a dumb, stupid ascetic self-sacrifice.

With our truer idea of a God do not you think that, if we had her strength of affection, i.e. her truth without her error, we should love Him even better than she loved her God? (BL Add. MSS 45843, f. 308)

As I conclude this study of the correspondence and friendship of Florence Nightingale and Mary Clare Moore, I am mindful of lines from T. S. Eliot's "The Love Song of J. Alfred Prufrock":

And I have known the eyes already, known them all—
The eyes that fix you in a formulated phrase,
And when I am formulated, sprawling on a pin,
When I am pinned and wriggling on the wall,
Then how should I begin
To spit out all the butt-ends of my days and ways?
  And how should I presume?

In presenting the letters of Florence Nightingale and Mary Clare Moore, I have tried hard not to fix these women in formulated phrases nor pin them to particular moments in their lives. This is obviously necessary where Clare Moore is concerned: she has often been fixed in a facile formulation by historians who have treated her as faceless, storyless, just another Catholic "Reverend Mother." By way of corrective, I hope that readers will find here convincing evidence of the attractiveness and quite special character of the woman whom Florence Nightingale was pleased to treasure as a friend. On a larger canvas, this small work might also go some way towards redressing the persistent neglect of the role of Catholic sisters in histories of nineteenth-century England.

Where Florence Nightingale is concerned I have especially wanted to be at the same time generous and realistic. In recent decades, scholars have sought to liberate her story from myths and ideologies that had burdened it for over a century. Their approach has been enormously beneficial for the historical record. I think particularly of the studies by Monica E. Baly, Zachary Cope, Anne Summers, and Rob van der Peet, as well as the two selections of letters edited by Sue M. Goldie and by Martha Vicinus and Bea Nergaard. The histories of women, of nursing, of military nursing, of nurses' training, of medicine, of public health, and of hospital design and administration are complex and nuanced stories that are ill served by inaccurate or excessive focus on, or adulation of, any one person's contribution. At the same time, as Leon Edel points out in *Writing Lives*, truthful interpretation of biographical subjects need not end by criticizing the subjects "for leading the lives they did." It "need not become . . . moral approval or disapproval of the life itself." Rather, there "enters into the process a quality of sympathy with the subject which is neither forbearance nor adulation; it is quite simply the capacity to be aware at every moment that the subject was human and therefore fallible" (Edel 182–83).[8]

The story I have told in the preceding pages is sympathetic to the temperament of Florence Nightingale and to the basic sincerity of her intellectual and religious pilgrimages. Hers was a long life; her thoughts and sentiments evolved over the course of it. She had her virtues and her faults and weaknesses. It would be particularly unfair to define so complex a person by a handful of selected episodes or turns of phrase in hastily-written letters. Moreover, what she wrote in 1850 or 1860 cannot safely be taken to signify what she thought and felt in 1870. The words and actions of the thirty-four-year-old super-intendent of nursing in the Crimea cannot be assumed to explain the thoughts and actions of the forty-eight-year-old reader of Catherine of Siena and John of the Cross.

As an example, her *Suggestions for Thought*, begun in 1851–1852 and privately printed in 1860 in a three-volume edition totaling over 800 octavo pages, cannot be regarded as an adequate presentation of Nightingale's religious views, unless one chooses to disregard her efforts in the early 1870s to formulate the "Stuff" anew, for her pro-posed anthology of excerpts from medieval and renaissance authors.[9] Moreover, that collection of unpublished manuscripts, many sheets of which were destroyed by Rosalind Smith Nash,[10] will itself—and would, even if all the sheets had been available—be modified by Night-ingale's religious writings from the 1880s and 1890s. Similarly, the religious views she expresses in her letters to Clare Moore cannot be taken as a final expression of her religious position; they do, however, represent a significant stage in the evolution of her religious philoso-phy and Christian faith—a stage that offered her the opportunity to shape a more mature expression of several key concepts: the will of God, purity of heart, and personal vocation in the context of Jesus Christ's continuing work.

That Mary Clare Moore was instrumental, both directly and in-directly, in Florence Nightingale's spiritual development is evident—in their correspondence and in Nightingale's religious writings. That Florence Nightingale was, at least from 1856 to 1874, a generous con-tributor to the work of the oldest foundation of Sisters of Mercy in England, as well as to one of its daughter houses, is also evident—in their correspondence and in the Annals of the Sisters of Mercy in Ber-mondsey.

When she was recording excerpts for her projected anthology of spiritual writers, Florence Nightingale chose to copy the fourth Solilo-quy in a group of seventeen "Soliloquies," or "Exclamations of the Soul to God," that Saint Teresa of Avila wrote in 1569. To Teresa's prayer, about recovering time lost in failing to love God, Florence attached a long footnote commenting on the word "happiness." She gave the prayer itself the following caption, evidently taken from the edition of Teresa's writings she was using: "Prayer to God that he may make us regain the time that we have not used in loving Him & serving Him."[11] This is the prayer, as Florence copied it, with her footnote:

My God, my soul seems to untire herself & to find rest in thinking what, if Thy mercy should render her so happy as to possess Thee some day, that joy will be; but I should wish her to have served Thee first, since it has been in serving us that Thou hast won the happiness* she presumes upon enjoying. What shall I do, my God? O how late I have waited before inspiring myself with the desire of loving Thee, & how hast Thou made haste on the contrary to give Thy gifts & to call me to Thee that I might employ all myself wholly in Thy service! O my Lord, can it be that Thou shouldst forsake a miserable being—can it be that Thou shouldst reject a poor beggar, when he comes to give himself to Thee? Thy greatness,—has it bounds? Thy goodness,—has it limits?

O my God & my mercy! how canst Thou show better what Thou art than by giving Thy knowledge to Thy servant? Great God, signalize Thy almightiness; cause it to be understood in my soul by making me regain thro' loving Thee all the time I have lost in failing to love Thee. But is this not an extravagance which I am saying, since all the world says that time lost can never be regained? My God, may all Thy creatures bless Thee!

*[12] This seems to be the very meaning of the word "perfect"—made through—"made perfect thro' suffering"—completed—& even the only idea we can form of the *Perfect Perfect*. We cannot really attach any meaning to *perfect* thought & feeling, unless its perfection has been attained by life & work, unless it is being realized in life & work. It is in fact a contradiction to suppose Perfection to exist except at work—to exist without exercise—without "working out"—i.e. we cannot conceive of *perfect* wisdom, perfect happiness except as having *attained*, attained perfection thro' work. The ideas of the Impassible, and of Perfection are contradictions.

"God in us"—"grieving the Holy Spirit of God"—"My Father worketh and I work"—these seem all indications of this truth.

Indeed it is rather that we cannot explain or conceive of Perfection except as having worked thro' Imperfection or sin than that we cannot conceive or explain how there can be sin if there is a Perfect Being. The Eternal Perfect almost presupposes the Eternal Imperfect. (BL Add MSS 45841, f. 75)

The aim of Florence Nightingale's life was not, in the first instance, to reform wretched conditions, but rather to love God well. In the call to love God well, she apparently heard, and with her sharp intellect apprehended, a call to discover with diligence the laws of

God's creation, the violations of which led to the wretched circumstances of human lives, and then to correct these violations. In this
analysis she was much better informed, both philosophically and sci-
entifically, than Clare Moore was.

Nevertheless, Florence believed that, beyond all this discovery
and correction, and all the grinding work and practice they entailed,
the end of all human life was to love the real God well. In Clare—
"a woman in whom is no one earthly failing that I ever could discover"[13]—Florence felt she had found such realistic and generous love
of God, pure and constant. Thus, the example of Mary Clare Moore in
life, and the memory of her after death, served a distinctive and enduring role in Florence Nightingale's religious development—a role
which she always gratefully acknowledged. And in Florence—"almost
the only one . . . to whom I can speak freely on religious subjects—I
mean my own feelings on them"[14]—Clare felt she had found a trusted
spiritual companion. Thus the friendship of Florence Nightingale, and
the numerous instances of her solicitude, constituted a distinctive and
enduring support in Clare Moore's religious life—a support which she
too always gratefully acknowledged.

On May 15, 1906, Mary Stanislaus Jones wrote to Florence Nightingale: "I am sending you my sincere congratulations and every good
wish for this anniversary of your birthday[15]. . . . I often think of
you and remember the little adventures of years ago." Florence was
now eighty-six. Of the Bermondsey sisters who had experienced those
"little adventures" in the Crimea, only Mary Stanislaus and Mary
Anastasia Kelly survived. Mary Stanislaus concludes her letter: "Dear
Miss Nightingale, I need not say how pleased I am to find that you are
pretty well—you have had a long life of labor and suffering and it is
my earnest prayer that God will reward you for all you have done to
benefit your fellow creatures."[16]

On Saturday, August 20, 1910, Florence Nightingale was buried
beside her parents in St. Margaret's churchyard in East Wellow, Hampshire. On that day Memorial Services were held at St. Paul's Cathedral
in London at noon, and at St. Thomas's Hospital at two o'clock in the
afternoon. The two services were identical. The antiphon sung before
Psalms 5, 23, and 27 was the supplication: "Make Thy way plain before my face" (Ps. 5.8).[17]

# Notes

*Preface*

1. Although "Moore" seems generally awkward now, the day may come when the use of surnames alone will be normal parlance in scholarly writing about members of religious congregations of women. However, I cannot imagine writers ever using "Benincasa" for Catherine of Siena or "de Ahumada y Cepeda" for Teresa of Avila.

2. The official name of these archives, located at the Convent of Mercy in Bermondsey, is the General Archives of the Institute of Our Lady of Mercy. For the sake of clarity and simplicity, especially for those unfamiliar with the present administrative organizations of the Sisters of Mercy in Great Britain—the Institute, the Union, and the Federation—in this book, where I am using only early, Bermondsey-related materials, I usually call these archives, simply, the Archives of the Sisters of Mercy in Bermondsey.

*Introduction*

1. In *Florence Nightingale and the Doctors* the physician Zachary Cope says that after the exhaustion of the Crimean experience and the self-imposed burden of her reform efforts, though not solely on the basis of these, Florence Nightingale "developed what is commonly called a neurosis, for that is the correct term to apply to her condition" (159). Cope says of her recovery:

> Though it would be wrong to say and unfair to think that Miss Nightingale ever consciously took advantage of her invalidity, it is certain that it was in some respects advantageous to her attaining the objects which she had at heart. It is probably true to say that she was able to achieve more by withdrawing herself from the world than she would have done if she had partaken of the ordinary social activities. (160)

2. Available biographies of Florence Nightingale and published collections of her letters are listed in the Works Cited at the end of this volume. Martha Vicinus and Bea Nergaard provide this estimate of the number of Nightingale's letters (1).

3. She was born in Florence, Italy, on May 12, 1820, during her parents' long sojourn abroad.

4. This biographical account is a revised version of material that appears in the introduction to Mary Clare Moore in my *Catherine McAuley and the Tradition of Mercy*, 77–84. Some biographers of Catherine McAuley, including Carroll, Burke Savage, and Degnan, and the artist who lettered the early pages of the Bermondsey Register, have used "Georgina" as Georgiana Moore's given name. The Bermondsey Annals entry for 1874, the year she died, also calls her "Georgina." However, in her "Last Will," dated January 16, 1860, she writes "I, Georgiana Moore . . .," and signs the will "Georgiana Moore." Moreover, her British passport for service as a nurse in the Crimean War, dated October 16, 1854, designates her as "Miss Georgiana Moore." The will and the passport are in the Archives of the Sisters of Mercy, Bermondsey, London.

5. Several biographers say Georgiana was born in Saint Andrew's parish, Townsend Street, Dublin. The Saint Anne's Parish referred to in the Bermondsey Register is the Church of Ireland parish on Dawson Street; after their conversion to the Catholic Church the family attended the nearby Saint Andrew's.

6. Mary Clare Moore to Mary Clare Augustine Moore, August 23, 1844. Autograph: Archives, Mercy International Centre, Baggot Street, Dublin. See note 16 below and Sullivan, ed. 85, for information about this series of letters.

7. I have not located an early source for this information, and Degnan does not indicate her source. Given her personality, Clare Moore would not have mentioned this herself, in her later reminiscences. Catherine McAuley's sister Mary married William Macauley, whose name was spelled thus.

8. Mary Clare Augustine Moore's letter to Mary Camillus Dempsey, then superior of the Bermondsey convent, was written on July 7, 1875. The autograph letter is in the Archives of the Sisters of Mercy, Bermondsey.

9. The appointment made in December 1841 lasted for six years, according to Bermondsey records, and then was extended for six more months until an election was held on June 8, 1848. The details of Mary Clare Agnew's unfortunate misinterpretation of the priorities of the Sisters of Mercy as set forth in the Rule and Constitutions, and of her subsequent departure from the community, are discussed in the Bermondsey Annals as well as in Carroll's *Life of Catherine McAuley* (407–22) and her *Leaves from the Annals* (2:84–94).

10. Mary Helen Ellis was elected superior in June 1851, but resigned in September 1852 to become superior of a new foundation made from Bermondsey in Brighton, England. From September 23, 1852 on, Clare Moore was re-elected every three years until she died in office in 1874. Every six years a rescript of dispensation (to permit her to remain superior beyond two consecutive years) was sought by the Bishop of Southwark and approved in Rome.

11. The convent and the parish church built in the 1830s both suffered irreparable damage during Nazi bombing on the night of March 2, 1945. The present structures were subsequently built on the same general site.

12. Unless otherwise noted, all references in this Introduction and in the following to the letters of Florence Nightingale are to the autographs in the Nightingale box in the Archives of the Sisters of Mercy, Bermondsey, London. The full texts of these autograph letters are presented in the section on "The Correspondence." Although the autograph is excerpted here, this letter of April 29, 1856 has

been previously published—for example, in Vicinus and Nergaard, eds., *Ever Yours, Florence Nightingale*, 156–57, where it is incorrectly dated April 26, 1856.

13. There is, to date, no full length modern biography of Mary Clare Moore, nor any published collection of her letters, although many of her autograph letters are preserved in the Archives of the Sisters of Mercy, Bermondsey. Volume 2 of Carroll's *Leaves from the Annals*, published in 1883, contains quotations from some of Clare's letters that are no longer extant.

14. The day of Clare Moore's death is given in the 1874 entry in the Bermondsey Annals. Carroll also says she died on December 14, 1874 (*Leaves* 1:228).

15. That is, a raincoat or rain garment.

16. The autographs of these letters are preserved in the Archives of the Sisters of Mercy, Dublin, at Mercy International Centre. They were written to Clare's sister, Mary Clare Augustine Moore, who was then residing at Baggot Street, Dublin. They are addressed to "Sister M. Clare" (or "Sister Mary Clare")—a shortened (and confusing!) form of Mary Clare Augustine's name which Catherine McAuley also used.

17. The Life of Catherine McAuley is contained in the first volume of the Bermondsey Annals, under the year 1841, the year of Catherine's death. However, the Life was entered into the Annals in 1849–1850, and then added to in 1868.

18. This was the first publication of Catherine McAuley's *Practical Sayings*. The story of its compilation, publication, and distribution to other convents of the Sisters of Mercy is contained in the Bermondsey Annals (for the year 1868), 2:[124]–[130]. See also Mary Hermenia Muldrey, RSM, *Abounding in Mercy*, 170–71, 302–3, 384–85, 423.

19. These letters are presented in Sue M. Goldie's edition of the Crimean War letters of Florence Nightingale. For a detailed discussion of this relationship from Mary Francis Bridgeman's perspective, see Evelyn (Mary Angela) Bolster's *The Sisters of Mercy in the Crimean War*.

20. Several notes in the following chapter provide detailed information on these books.

21. F. B. Smith, *Florence Nightingale: Reputation and Power*, 183. Broad assertions of this type, or of a psychoanalytical nature, are frequent in Smith's book and weaken confidence in the trustworthiness of the narration.

## The Friendship

1. British Library Add. MSS 45783, ff. 2–13 is a typescript, not Nightingale's original autograph letter to Jowett. Extracts from the letter have been published in *Dear Miss Nightingale*, Quinn and Prest, eds., but not this paragraph. Unfortunately, as Quinn and Prest indicate in a footnote, the British Library typescript is a "copy of an original now perished" (17). Because the original is not available, because some of the British Library typescripts of Nightingale letters can be shown to contain errors (when the original autographs are available, as in the case of the autographs in the Archives of the Sisters of Mercy, Bermondsey) and because Nightingale's handwritten *n*'s, *v*'s, and *r*'s are often difficult to read, I have changed "correct" (in the typescript) to "convert" (the word I presume was in the autograph). The word

"convert" makes much more sense in this context and is, I believe, the word Nightingale wrote. For similar reasons, I have also changed "lays a grain of truth" to "says a grain of truth" in my later use of this typescript.

2. Handwritten copies of this manuscript are available in several archives in Ireland and England, but Clare Moore's original manuscript, in her own handwriting, does not appear to be among them. It is conceivable that Clare loaned this manuscript to Florence Nightingale and that, in time, it may be discovered somewhere among the Nightingale papers.

3. In the five years immediately following her return from the Crimea in 1856, Nightingale's all-consuming goal was to do justice to "my poor men who endured so patiently," now "lying in your Crimean grave," especially the "73 per cent in eight regiments during six months from disease alone" (Vicinus and Nergaard, eds. 171). Through Sidney Herbert and others, she succeeded in getting a Royal Commission and four sub-commissions established to investigate and recommend reforms concerning the sanitary conditions of the Army, Army medical statistics, Army medical training, and the functioning of the Army Medical Department. Herbert, who chaired all four sub-commissions, worked on these reforms to within a month of his death from kidney failure on August 2, 1861. But he had not succeeded in reforming the War Office, which oversaw the implementation of these reforms and had the power to frustrate them. Nightingale took years to recover from the loss of his leadership, claiming in August 1861, somewhat inaccurately, "Now, not one man remains (that I can call a man) of all those whom I began work with, five years ago" (Vicinus and Nergaard, eds. 223). She was passionately torn between lamenting Herbert's death and blaming him for leaving her alone, with the work undone.

4. Since Florence Nightingale uses both parentheses and square brackets in her writing, I use double square brackets to indicate my insertions of clarifications and queries in her texts. Nightingale also uses single and double quotation marks; I have followed her usage exactly.

5. Missing word: the typescript reads, "I that might be. . . ." See note 1.

6. By 1841 the religious vows of the Sisters of Mercy contained these words ("the service of the poor, the sick, and the ignorant"), expressive of the particular works of the congregation.

7. This essay, in Catherine McAuley's handwriting, is actually a revised and much abbreviated transcription of an English translation of an early seventeenth-century Spanish treatise by Alonso Rodriguez, SJ, contained in his *Practice of Christian and Religious Perfection*. See Sullivan, "Catherine McAuley's Theological and Literary Debt to Alonso Rodriguez."

8. A small copybook of handwritten "Notes of Lectures," in what appears to be Clare Moore's hand, is preserved in the Archives of the Sisters of Mercy, Bermondsey, London. Traditionally, the Sisters of Mercy observed the first Sunday of each month as a day of prayer and reflection. Clare Moore, as the superior of her community, evidently prepared these notes for lectures on such occasions.

9. Missing words in the autograph: it reads, "Without the occasion . . ."

10. Mary Clare Augustine Moore to Mary Camillus Dempsey, July 7, 1875. This autograph letter is preserved in the Archives of the Sisters of Mercy, Bermondsey, London.

11. Mary Clare Augustine Moore to Mary Camillus Dempsey, July 7, 1875.

12. The word—beginning, I believe, with "a"—is at the frayed right edge of the stationery and cannot now be deciphered.

13. Mary Clare Augustine Moore to Mary Camillus Dempsey, July 7, 1875.

14. The particular edition or editions of the life and writings of John of the Cross that Clare loaned her and to which Florence here refers cannot be named with certainty. However, a strong case can be made for the four-volume French edition of the *Oeuvres très complètes de Saint Thérèse . . . des oeuvres complètes de S. Pierre d'Alcantara, de S. Jean de la Croix, et du Bienheureux Jean d'Avila*, translated from the Spanish by Arnaud d'Andilly et al., and edited and published by Abbé J.-P. Migne (Paris, 1860). This set of volumes is large-sized, with small print, which may correspond with Florence Nightingale's comment (in her letter of December 15, 1863) about the difficulty of reading Teresa of Avila at night (or any other "large, close-printed book"). Volumes 1 and 2 of this edition are devoted to the works of Teresa of Avila, and Nightingale speaks of having on loan from Clare a "first" and a "second" volume. Several quotations from the writings of Teresa of Avila are included in BL Add. MSS 45841, Nightingale's draft anthology of the writings of "Devotional Authors." Volume 3 of this set contains four works by John of the Cross, including *La nuit obscure de l'âme*, which may account for Nightingale's references to his "Obscure Night" (in her letter of January 9, 1865). In fact, Nightingale copies from this volume (p. 616), in French and in slightly abbreviated form, a long passage on the second degree of love, from Book II, Chapter 19, of John's *La nuit obscure de l'âme* (BL Add. MSS 45841, f. 83). Volume 4 contains the writings of John of Avila, whom Florence Nightingale quotes in French (letters of August 20 and September 8, 1868). The Bermondsey community may have received these four large volumes as a gift, possibly from Thomas Grant, Bishop of Southwark.

Clare may also have loaned Florence a smaller edition of the writings of John of the Cross, although Florence's reference (in March 1867) to "your little S. John of the Cross" may not be to a book, but to a small card or transcription.

After the Second Vatican Council, the feast day of John of the Cross was changed from November 24 to December 14.

15. The life of Catherine of Genoa (1447–1510) to which Florence refers may be *Vie de Sainte Catherine de Gènes, . . . suivie de son Traité du Purgatoire, ouvrage traduit du Latin, des Bollandistes*, published by the Vicar General of Evreux (n.p., 1840). On pp. 60ff. of this book is an account of the "injures" Catherine suffered at the hands of the hospital workers and the mistreated and incurable patients at the Pammatone Hospital in Genoa, and of her patient bearing of these insults. On p. 83 is the excerpt from Catherine's *Dialogue* that Florence Nightingale quotes in her next letter to Clare (Christmas Eve, 1863): "Dieu s'est fait homme pour me faire dieu." Since Catherine of Genoa was one of the patron saints of the Sisters of Mercy, it is likely that some French edition of her life and writings, if not this one, was in the Bermondsey community library. Clare Moore herself was a proficient reader of French.

16. I have not been able to identify the particular French edition of the life or writings of Catherine of Siena (1347–1380) that Clare Moore loaned Florence Nightingale. Florence's references to Catherine, whether in letters to Clare or in numerous entries and comments in her draft anthology of "Notes from Devotional Authors" (BL Add. MSS 45841), are all quotations from Catherine's spoken and

recorded prayers, and these prayers can be found in various translations and biographies based on the original Italian and Latin sources. The prayer that Florence quotes in French in her letter of Christmas Eve 1863, and again in her letter of January 23, 1865, is, according to Suzanne Noffke, OP, the last recorded prayer of Catherine's life, uttered three months before her death in Rome in 1380 (224). Noffke's translation of this section of Prayer 26 is as follows:

> To you, eternal Father,
> I offer once again my life,
> poor as I am,
> for your dear bride.
> As often as it pleases your goodness,
> drag me out of this body
> and send me back again,
> each time with greater suffering than before,
> if only I may see the reform
> of this dear bride, holy Church. (Noffke, ed. 225)

A respected nineteenth-century French biography of Catherine of Siena which may have been in the Bermondsey community library is Emile Chavin de Malan's two-volume *Histoire de Sainte Catherine de Sienne* (Paris: Sagnier et Bray, 1846). However, a search in this biography has not uncovered the passages Florence Nightingale quotes. In the early eighteenth century, Girolamo Gigli published a four-volume Italian edition of *L'opere della Serafica Santa Caterina da Siena* (Siena, 1707), containing, in Volume 4, many of Catherine's prayers. Subsequent biographies of Catherine presumably relied in part on this edition and on Raymond of Capua's *Legenda Major*.

17. See note 14 above.

18. Nightingale occasionally finds fault with Teresa of Avila's theology in some of the passages she copies into her draft anthology: for example, she finds Teresa's God harsh, and she does not accept what she regards as Teresa's excessive reliance on God's intervening grace. However, she finds comfort in Teresa's claim that she has been tardy in loving and serving God and in her belief that one comes to perfection through works of love (BL Add. MSS 45841, ff. 75–76).

Undoubtedly, many excerpts from Teresa's writings that Nightingale recorded for her anthology, as well as many passages from other authors, were later destroyed, as Rosalind Smith Nash explains at the end of BL Add. MSS 45841: "The book of translations from the Mystics projected by F.N. was not finished. [In 1937] I submitted the MS. sheets to the S.P.C.K. [Society for Promoting Christian Knowledge] and asked if they considered any part of them suitable for publication. They said not, as I expected, and accordingly I destroyed them." Presumably the many folios remaining in BL Add. MSS 45841 were not chosen for submission to the S.P.C.K.

19. I have not been able to identify the particular books on Mary Magdalen de Pazzi (1566–1607), Francis Xavier (1506–1552), and Francis de Sales (1567–1622) that Clare loaned Florence, and to which Florence refers in these letters. It is also

not clear from her correspondence whether these works were in French or English. Francis Xavier and Francis de Sales were among the patron saints of the Sisters of Mercy, and Mary Magdalen de Pazzi was the patron saint of one of the earliest Sisters of Mercy, Mary de Pazzi Delany, a close friend of Clare Moore. It is thus likely that biographies of these saints were in the Bermondsey library. In addition to the reference to Mary Magdalen de Pazzi in her January 3, 1864 letter to Clare, Nightingale also quotes this sixteenth-century Italian Carmelite nun in her "Notes from Devotional Authors": " 'I offer myself to God,' says Mary Magdalene de' Pazzi, in a humbler strain [[than St. Paul (Gal. 6.14) whom Nightingale has just quoted]], 'that I may never seek anything but Him crucified—but to keep my soul united to Him' (that is, 'in that Cross' where Bernard truly says He is alone to be found) '& to do my utmost to qualify myself for His service' " (BL Add. MSS 45841, f. 43).

20. Louis Lallemant, SJ (1588–1635) was the leading French Jesuit teacher of mystical theology in the early seventeenth century. Although he did not publish his doctrine, his teachings were recorded by his pupils, Jean Rigoleuc, SJ (1596–1658) and Jean-Joseph Surin, SJ (1600–1665). Their notes of Lallemant's conferences and lectures were subsequently published in Pierre Champion's *La vie et la doctrine spirituelle du Père Louis Lallemant* (Paris: Michallet, 1694). An English translation of this work was edited by Frederick W. Faber and published in 1855. In 1856 L'Abbé Migne edited and published in Paris a three-volume *Oeuvres complètes de [Henri-Marie] Boudon*, in Volume 3 of which is Boudon's *L'homme de Dieu en la personne du Rév. Père Jean-Joseph Seurin* (first published in 1689). Boudon (1624–1702) was Surin's younger contemporary.

From Florence Nightingale's references to books by or about these writers it appears that Clare Moore had loaned her Migne's third volume of *Oeuvres complètes de Boudon*: the first work in this volume is Boudon's biography of Surin (generally spelled "Seurin" in this work), and chapter 2 in part 3 is titled "De la pureté de son zèle." Surin himself was known to have suffered from depression and attendant mental illnesses.

The second book Clare loaned Florence may have been Faber's English edition of Pierre Champion's *La vie et la doctrine spirituelle du Père Louis Lallemant: The Spiritual Doctrine of Father Louis Lallemant* (London: Burns & Lambert, 1855). Since Clare loaned her another book by Faber (see below) it is possible that the Bermondsey community had a Faber collection. Faber's edition of Lallemant's teachings contains, in English translation, Pierre Champion's account of Lallemant's life, Champion's text of Lallemant's doctrine based on the notes of Jean Rigoleuc, and—as "Additions" to the text—"Certain Thoughts of Father Lallemant, Collected by Father John Joseph Seurin. . . ." This edition is probably the account of Lallemant's thought to which Florence Nightingale refers. Her reference to "the absolute brief compressed precept of the part by P. Seurin" corresponds well with the character of the "Certain Thoughts . . . Collected by Father John Joseph Seurin" (327ff.).

In commenting on these French writers I have found the *Dictionnaire de spiritualité* and Jordan Aumann's *Christian Spirituality in the Catholic Tradition* very helpful.

21. Frederick William Faber's *Spiritual Conferences* was first published in 1859. "Wounded Feelings" is a particularly interesting essay for Florence Nightingale to

have focused on. In this essay, Faber speaks of "easily wounded feelings, the gift or the curse of sensitiveness" (278); he counsels that "Sensitiveness is neither a virtue nor a vice" (278) and that the mortification of sensitiveness "is a brave making use of the torture of our wounded feelings to get nearer God and to be kinder to men" (282). Faber was founder of the London Oratory, a community of the religious congregation founded by Saint Philip Neri.

Jean-Jacques Olier (1608–1657), founder of the company of priests of the Seminary of Saint-Sulpice, published works in French on priestly and lay spirituality (Aumann 227). He focused on the Eucharist "as the most effective means of union with Christ" and believed, according to Aumann, that "we should become annihilated in regard to our own interests and self-love so that we can be clothed with Jesus Christ and, in keeping with the mystery of the Incarnation, be completely consecrated to the service of God" (228). In her letters Florence Nightingale does not record her reaction to the life of Olier; however, in her "Notes from Devotional Authors" she copies a long passage on Olier's peaceful attitude toward his own death: he gave "himself up without reserve, in union with Jesus Christ dying on Calvary . . . content to be forsaken & neglected even untill death, for the end of honouring that of Jesus Christ, who was forsaken by almost all his friends" (BL Add. MSS 45841, f. 60). A. de Bretonvilliers, Olier's disciple and successor at Saint-Sulpice, wrote a manuscript life of Olier which served as the basis for future biographies: for example, F. C. Nagot's *Vie de M. Olier* (Versailles, 1818) and E.-M. Faillon's *Vie de M. Olier* (1841) and two abridgements thereof (Paris-Le Mans, 1843; Montreal, 1847). Perhaps Clare loaned Florence one of these books. Although the book in question may have been in English, Florence's reference to "M[onsieur, or Monsignor] Olier" suggests that it was in French.

22. The sentence Florence quotes (with a slight modification) is in Faber's long essay on "Kindness" in his *Spiritual Conferences* (1–58). He writes:

> Devout people are, as a class, the least kind of all classes. This is a scandalous thing to say; but the scandal of the fact is so much greater than the scandal of acknowledging it, that I will brave this last, for the sake of a greater good. Religious people are an unkindly lot. Poor human nature cannot do everything; and kindness is too often left uncultivated, because men do not sufficiently understand its value. Men may be charitable, yet not kind; merciful, yet not kind; self-denying, yet not kind. . . . There is a sort of spiritual selfishness in devotion, which is rather to be regretted than condemned. I should not like to think it is unavoidable. (17)

23. I have not been able to identify the particular book on Saint Gertrude the Great that Clare loaned Florence. However, in "Thoughts on St. Gertrude," Aubrey de Vere reviewed the recently published *Life and Revelations of St. Gertrude, Virgin and Abbess, of the Order of St. Benedict*, a work he says "has now first appeared in an English version." This English translation, by "a Religious of the Order of Poor Clares," was not made from the then recently published French translation—*La vie et les révélations de Sainte Gertrude, Vierge, et Abbesse de l'Ordre de Saint-Benoît* (Avignon: Seguin Aîné, 1842)—but from the Latin. In his review, de Vere notes that the

"Revelations" of Saint Gertrude of Helfta (1256–1302) "were first translated into Latin [from the original German] . . . by Lamberto Luscorino in 1390" and later published, "under the name of *Insinuationes Divinae Pietatis*, by Lanspergius, who wrote at the close of the fifteenth and the beginning of the sixteenth century."

The book Clare Moore shared with Florence Nightingale may have been the 1842 French edition or the more recently published English translation of the *Life and Revelations of St. Gertrude*. However, de Vere also reports that "Two [other] works by the Saint, her *Prayers* and her *Exercises*, have lately appeared in an English version" (222). Possibly the book was one of these. In her October 21, 1863 letter to Clare, prior to publication of the 1865 English edition, Florence says: "I began a letter to you some days ago to tell you that one of the bright jewels in your crown will be your conduct in the Crimean War (to use St. Gertrude's phraseology)." This reference suggests that Florence had been reading some edition of Saint Gertrude's life or writings published prior to 1865.

24. I cannot identify these Advent Meditations. Possibly they are Frederick W. Faber's collection, entitled *Bethlehem*.

25. See note 14 above.

26. See Cook, *The Life of Florence Nightingale* 1:249, and Ramsay, *Thomas Grant, First Bishop of Southwark* 165–66.

27. *Il Combattimento* (*The Spiritual Combat*) is a sixteenth-century classic of Italian spiritual theology and is attributed to Lorenzo Scupoli. It was first published in 1589 and then "enlarged in later editions" (Aumann 305 n. 71). According to Jean Pierre Camus, this book was Francis de Sales's "own favourite, his 'dear book.' He has often told me that he had carried it eighteen years or more in his pocket, and read some chapters, or at all events some pages, daily. He used to recommend it to all under his guidance, as most attractive and most practical" (*The Spirit of S. Francis de Sales* 37). Evidently Florence Nightingale felt a similar attraction to this book: in giving it to Clare she says, "It was all to pieces, and I had had it bound" (May 12, 1864).

28. Caroline Walker Bynum's *Jesus as Mother: Studies in the Spirituality of the High Middle Ages* provides an excellent account of the nuns of Helfta and of the writings of these women. Her treatment of the writings of Gertrude (170–209) is particularly relevant to this study. Contrary to an error that persisted into the nineteenth century and beyond, as reflected in various editions of Gertrude of Helfta's writings, the abbess of Helfta was Gertrude of Hackeborn, Mechtild's sister, not Gertrude of Helfta.

29. Both of these books have been recently published in the Cistercian Fathers Series: *Legatus divinae pietatis*, translated by Alexandra Barratt as *The Herald of God's Loving-Kindness*, and *Exercitia spiritualia* (*Spiritual Exercises*), translated by Gertrud Jaron Lewis and Jack Lewis.

30. See notes 23 and 28 above.

31. See folios 66, 67, 68, 69, 70, 71, and 72, for example. Folio 66 contains Nightingale's almost verbatim transcription of a passage on page 35 of the 1865 English edition of *The Life and Revelations of Saint Gertrude*. In this passage, as Nightingale records it, Gertrude says, in part: "This solitude is nothing else than the state of infirmity & illness when our Lord speaks to the heart & not to the ear of

his beloved." Nightingale evidently took comfort in Gertrude's interpretation of the solitude that accompanies illness.

32. Again, see note 23 above.

## The Correspondence

1. The Annals for 1854, 1855, and 1856 of the Convent of the Sisters of Mercy in Bermondsey, London (on Parker's Row, Dockhead) devote one hundred pages to their Crimean War experience, from the departure of the first group to the return of all eight sisters in the summer of 1856.

2. Georgiana Ffarington Barrie was born on June 25, 1825 at Lowstock Hall, near Preston in Lancashire. Her parents were Protestants. Her father, Sir Robert Ffarington Barrie, was Governor of Upper Canada from 1813 to 1835. On October 4, 1846, Georgiana was received into the Catholic Church, and two years later she entered the Convent of the Sisters of Mercy, Bermondsey, London, taking the name Mary Gonzaga. In 1854, when the Bermondsey Sisters were asked to offer their services for the military hospitals in the Crimea, she quickly volunteered.

In Scutari, Mary Gonzaga worked in the General Hospital, a short distance from the Barrack Hospital where Florence Nightingale had her main headquarters and where Clare Moore was based. Some of her experiences are recounted in letters to her sister Juey. In one of them she describes the daily walk from the Barrack Hospital, where she lived, to the General Hospital: "We are close to the great Turkish Cemetery but it is not safe to walk on account of the dogs. . . . Seven of them escorted us yesterday, walking around us and sniffing and showing their long fangs in a very ugly way. Not long ago they killed and nearly devoured a soldier." Florence Nightingale had great affection for her, and their friendship continued until Gonzaga's death.

After her return to England in 1856, Mary Gonzaga Barrie was appointed superior of the new Hospital of St. Elizabeth of Hungary on Great Ormond Street, London. Later she nursed Cardinal Wiseman during his last illness. In November 1867, Mary Gonzaga returned to the convent in Bermondsey. She then shared in the work of nursing the sick poor in their own homes, until her death from typhus on April 16, 1873.

3. Mary de Chantal Hudden was born Maria Monica Hudden in 1824 in Hackney, London. She became a Sister of Mercy in Bermondsey in 1851 and professed her vows in November 1853. Less than a year later she accompanied Clare Moore and three other sisters to Turkey to nurse the wounded in the Crimean War.

She served first in the Barrack Hospital, Scutari, and then in the General Hospital, Balaclava. References to her in Florence Nightingale's letters to Clare Moore indicate that her nursing skills were well respected by those with whom she worked.

After her return from the Crimea, she accompanied Mary Martha Beste, the superior, on a new foundation of Sisters of Mercy to Wigton, Cumberland, in 1857. In 1897 she received from Queen Victoria the Royal Red Cross in recognition of her service in the Crimean hospitals. Having lived and worked in Wigton for almost fifty years, she died there on January 2, 1906.

4. Mary Stanislaus Jones was born Margaret Jones in 1822, in the Marylebone district of London. She entered the Sisters of Mercy in Bermondsey on July 21, 1846, and professed her vows in February 1849.

When the call for nurses for the Crimean hospitals came in October 1854, she was chosen to be in the first group to go from Bermondsey. She served in the Barrack Hospital, Scutari, and in the General Hospital, Balaclava, and her skill as a nurse was praised by Florence Nightingale. After her return to England, their friendship continued, and some correspondence between them is preserved.

In 1856, Mary Stanislaus helped to found the new Hospital of St. Elizabeth of Hungary, and she worked there for many years, before moving to the orphanage in Walthamstow. In 1897, she was one of the four surviving Bermondsey sisters to receive the Royal Red Cross from Queen Victoria for their service in the Crimea. She died on April 16, 1913, and is buried in the cemetery at Kensal Green, London, beside Clare Moore.

5. Sarah Kelly was born in 1827 in Rotherhithe, in southeast London, the daughter of Michael and Bridget Kelly. She entered the Sisters of Mercy in 1842, when she was only fifteen years old, taking the name Mary Anastasia, and professed her vows on October 21, 1846.

During the Crimean War, she served first in the Barrack Hospital, Scutari. In April 1856, she went to the General Hospital in Balaclava, where she remained until it was evacuated at the end of June. Florence Nightingale said of her in a letter to Clare Moore: "Sister Anastasia is such a very steady, quiet worker."

On her return from the war, Mary Anastasia was selected by Clare Moore to be one of the team of nurses in the new Hospital of St. Elizabeth of Hungary. Together with Mary Stanislaus Jones, Mary Helen Ellis, and Mary de Chantal Hudden, she received the Royal Red Cross from Queen Victoria in 1897. She died on October 20, 1911.

In her official report on Mary Anastasia Kelly, Mary Stanislaus Jones, and Mary de Chantal Hudden, written at the end of the Crimean War, Florence Nightingale said: "these 'Sisters' have done their work well & nobly—have 'held fast their integrity nor let their hearts reproach them as long as they live'" (BL Add. MSS 43402, f. 22).

6. For a fuller understanding of these tensions, see Arnstein, *Protestant Versus Catholic* (1–9). Moreover, the Sisters of Mercy traveled to the Crimea in their religious habits. In a letter written home to Bermondsey, Clare Moore remarks: "it is a comfort to know that the Protestant Government has consented to employ poor Nuns *as Nuns*" (BA 1:[223]).

7. By the following Christmas, Nightingale had sent all five of the Norwood Sisters home: "their order being enclosed they had little experience with regard to the manner of going amongst the sick, their Habit too was very remarkable, and after some weeks it was considered best they should return to England" (BA 1:[231]).

8. The "Matron" referred to here is Mrs. Clarke, who had evidently been

Florence Nightingale's housekeeper at an "Establishment for Gentlewomen during
Illness" (Cook 1:133) on Harley Street, London (where Nightingale was superintendent before going to the Crimea), and whom she brought with her to Scutari.
Other nurses wrote home about the "tyrannical behaviour" of Mrs. Clarke (Goldie,
ed. 42).

9. In *The Sisters of Mercy in the Crimean War*, Evelyn (Mary Angela) Bolster,
RSM, has focused primarily on this group of fifteen Sisters of Mercy, and has presented a thorough account of their agreement with the War Office and of their
experience in Turkey (at Scutari and Koulali) and in the Crimea (at Balaclava).
Her study amply presents their situation, especially from the perspective of Mary
Francis Bridgeman and the Irish sisters. Mary Francis Bridgeman (1813–1888), the
superior of the Sisters of Mercy in Kinsale, Ireland, was the designated religious
superior of the fifteen sisters (eleven from Ireland, three from Liverpool, and one
from Chelsea) who constituted the second group of Sisters of Mercy to come to the
Crimea to nurse the wounded. The eleven Irish sisters had been recruited chiefly
by Mary Vincent Whitty, the superior of the Sisters of Mercy on Baggot Street in
Dublin. By October 24, 1854, they had assembled in Dublin—from Carlow, Charleville, Cork, and Kinsale, as well as Baggot Street—and were ready to depart for
the Crimea.

Although Thomas Grant, Bishop of Southwark, had made an initial appeal
for volunteer nurses to the Irish bishops, the actual arrangements for this second
group of sisters were made by Dr. Robert Whitty (Mary Vincent's brother) and
Monsignor William Yore, the vicars general of the dioceses of Westminster and
Dublin respectively, with the assistance of Dr. Henry Manning in negotiations with
the War Office, and with the support and advice of the respective archbishops,
Nicholas Wiseman and Paul Cullen, who were then at a convocation in Rome. On
November 3, Mary Francis Bridgeman and Mary Vincent Whitty went to London
to finalize these arrangements. After some delay on the part of the War Office, the
sisters waiting in Dublin were sent for, and they reached London on November 30,
where they were joined by three sisters from Liverpool and one from Chelsea.
They departed from London with Mary Stanley's party of volunteers on December 2, and reached Constantinople on December 17 (Bolster 49–68).

There were, in varying degrees, failures of judgment and conciliation on both
sides of the complex dispute between Florence Nightingale and Mary Francis
Bridgeman, but in the end one must say that, as superintendent of nursing, Florence
Nightingale bore greater, though not complete, responsibility for the unfortunate
outcome: the Irish sisters' increasing disaffection from her, their finding work
where they could, and their eventual resignation and departure from Balaclava in
April 1856. Mixed in the dispute were Irish-English and Catholic-Protestant prejudices and fears, as well as tensions between medical officers and Florence Nightingale and confusing, if not inconsistent, messages from ecclesiastical and government officials at home. The theater of war, with its constant pressures and crises and
its great distance from England and Ireland, was an unpropitious place in which
to try to sort out misunderstandings and personal conflicts. Some sympathy may
be reasonably accorded to the young, relatively inexperienced superintendent of
nursing who was seeking, through trial and error, with both help and opposition,

to manage her assigned responsibilities. Mary Angela Bolster's final commentary on the situation provides a useful summary:

> The integrity of her [Mary Francis Bridgeman's] community [i.e., the fifteen sisters] and the right to minister in a spiritual way to the Catholics was, at the outset, officially confirmed by Sidney Herbert. One can scarcely condemn Mother Bridgeman, therefore, for endeavouring to maintain that integrity with all the ardour of her Irish nature. It was unfortunate, if not disastrous, that assertiveness at times outweighed Mother Bridgeman's more admirable characteristics; it was little less than catastrophic that the same was also true of Florence Nightingale. Under the circumstances, a clash of personalities was inevitable sooner or later. That it came so early in their relationship is regrettable: a proper handling of the situation could have produced some excellent team-work between the Sisters, Miss Nightingale and the medical officers. (Bolster 295–96)

10. Amelia Ellis was born in Bermondsey, London, in 1817 and entered the Sisters of Mercy on November 21, 1840, taking the name Mary Helen.

In 1851, she was chosen superior of the Bermondsey community, but a year later, she was chosen to head a new foundation in Brighton. However, she returned to Bermondsey before the outbreak of the Crimean War. When Florence Nightingale requested additional sisters from Bermondsey in late 1855, Mary Helen Ellis was among the second group selected by Clare Moore. She arrived in Turkey in January 1856, accompanied by Mary Joseph Hawkins and Mary Martha Beste. Most of her nursing service was in the hut hospitals of the Land Transport Corps near Karani.

On returning to London, Helen was sent to help found the new Hospital of St. Elizabeth on Great Ormond Street, London. After some years at the Hospital, she was sent to serve at the orphanage in Walthamstow. She died there on September 18, 1897, having received the Royal Red Cross from Queen Victoria two months earlier.

11. Catherine Beste was born in Bath, Somerset, in 1831, the daughter of John and Harriet Digby-Beste. At the age of twenty-one, she entered the Convent of Mercy, Bermondsey, taking the name Mary Martha. She professed her vows on September 24, 1855.

Toward the end of 1855, when Florence Nightingale asked Clare Moore to allow three more sisters to join the five sisters already serving in the Crimea, Mary Martha volunteered. She arrived in Turkey in January 1856, and served first in the Barrack Hospital, Scutari, and then in the General Hospital, Balaclava. She became seriously ill with typhus in the spring of that year, but gradually recovered, thanks to Florence Nightingale's personal nursing care.

On her return to England, Mary Martha was sent on the new foundation to Wigton in 1857. For the next eighteen years, until her death in Wigton on April 26, 1875, she taught in the Catholic school, served in the orphanage, and visited the sick in their homes and in the workhouse.

Writing to her sister Parthenope from Balaclava on June 2, 1856, Florence

Nightingale said of Mary Martha Beste, then twenty-five: "I love her the most of all the Sisters. She is a gentle, anxious, depressed, single-hearted, single-eyed, conscientious girl, not energetic, but a worker & no talker. I am very fond of her. And she is honest & true. She is very interesting, almost too patient & diffident. And she has been rescued from Death's door. She is heavy & stupid—trustworthy & noble" (Goldie, ed. 269).

12. Sarah Hawkins was born in Bermondsey in 1819, the daughter of Benjamin and Elizabeth Hawkins. She entered the newly founded Convent of Mercy in Bermondsey on November 26, 1839, and on December 12, 1839, received the habit from Catherine McAuley herself, taking the name Mary Joseph. According to the Bermondsey Annals for 1882, "her appearance indicated the childlike innocence & simplicity which were the most striking points in her character."

She was selected to go to Scutari in the second group of Sisters leaving Bermondsey in January 1856. She worked for a short while in the Barrack Hospital and then was transferred to the hut hospitals in Karani. She remained there several months until the wounded were evacuated.

In her later years in Bermondsey she was crippled with rheumatism, and was sent to Eltham because the air there agreed with her and in some measure relieved her sufferings. Here she devoted herself to the care of the children in the industrial school. She died on February 23, 1882.

In her official report on Mary Helen Ellis, Mary Martha Beste, and Mary Joseph Hawkins, written at the end of the Crimean War, Florence Nightingale said: "It is impossible to estimate too highly the unwearied devotion, patience & cheerfulness, the judgment and activity, & the single-heartedness with which these 'Sisters' (who are from Bermondsey) have labored in the service of the sick" (BL Add. MSS 43402, f. 10).

13. Florence Nightingale did not return to the Crimean peninsula on March 16 (as in Goldie, ed. 230), but a week later, on Good Friday, March 21 (Goldie, ed. 235).

14. The Land Transport Corps hospitals on the Crimean peninsula consisted of huts and were located near Karani, about five miles from the "Genoese heights" above Balaclava (Cook 1:254).

15. Alexis Soyer (1809–1858) was formerly the French chef of the Reform Club in London. He went to the Crimea as a volunteer in March 1855, and Florence Nightingale enlisted his expertise to make army rations more palatable for the sick. See also note 41 below.

16. The emphasized "o," substituted for the "a" in "sacrifice" and "sacrifices," is Florence Nightingale's own deliberate imitation of Mary Francis Bridgeman's Irish pronunciation of this word.

17. "I have learned a little of the skill [technique, craft]" of the "thief." I am grateful to Antonietta Nasello for her translation of this passage from Alessandro Manzoni's I Promessi Sposi.

18. For another perspective on some of the Catholic chaplains in Turkey and the Crimea, please see Bolster 180–92, 281–82.

19. Michael Cuffe was senior Catholic chaplain in Turkey.

20. Dr. George Taylor, the principal medical officer of the Land Transport Corps hospitals (Goldie, ed. 5, 325).

21. For Mary Francis Bridgeman's perspective on Nightingale's description, see Bolster 260–68.

22. Thomas Unsworth and Michael Gleeson (Bolster 186, 192).

23. Vickery was evidently an aide or servant to Mai Smith in Florence Nightingale's quarters in Scutari.

24. Thomas Moloney. See Bolster 192.

25. I have not been able to identify this child or her circumstances.

26. I presume that this sentence contains an idiomatic expression (a double negative) and is to be understood now as if "but" were inserted before "only": i.e., "I did not send you that life . . . but only to give you pleasure"; or, "I sent you that life . . . only to give you pleasure"; or, "The only reason I sent you that life . . . was to give you pleasure." Perhaps Clare feared that Florence suspected an ulterior motive, such as a covert effort to move her toward the Roman Catholic Church.

27. See note 14 in "The Friendship," p. 193.

28. Jeanne Charlotte de Bréchard (1580–1637) was one of the first companions of Jane Frances de Chantal at the founding of the Order of the Visitation in 1610 in Annecy, France. She became the superior of the Visitation Convent in Moulins in 1616. I have not been able to identify the book that was the source of Florence Nightingale's knowledge of Mère de Bréchard. However, in 1924 the Sisters of the Visitation in Harrow, England published the first life of Mère de Bréchard in English, drawing on the early French sources. This volume contains in English translation the statement of Mère de Bréchard to which Nightingale is probably referring. In a letter to another superior about the burdens of the role of superior, Mère de Bréchard writes: "Our imagination . . . makes us fancy that it would be more advantageous for our own souls if we had less to do with those of others. But anyone can see through this fallacy. In carrying out such charges as ours we have far more opportunities of humbling, mortifying, and denying ourselves and of trusting wholly to God than when we are free of responsibility" (Sisters 115).

29. See note 15 in "The Friendship," p. 193.

30. See note 14 in "The Friendship," p. 193.

31. See note 15 in "The Friendship," p. 193.

32. This quotation from Catherine of Siena is actually a selection of two passages in Catherine's Prayer 26 (see note 16 in "The Friendship," pp. 193–94). Suzanne Noffke's English translation of the original Latin and Italian versions of these sentences is as follows: "I offer and commend to you my children, whom I so love, for they are my soul. . . . To you, eternal Father, I offer once again my life, poor as I am, for your dear bride. As often as it pleases your goodness, drag me out of this body and send me back again, each time with greater suffering than before, if only I may see the reform of this dear bride, holy Church" (Noffke, ed. 226, 225).

33. See note 19 in "The Friendship," pp. 194–95.

34. "Each time I permit that to happen to him [her], so that he [she] might be more attentive to flee from himself [herself], and to come and have recourse to me . . . and that he [she] might consider that through love I give him [her] the means to develop a mastery of true humility, reputing himself [herself] unworthy of peace and repose of thought, like my other servants—and on the contrary, regarding himself [herself] worthy of the pains that he [she] suffers." I have not been

able to identify the particular source of this quotation from Catherine of Siena. I am grateful to Gratia L'Esperance, RSM, for her translation. See note 15 in "The Friendship," p. 193.

35. See note 19 in "The Friendship," pp. 194–95.

36. See notes 14 and 19 in "The Friendship," pp. 193, 194–95.

37. "Foxes have holes, and birds of the air have nests; but the Son of Man has nowhere to lay his head" (Matt 8.20). In one of her notes on religious topics Nightingale wrote: "Foxes have holes & the birds of the air have nests etc. Jesus never intended by this to attract compassion; he wishes to describe his normal position" (BL Add. MSS 45841, f. 79)—that is, his work, like hers, required movement and the forgoing of permanent housing.

38. Nightingale was revered in Italy, as a consequence of the Crimean War, and she was sympathetic to Garibaldi's cause, but she wished him to bide his time, and she was not impressed with his personal capacity to administer the practical affairs of the kind of Italian government he sought. He had visited her on April 17, 1864, at 115 Park Street. Though she tried to keep the visit a secret, the London newspapers published the event (Cook 2:90–91).

39. See note 27 in "The Friendship," p. 197, on *Il Combattimento* (*The Spiritual Combat*) by Lorenzo Scupoli. "Reflecting as it does a period of Church reform and renewal, *The Spiritual Combat* aims primarily at conversion from sin and the cultivation of an interior life. It states as a fundamental principle that the spiritual life does not consist essentially in external practices but in the knowledge and love of God" (Aumann 209).

40. See note 20 in "The Friendship," p. 195.

41. Nightingale evidently had personal copies of the recipes (receipts) for nutritious quantity cooking that Alexis Soyer had used in the Crimea. Before his death in 1858, he published *Soyer's Culinary Campaign, being Historical Reminiscences of the late War, the plain Art of Cookery for Military and Civil Institutions, the Army, Navy, Public, etc.* (London: Routledge, 1857). I have not been able to identify Warriner. Clare Moore had apparently asked Nightingale for recipes that Sisters of Mercy who were responsible for feeding large numbers of people might use. See also Letter 44.

42. Nightingale's reference to "the 2nd Vol." may refer to the second volume of the works of Teresa of Avila, or to a second volume of the works of John of the Cross (see note 14 in "The Friendship," p. 193). If she is referring to the latter, this may suggest that Clare had lent her the two-volume edition of *The Complete Works of Saint John of the Cross*, edited by David Lewis (London: Longman, Green, Longman, Roberts & Green, 1864). The first volume of this edition is still in the Archives of the Sisters of Mercy, Bermondsey, but the second volume is missing. The first volume contains *The Obscure Night of the Soul*.

43. "On Christmas Eve 1864 there appeared in *The Times* a letter from James Shuter under the caption 'Horrible Case of Union Neglect' which referred to the death of Timothy Daly in the Holborn Workhouse. Miss Nightingale promptly wrote to Charles Villiers, the President of the Poor Law Board," recommending an inquiry into workhouse nursing (Baly 85).

44. See note 16 in "The Friendship," pp. 193–94. In her "Notes from Devotional Authors of the Middle Ages" Nightingale copied in French this entire, long

"dying" prayer of Catherine of Siena (BL Add. MSS 45841, f. 62), and then commented on it:

> There is scarcely a word of herself all through in this dying prayer—the "egotism of death," as some one so truly calls it—& which reigns almost unmixed in all the death-bed prayers which people think so beautiful.
>
> Here it is all the "reformation of God's church," it is God's "children," for whom she would give "her *soul*," which occupy her dying thoughts.
>
> There is not even a desire for release (which is more than I can say for myself) but on the contrary she offers to suffer the continually rallying from a dying state (& how great an offering that is none can tell like me!) with ever greater pain "every time"—& still she ascribes this to God's goodness—if only she can do anything for God's children.
>
> She did not live to see "la réformation" of God's church: no more shall I. But at least we can all work towards it. (BL Add. MSS 45841, f. 63)

Nightingale was very fond of this prayer of Catherine of Siena and quoted from it often, as in this letter to Clare Moore, where she likens Cardinal Wiseman's temporary recovery to Catherine's experience: God's withdrawing the soul from the body & restoring it to the body "always with greater pain one time than the other."

45. In Denis Gwynn's *Cardinal Wiseman* there is a single reference to "the nuns" who attended Wiseman's death-bed (190). Brian Fothergill's *Nicholas Wiseman* does not mention the sisters who nursed Wiseman during his last illness. Wilfrid Ward's *The Life and Times of Cardinal Wiseman* mentions "the Reverend Mother of the Hospital, who nursed him" (2:512). Yet in volume two of her *Leaves from the Annals of the Sisters of Mercy*, Mary Austin Carroll devotes eleven pages (2:227–36, 242) to an account of Mary Gonzaga Barrie's service as Wiseman's nurse and secretary during the last five weeks of his life, including excerpts from many of her letters about his condition, written to his relatives in Ireland and to the sisters in Bermondsey. In addition, four of Gonzaga's letters to Clare Moore during this period, now preserved in the Bermondsey archives, describe Wiseman's illness and her nursing service in some detail.

46. Here the verb "doubt" is used in the sense of "suspect" or "anticipate with apprehension" (OED).

47. See notes 21 and 22 in "The Friendship," pp. 195–96. Nightingale's reference to Faber's "Conference on 'Sensitiveness' " is actually to his chapter on "Wounded Feelings."

48. These letters of Wiseman are in the Archives of the Sisters of Mercy, Bermondsey. Further research is needed to establish whether there is any other "G_____" to whom Mary Gonzaga could possibly be referring.

49. This is probably an allusion to Jean-Joseph Surin, who, Nightingale said, offered himself to "the humiliation of madness (if the will of God)." See note 20 in "The Friendship," p. 195 and Nightingale's reference to him in Letter 41. About the time of Cardinal Wiseman's death, there was "illness and death" in the hospital community (BA 2:[84]), which may explain the reference to "the poor Postulant Sister" who died.

50. I have not been able to identify the prayer of Cardinal Wiseman to which Nightingale refers.

51. See note 21 (first paragraph) and note 22 in "The Friendship," pp. 195–96.

52. See note 21 (second paragraph) in "The Friendship," p. 196.

53. Walter L. Arnstein's *Protestant Versus Catholic in Mid-Victorian England: Mr. Newdegate and the Nuns* is extremely helpful in understanding the "nunneries bills." See especially pp. 62–73. There were then "thirty-two Roman Catholic M.P.s (thirty-one from Ireland, one from England)" (Arnstein 67). Sir George Grey's joke may have been his dry comment, in response to the broad allegations in the debate: "We do not appoint committees merely to gratify curiosity" (Arnstein 69).

54. See note 48 above.

55. Florence Nightingale's cousin, Hilary Bonham Carter, died on September 6, 1865 (Vicinus and Nergaard, eds. 265).

56. Beatrice Shore Smith, the daughter of Aunt Mai Smith.

57. See Letter 57.

58. As will be seen later, Mary Gonzaga Barrie resigned as superior of the hospital community in 1866.

59. The Congregation for the Propagation of the Faith was the department of the Roman curia then responsible for the missions of the Roman Church and for the religious congregations enjoying pontifical approval, such as the Sisters of Mercy. "Direct Papal authority in England in practice meant government by the Sacred Congregation of Propaganda Fide, under whose jurisdiction, as a missionary territory, the country was placed throughout the nineteenth century." However, by the late 1880s the English bishops had established their own relations with the various other curial congregations and their tie to Propaganda Fide became "scarcely important" (Norman, *The English Catholic Church* 72–75).

60. Five sides of writing in pencil compose this letter: four sides on a folded full sheet of black-bordered blue-gray paper, and one side on a half sheet of the same paper. The last sentence of the letter ("Pray for me. . . ."), the closing, the date, and the postscript are all on the half sheet. (The British Library typescript of the half sheet is unconnected to any other fragment, and there is no British Library typescript of the full sheet.)

I believe these two pieces may belong together and constitute a single complete letter. No other autographs or fragments in the Nightingale collection in the Bermondsey archives of the Sisters of Mercy match the paper and the pencil writing of these two sheets. However, the dates given are a problem: "May 11/66" at the beginning of the full sheet, and "Holy Thursday/66" on the half sheet. Is this simply a mistake on Nightingale's part? Does she mean "Ascension Thursday" when she writes "Holy Thursday"? And does she mean May 10 when she writes, I think, May 11? In 1866, Holy Thursday was on March 29 and Ascension Thursday was on May 10. It remains, of course, possible that these two pieces do not go together.

61. The feast day of Saint John of the Cross was then November 24.

62. These words of Teresa of Avila may be translated: "Our Lord said to me: that it was not these wounds [of the Passion] which ought to have afflicted me, but those which people were doing to him presently." I have not yet located this exact quotation in Teresa's writings, but a passage in Teresa's *Interior Castle*, Book 5, chap-

ter 2, is similar in content: "Well then, how is it, Lord, that You weren't thinking of the laborious death You were about to suffer, so painful and frightful? You answer: 'No, my great love and the desire I have that souls be saved are incomparably more important than these sufferings; and the very greatest sorrows that I have suffered and do suffer, after being in the world, are not enough to be considered anything at all in comparison with this love and desire to save souls.' . . . And what kind of life must He have suffered since all things were present to Him and He was always witnessing the serious offenses committed against His Father? I believe without a doubt that these sufferings were much greater than were those of His most sacred Passion" (Kavanaugh and Rodriguez, eds. 2:346–47). The reality of the present sufferings of Christ is a prevalent theme in Teresa's writings, and one that would have appealed to Florence Nightingale. If Nightingale is citing the passage above, the differences in wording may be due to the translations from the original Spanish.

63. See Letter 59.

64. Mary Helen Ellis and, years later, Mary Stanislaus Jones, were among these (*Trees of Mercy* 23).

65. Mary Clare Augustine Moore to Mary Camillus Dempsey, July 7, 1875. The autograph is in the Archives of the Sisters of Mercy, Bermondsey.

66. According to the Rule of the Sisters of Mercy, the eight days preceding the feast of the Assumption of Mary (August 15) were annually devoted to a spiritual retreat in each community: a period of silence, reflection, and prayer. As superior of her community, Clare Moore would have had individual and group conferences with the members of the community at this time—especially if they had not secured a priest to serve as retreat director, as was the case in 1868.

67. This undated fragment is preserved in the Bermondsey archives. It was probably written sometime in 1867 or 1868, perhaps as an enclosed note in another letter; the cream-colored paper of the fragment matches the paper of other letters Florence wrote to Clare or Gonzaga in those years.

68. In his *Protestant Versus Catholic in Mid-Victorian England*, Walter Arnstein provides a detailed and objective discussion of "The Great Convent Case"—i.e., the Hull case (108–22). However, he does not identify the community in question as the Sisters of Mercy.

69. See Arnstein 123–35.

70. A wheel chair.

71. Although Nightingale says that Mary Gonzaga died of typhoid fever, the Bermondsey Annals clearly say that her disease was typhus. The pathological differences between these diseases had been pointed out by William Wood Gerhard earlier in the century, but some confusion of terminology remained. William Budd's treatise, *Typhoid Fever: Its Nature, Mode of Spreading, and Prevention* was published in 1873 (Talbott 734–37).

72. Sidney Herbert.

73. For further information on Clare Moore's work to correct the conditions at the industrial school and on her kindness to the girls, please see the Introduction to this volume, especially pp. 10–12.

74. In this era, Sisters of Mercy normally observed silence at all their meals (usually with readings during dinner and supper). However, on major feasts of the

Church, the feast days and jubilees of the sisters, and the anniversaries of the religious congregation, "recreation," that is, conversation, occurred.

75. Writing to the sisters in Chelsea on August 16, 1847, four days after the death of Bishop Thomas Griffiths, whom she had nursed, Clare reported that he had said: "if I would cause the Holy Name of Jesus to sound in his ears, when he was dying, he would make me hear it at my death."

76. Although the Bermondsey Annals do not give the date of her burial, the undertaker, Charles McCarthy, wrote a document, now in the Bermondsey archives, "to certify that I attended the interment of Reverend Mother Mary Clare Moore on Friday the 18th day of December and that she was buried in St. Marys Cemetery Kensal Green."

77. Mary Catherine Maher addressed this letter to Mary Gonzaga Barrie at the Bermondsey convent, not realizing (or not remembering) that Gonzaga had died. The autograph is in the Archives of the Sisters of Mercy, Bermondsey. Several other letters written in response to Clare's death are also preserved in the Bermondsey archives.

78. I am very grateful to Geoff Pick, Manager of the Reader Services Division of the London Metropolitan Archives, who transcribed this letter for me. "Bronchitis" may be the correct diagnosis of Clare Moore's final illness, but the Bermondsey Annals say it was "violent pleurisy" (2:[225]).

79. I have not been able to find the autograph. Evidently "Smith" (the correct spelling) was inadvertently changed to "Smyth" in the course of transcription.

80. This oil portrait is still hanging in the Convent of Mercy, Parker's Row, Dockhead, Bermondsey, London.

## Epilogue

1. The five letters of Mary Stanislaus Jones to Florence Nightingale are in the Nightingale Collection of the Florence Nightingale Museum Trust at the London Metropolitan Archives: HI/ST/NC2—V2/89, V7/97, V11/97, V13/97, and V1/06. The six letters from Nightingale to Jones are part of the archives of the Sisters of Mercy, St. John's Wood, preserved by the Union of the Sisters of Mercy in Great Britain. Through the courtesy of Anna Moloney, RSM, archivist, photocopies of these Nightingale letters are available at the Archives of the Sisters of Mercy, Bermondsey.

2. By 1899 the Hospital of St. John and St. Elizabeth on Great Ormond Street had moved to St. John's Wood in northwest London.

3. I am grateful to Martha Vicinus and Bea Nergaard's *Ever Yours, Florence Nightingale* (377, 421) for these dates.

4. See Vicinus and Nergaard, eds. 40–41, and Cook 1:96–103.

5. Sara Ruddick's *Maternal Thinking: Towards a Politics of Peace* offers an extended analysis of "maternal work" and the three demands that constitute it: "*preservation, growth,* and *social acceptability* . . . to be a mother is to be committed to meeting these demands by works of preservative love, nurturance, and training" (17).

6. Elizabeth Fry (1780–1845), a Quaker, was an important nineteenth-century prison reformer in England. In London she formed a group of Quaker volunteers devoted to improving the lives and penal conditions of women prisoners and their children in Newgate prison, but her reform work also extended to northern England and Scotland.

7. "Oh my God, it must be so great a favor to be so little esteemed." I have not been able to find this quotation in the works of Teresa of Avila.

8. In his essay on Florence Nightingale (as in his essays on other Victorian subjects), Lytton Strachey, who "allowed his hostility to the Victorians to color much of his work," founded a "debunking" style of biography (Edel 181–82). A renewal of this style characterizes some commentary on Nightingale. But it is hard to believe that the greater biographical and historical accuracy at which writing such as this supposedly aims is actually achieved by so merciless a use of language. For as Edel notes, irony in biographical writing "can distort as well as it can illuminate" (182). The hermeneutic of suspicion—as corrective as it may often be—is an interpretive method that has its own temptations to inaccuracy and excess. In treatments of Nightingale, one can, on occasion, find categorical dismissal of the face value of her words and actions, insinuation in regard to her inner motives, and an unsparingly hostile rhetorical style. On the other hand, the work of those who find such approaches incompatible with their research findings and intellectual habits may be regarded as methodologically naive or obsolete, or worse, "hagiographical"—a term currently used pejoratively, and rather more broadly than is useful.

9. The publication of *Suggestions for Thought by Florence Nightingale: Selections and Commentaries*, edited by Michael D. Calabria and Janet A. Macrae (1994) is enormously helpful for understanding Nightingale's early religious perspectives, and as an accessible guide to the major themes in the longer three-volume work (of which there were, apparently, only six printed copies).

10. See the second paragraph of note 18 in "The Friendship," p. 194.

11. I have not yet identified the particular edition of Teresa's works that Nightingale is here using. In the second edition of volume one of Kieran Kavanaugh and Otilio Rodriguez's *The Collected Works of St. Teresa of Avila*, the fourth Soliloquy is simply titled, "Recovering lost time" (446–47). The slight awkwardness of some phrases in the text as Nightingale copies it may suggest that she is translating from a French edition.

12. This is Nightingale's footnote on the word "happiness"; it follows immediately after the prayer.

13. Florence Nightingale to Elizabeth Herbert, [May 13], 1858. Typescript fragment. BL Add. MSS 43396, f. 59.

14. Mary Clare Moore to Florence Nightingale, December 28, 1862. LMA, HI/ST/NC2—V31/62.

15. Florence Nightingale's birthday was actually May 12.

16. Mary Stanislaus Jones to Florence Nightingale, May 15, 1906. Photocopy, Archives of the Sisters of Mercy, Bermondsey.

17. The programs for these two Memorial Services are preserved in the London Metropolitan Archives (HI/ST/NC—10/3). The opening hymn was "The Son

of God goes forth to war, / A Kingly crown to gain" (No. 439); after Psalms 5, 23, and 27, the Benedictus was sung, with the antiphon, "I am the resurrection and the life"; the Lesson was 1 Corinthians 15.20; following several other prayers, the closing hymn was "The King of love my Shepherd is, / Whose goodness faileth never" (No. 197).

# Works Cited

The following list—of works cited in this volume, or consulted in its preparation—does not include the many works examined in an effort to identify the precise editions of the religious books Mary Clare Moore lent to Florence Nightingale. Notes 14–16, 19–24, 27, 29, and 31 in "The Friendship," notes 28, 32, 39, 42, and 62 in "The Correspondence," and note 11 in the Epilogue present bibliographical information about editions of these works that were, or may have been, available to Clare Moore, and through her, to Florence Nightingale. The reader is invited to consult these notes for the probable or possible sources of Nightingale's references to and quotations from spiritual writers, as found in her letters to Clare Moore and in her other papers.

### PRINCIPAL MANUSCRIPTS

Annals of the Convent of Our Lady of Mercy, Bermondsey [London]. Volume I: 1839–1856; Volume II: 1857–1905. Archives of the Sisters of Mercy, Parker's Row, Dockhead, Bermondsey, London. Generally called the Bermondsey Annals.

Barrie, Mary Gonzaga. Letters to Mary Clare Moore, and other correspondents, 1854–1865. Archives of the Sisters of Mercy, Parker's Row, Dockhead, Bermondsey, London.

Claydon Collection (photocopies) of Nightingale and Verney Papers. Western Manuscripts Department. Wellcome Institute for the History of Medicine, Euston Road, London.

Grant, Thomas. Letters to Mary Clare Moore, 1851–1870. Archives of the Sisters of Mercy, Parker's Row, Dockhead, Bermondsey, London.

Jones, Mary Stanislaus. Letters to Florence Nightingale, 1889–1906. Nightingale Collection of the Florence Nightingale Museum Trust. London Metropolitan Archives, Northampton Road, London.

Moore, Mary Clare. Letters to Thomas Grant, and other correspondents, 1839–1874. Archives of the Sisters of Mercy, Parker's Row, Dockhead, Bermondsey, London.

———. Letters to Florence Nightingale, May–December 1862. Nightingale Collection of the Florence Nightingale Museum Trust. London Metropolitan Archives, Northampton Road, London.

————. Letter to Florence Nightingale, 17 May 1858. Add. MSS 45797, ff. 13–15. Department of Manuscripts. British Library, St. Pancras, Euston Road, London.

Nightingale, Florence. Letters to Mary Clare Moore, Mary Gonzaga Barrie, Mary Stanislaus Jones, and other correspondents, 1855–1899. Archives of the Sisters of Mercy, Parker's Row, Dockhead, Bermondsey, London.

Nightingale Collection of the Florence Nightingale Museum Trust. London Metropolitan Archives, Northampton Road, London.

Nightingale Collection. Western Manuscripts Department. Wellcome Institute for the History of Medicine, Euston Road, London.

Nightingale Papers. Add. MSS 43393–43403, 45750–45849, 47714–47767. Department of Manuscripts. British Library, St. Pancras, Euston Road, London.

Wiseman, Nicholas. Letters to Mary Gonzaga Barrie, 1856–1864. Archives of the Sisters of Mercy, Parker's Row, Dockhead, Bermondsey, London.

OTHER WORKS

Anderson, George M. "Elizabeth Fry (1780–1845): Timeless Reformer." America, 14 October 1995: 22–23.

Arnstein, Walter L. Protestant Versus Catholic in Mid-Victorian England: Mr. Newdegate and the Nuns. Columbia: University of Missouri Press, 1982.

Aumann, Jordan. Christian Spirituality in the Catholic Tradition. London: Sheed & Ward, 1985.

Baly, Monica E. Florence Nightingale and the Nursing Legacy. London: Croom Helm, 1986.

Beck, George Andrew, ed. The English Catholics, 1850–1950. London: Burns Oates, 1950.

Bolster, Evelyn [Mary Angela, RSM]. The Sisters of Mercy in the Crimean War. Cork: Mercier Press, 1964.

Bourne, Francis et al. Catholic Emancipation, 1829 to 1929. London: Longmans, Green and Co., 1929.

Bullough, Vern, Bonnie Bullough, and Marietta P. Stanton, eds. Florence Nightingale and Her Era: A Collection of New Scholarship. New York and London: Garland, 1990.

Burke Savage, Roland, SJ. Catherine McAuley: The First Sister of Mercy. Dublin: M. H. Gill and Son, 1949.

Bynum, Caroline Walker. Jesus as Mother: Studies in the Spirituality of the High Middle Ages. Berkeley and Los Angeles: University of California Press, 1982.

Camus, Jean Pierre. The Spirit of S. Francis de Sales. London: Longmans, Green, and Co., 1904.

[Carroll, Mary Austin, RSM]. Leaves from the Annals of the Sisters of Mercy. 4 vols. Vol. 1, Ireland. New York: Catholic Publication Society, 1881. Vol. 2, England, Crimea, Scotland, Australia and New Zealand. New York: Catholic Publication Society, 1883. Vol. 3, Newfoundland and the United States. New York: Catholic Publication Society, 1889. Vol. 4, South America, Central America and the United States. New York: P. O'Shea, 1895.

———. *Life of Catherine McAuley*. New York: D. & J. Sadlier, 1866.

Cartwright, Frederick F. *Disease and History*. New York: Thomas Y. Crowell, 1972.

Catherine of Siena. *The Prayers of Catherine of Siena*. Ed. Suzanne Noffke, OP. Ramsey, N.J.: Paulist Press, 1983.

[Coleridge, Henry J., SJ]. "The First Sister of Mercy." *The Month* 4 (February 1866): 111–27.

Cook, Edward. *The Life of Florence Nightingale*. 2 vols. London: Macmillan, 1913.

Cope, Zachary. *Florence Nightingale and the Doctors*. Philadelphia: J. P. Lippincott, 1958.

———. *Six Disciples of Florence Nightingale*. London: Pitman Medical Publishing Co., 1961.

Degnan, Mary Bertrand, RSM. *Mercy Unto Thousands: Life of Mother Mary Catherine McAuley, Foundress of the Sisters of Mercy*. Westminster, Md.: Newman Press, 1957.

De Vere, Aubrey. "Thoughts on St. Gertrude." *The Month* (September 1865): 221–39.

*Dictionnaire de spiritualité*. Fondé par M. Viller . . . Continué par A. Derville . . . de la Compagnie de Jésus. Paris: Beauchesne, 1990.

Dingwall, Robert, Anne Marie Rafferty, and Charles Webster. *An Introduction to the Social History of Nursing*. London: Routledge, 1988.

Edel, Leon. *Writing Lives: Principia Biographica*. 1959. New York and London: W. W. Norton, 1984.

Faber, Frederick W. *Bethlehem*. London: Thomas Richardson and Son, 1860.

———. *Spiritual Conferences*. London: Thomas Richardson and Son, 1859.

———, ed. *The Spiritual Doctrine of Father Louis Lallemant*. London: Burns & Lambert, 1855.

Fothergill, Brian. *Nicholas Wiseman*. London: Faber and Faber, 1963.

Gertrud the Great of Helfta. *The Herald of God's Loving-Kindness*. Books One and Two. Trans. Alexandra Barratt. Kalamazoo, Mich.: Cistercian Publications, 1991.

———. *Spiritual Exercises*. Trans. Gertrud Jaron Lewis and Jack Lewis. Kalamazoo, Mich: Cistercian Publications, 1989.

[Grant, Thomas]. *Meditations of the Sisters of Mercy before Renewal of Vows*. London: Keating & Co., 1863.

Gwynn, Denis. *Cardinal Wiseman*. Dublin: Browne & Nolan, 1950.

Hebert, Raymond G., ed. *Florence Nightingale: Saint, Reformer, or Rebel?* Malabar, Fl.: Krieger, 1981.

Holmes, J. Derek. *More Roman Than Rome: English Catholicism in the Nineteenth Century*. London: Burns & Oates, 1978.

Huxley, Elspeth. *Florence Nightingale*. New York: G. P. Putnam's Sons, 1975.

Jowett, Benjamin. *Dear Miss Nightingale: A Selection of Benjamin Jowett's Letters to Florence Nightingale, 1860–1893*. Ed. Vincent Quinn and John Prest. Oxford: Clarendon Press, 1987.

Leslie, Shane. *Henry Edward Manning: His Life and Labours*. New York: P. J. Kenedy and Sons, 1921.

McAuley, Catherine. *The Letters of Catherine McAuley, 1827–1841*. Ed. Mary Ignatia Neumann, RSM. Baltimore: Helicon, 1969.

———. *A Little Book of the Practical Sayings, Advices and Prayers of Our Revered Foundress, Mary Catharine [sic] McAuley*. Ed. [Mary Clare Moore]. London: Burns, Oates & Co., 1868.

Muldrey, Mary Hermenia, RSM. *Abounding in Mercy: Mother Austin Carroll*. New Orleans: Habersham, 1988.

Nightingale, Florence. *Ever Yours, Florence Nightingale: Selected Letters*. Ed. Martha Vicinus and Bea Nergaard. London: Virago Press, 1989.

———. *"I have done my duty": Florence Nightingale in the Crimean War, 1854–56*. Ed. Sue M. Goldie. Manchester: Manchester University Press, 1987.

———. *Notes on Hospitals*. 1858. Third ed. London: Longman, Green, Longman, Roberts, and Green, 1863.

———. *Suggestions for Thought by Florence Nightingale: Selections and Commentaries*. Ed. Michael D. Calabria and Janet A. Macrae. Philadelphia: University of Pennsylvania Press, 1994.

Norman, Edward R. *Anti-Catholicism in Victorian England*. New York: Barnes & Noble, 1968.

———. *The English Catholic Church in the Nineteenth Century*. Oxford: Clarendon Press, 1984.

O'Malley, I. B. *Florence Nightingale, 1820–1856*. London: Thornton Butterworth, 1931.

Perkin, Joan. *Victorian Women*. London: John Murray, 1993.

Ramsay, Grace [Kathleen O'Meara]. *Thomas Grant, First Bishop of Southwark*. London: Smith, Elder, & Co., 1874.

A Religious of the Order of Poor Clares, trans. *Life and Revelations of St. Gertrude, Virgin and Abbess, of the Order of St. Benedict*. London: Burns, Lambert, & Oates, 1865.

Rodriguez, Alonsus, SJ. *The Practice of Christian and Religious Perfection*. Trans. from the French copy of M. l'Abbé Regnier des Marais. 3 vols. Kilkenny: John Reynolds, 1806.

Ruddick, Sara. *Maternal Thinking: Towards a Politics of Peace*. London: Women's Press, 1989.

Sheldrake, Philip. *Spirituality and History*. New York: Crossroad, 1992.

Sisters of the Visitation. *The Life of Jeanne Charlotte de Bréchard*. London: Longmans, Green and Co., 1924.

Smith, F. B. *Florence Nightingale: Reputation and Power*. New York: St. Martin's Press, 1982.

Soyer, Alexis. *Soyer's Culinary Campaign, being Historical Reminiscences of the late War, the plain Art of Cookery for Military and Civil Institutions, the Army, Navy, Public, etc.* London: Routledge, 1857.

Strachey, Lytton. "Florence Nightingale." *Eminent Victorians: Cardinal Manning, Dr. Arnold, Florence Nightingale, General Gordon.* London: Chatto & Windus, 1918. 115–77.

Sullivan, Mary C., RSM. *Catherine McAuley and the Tradition of Mercy.* Dublin: Four Courts Press, 1995; Notre Dame, Ind.: University of Notre Dame Press, 1995.

————. "Catherine McAuley's Theological and Literary Debt to Alonso Rodriguez: The 'Spirit of the Institute' Parallels." *Recusant History* 20 (May 1990): 81–105.

Summers, Anne. *Angels and Citizens: British Women as Military Nurses, 1854–1914.* London and New York: Routledge & Kegan Paul, 1988.

Talbott, John H. *A Biographical History of Medicine.* New York and London: Grune and Stratton, 1970.

Teresa of Avila. *The Collected Works of St. Teresa of Avila.* Ed. Kieran Kavanaugh, OCD and Otilio Rodriguez, OCD. Vol. 1, second ed., Washington, D.C.: Institute of Carmelite Studies Publications, 1987; vol. 2, Washington, D.C.: Institute of Carmelite Studies Publications, 1980.

*Trees of Mercy: Sisters of Mercy of Great Britain, from 1839.* Wickford, Essex: Sisters of Mercy, 1993.

Valerio, Adriana. "Women in Church History." *Women—Invisible in Theology and Church* (Concilium 182). Ed. Elizabeth Schüssler Fiorenza and Mary Collins. Edinburgh: T. and T. Clark, 1985. 63–71.

van der Peet, Rob. *The Nightingale Model of Nursing.* Edinburgh: Campion Press, 1995.

Walton, John, Paul B. Beeson, and Ronald Bodley Scott, eds. *The Oxford Companion to Medicine.* 2 vols. Oxford and New York: Oxford University Press, 1986.

Ward, Wilfrid. *The Life and Times of Cardinal Wiseman.* 2 vols. Second ed. London: Longmans, Green, and Co., 1897.

Whatmore, L. E. *The Story of Dockhead Parish.* Rome: Congregation of Rites, 1960.

Widerquist, JoAnn G. "Dearest Rev'd Mother." *Florence Nightingale and Her Era: A Collection of New Scholarship,* ed. Vern Bullough, Bonnie Bullough, and Marietta P. Stanton. New York: Garland, 1990.

# Index